The Hidden Role of Softv in Educational Research

Educational research often discounts the uniqueness and ubiquity of soft-ware and the hidden political, economic and epistemological ways it impacts teaching and learning in K-12 settings. Drawing on theories and methodologies from English education, critical discourse analysis, multimodal semiotics and digital humanities, this volume exposes the problems of technology in schools and refocuses the conversation on software. This shifting of focus invites more nuanced questions concerning the role of software in school reform and classroom instruction, and takes a critical stance on software's role in education.

This volume explores the ontology of software and the ways it is construed within educational policy discussions. It is beneficial to schools, companies, policy makers and practitioners seeking a unique theoretical framework for technology in education.

Tom Liam Lynch is Assistant Professor of Education Technology at Pace University, USA.

Routledge Research in Education

For a full list of titles in this series, please visit www.routledge.com

The Hidden Role of Software in Educational Research

Policy to Practice

Tom Liam Lynch

Routledge
Taylor & Francis Group

LONDON AND NEW YORK

MT

First published 2015 by Routledge

2 Park Square, Milton Park, Abingdon, Oxon OX14 4RN
711 Third Avenue, New York, NY 10017, USA

Routledge is an imprint of the Taylor & Francis Group, an informa business

First issued in paperback 2017

Library of Congress Cataloging-in-Publication Data

Lynch, Tom Liam.
    The hidden role of software in educational research : policy to practice / by
Tom Liam Lynch.
        pages cm. — (Routledge research in education ; 143)
    Includes bibliographical references and index.
  1. Education—Data processing.   2. Educational evaluation.
3. Telecommunication in education.   4. Education—Standards.   I. Title.
    LB1028.43.L96 2015
    379.1'58—dc23
    2015001117

ISBN: 978-1-138-80729-7 (hbk)
ISBN: 978-1-138-08493-3 (pbk)

Typeset in Sabon
by Apex CoVantage, LLC

2/28/18

To my wife, Kerry McKibbin, and our son Declan. Thank you for your love, patience, understanding, and presence.

Contents

Tables and Figures

Tables

Figures

Acknowledgements

I would like to thank many others who supported me in the writing of this manuscript.

It is because of the thoughtfulness and enthusiasm of Allen Webb that I had the opportunity to take the idea for this book into reality. Allen not only supports my ideas and passions, but also paired me with a fine team at Routledge who were looking for new talent. At Routledge-Taylor Francis, many thanks to Stacy Noto, Lauren Verity, and Merritt Duncan.

My work at two institutions were essential for the ideas and experiences herein. At the Pace University School of Education, the completion of this manuscript would not have been possible without the support of Drs. Penny Spencer, Xiao-Lei Wang, and Brian Evans. At the New York City Department of Education, I wish to offer my thanks to those with whom I've had the honor to work and speak, including Courtney Allison, Cricket Heinze, Michael Weinraub, Viraj Kamdar, Angie Bedford Jack, Casi Graddy-Gamel, Britt Neuhaus, Seth Schoenfeld, Kathy Tsamasiros, and Hal Friedlander.

I am grateful to those academic colleagues who have expressed interest in and feedback to the ideas in this book, including Drs. Ellen Meier, Ruth Vinz, Noah Golden, Nadia Behizadeh, Julie and Dave Gorlewski, Shobana Musti, Gerald Ardito, Sandra Schamroth Abrams, Hannah Gerber, Troy Hicks, and Tony Picciano. Also to Shellie Elson at NCTE who helped me navigate the process of securing permissions for reprinted materials.

1   Silicon Bullets in New York

"Both [authors] move me to reach into my own story, into the ambivalence of my own choosing to act in such a way that I break loose from anchorage and that I stir others to break loose along with me, so that we all become different, that we all engage in a dialectic to reach beyond where we are."

—*Maxine Greene in "Teaching for Openings,"*
Releasing the Imagination, p. 110

One winter morning, a group of people met around a grand wooden table. Leaders from both New York City public schools and a large philanthropic organization gathered in what was once a 19th-century townhouse blocks from city hall and just south of the Brooklyn Bridge. The city had recently been awarded a multi-million dollar grant to implement a professional development initiative that leveraged online learning to support 75,000 teachers. As an advisor to the city's central office, I designed and co-wrote the proposal the group gathered to discuss.

When I arrived, the meeting had been in progress for a couple hours. I settled into a chair, apologized for my lateness, and stirred a porcelain cup of coffee. Attendees were in the midst of assessing the city's preparedness to implement the ambitious plans before it. After some time, members of the group began excitedly talking about how the proposed use of technology could provide new insights into teachers' professional needs and help them find resources like curricula, online courses, and other colleagues. Speakers interrupted each other enthusiastically and the room filled with energy. Words like *data feeds, metadata,* and *personalization* buzzed high into the air aside dust balls and crown molding. "Let's stay focused on the very human nature of our work," I said after voices settled down. "We should take a moment to remember that there is no silver—or better—*silicon* bullet that will solve challenges in teacher development."

Silence followed with some smiles, some furrowed brows, and some looks of loss as attendees peered up from their mobile phones, their focus and multitasking stalled. The phrase *silicon bullet* resonated. It conveyed my criticism of the idea that we should speak in terms of single solutions to perceived problems. I like to think the term wittily capitalized on market-based education reformers' belief in the fundamental goodness of their agenda. After all, no one wants to be associated with weaponry or werewolves.

Interjecting in settings like this one, where dedicated and smart people wax prophetic about the untapped potential of technology, is a language game tactic I learned working in the city schools. In 2009, after six years teaching high school English and serving as my school's technology coordinator, I joined a $50 million online learning project at the central offices called iLearnNYC. The *New York Post* referred to iLearnNYC as "a boom in online learning that could see as many as 80 public schools delivering a large chunk of their instruction via the Internet in the coming school year" (Gonen, 2010, para. 2). iLearnNYC and other technology-related initiatives were a key component of then-mayor Michael Bloomberg and schools chancellor Joel Klein's reform strategy. The popular education news site Gotham Schools ran a piece in which they note the importance of virtual schooling to the Bloomberg-Klein administration, calling it "a major focus of Klein's tenure at the Department of Education" (Phillips, 2010, para. 2). Unlike other online learning programs in which a district partners with a single online learning company, iLearnNYC used one online platform that integrated with dozens of other companies to provide schools access to more resources, an impressive technical achievement in its own right. The idea was to give schools curricular choice across multiple vendors rather than locking them into contracts with just one or two.

For two years, I managed and directed iLearnNYC's implementation. My day-to-day work consisted of meeting with educators, companies, and members of our IT division. It was a crash course in information technologies and business processes. As a lover of words I began to hone in on the language being used to discuss the project. At one meeting, I remember holding my phone under the table as I discreetly tried to Google "deliverable" to ascertain if it was an actual word. Or, at another "high-level" meeting, I used an acronym search engine to come up with working definitions for "COB" and "MOU" and "BAFO" ("Close of Business," "Memorandum of Understanding," and "Best and Final Offer," respectively.) This was the lexicon that comprised my work. I found it endearing, initially. But beneath it flowed an underlying discourse and ideological perspective with which I was less comfortable. The project plans, the conference calls, the meetings, and the PowerPoint "decks" all fueled an assumption about the ends of education and technology's place in our schools and districts.

EDUCATION REFORM

For the past 20 years, efforts to reform education have begun to sound and look the same regardless of whether liberals or conservatives have led the charge. Whereas the two sides of the political aisle once disagreed vehemently over sociocultural matters like how to teach the Civil War or evolution, both sides seem to have agreed on an education strategy that attempts to skirt such knotty social issues in favor of a more palatable alternative. I shall refer to this alternative strategy as *neoliberal education reform* or simply *neoliberal* in adjectival form. Not all scholars use this term, perhaps because they disagree with its usage or because they fear it will be misread as simply liberal or Democratic. The values promoted via the neoliberal reform agenda transcend party lines due to its emphasis on market-based logic as the solution to institutional woes, including championing things like accountability, standards, choice, transparency, data, and the involvement of private enterprise in public education. This perspective appeals to quintessential conservatives who disagree with liberals on many social issues but value the emphasis on economic prosperity; it appeals to quintessential liberals who view it as a way to bolster the economy while purporting to support populations who struggle most in our public schools. I am making a thin summary out of what is a rich and expansive topic. The point is to note the fact that for at least the last two decades, public education has been first slowly and now quite rapidly steered by a reform agenda that is largely driven by political and economic ideologies. I experienced the operationalization of the neoliberal reform agenda at its prime while working as a teacher and schools official in New York City in the early 2000s. I witnessed the division of large schools into smaller ones, children and their families required to "choose" the new small school to which their child would go (not uncommonly outside their neighborhood), "data-driven" instruction mandated across the city, teachers forced to "share" their classrooms because preparation periods and a quiet space were considered an inefficient use of resources, and coercive attempts to script curricula. When I left the classroom to work on iLearnNYC, I witnessed not only the effects of the neoliberal agenda but worked closely with the men and women who believed it was the right thing to do, sometimes out of conviction and sometimes out of arrogance. In all such cases, out of naiveté. There are three aspects of the neoliberal agenda most relevant to our current purposes: accountability and standards, data, and technology.

ACCOUNTABILITY & STANDARDS

The idea that public institutions should be accountable to the public is difficult to dispute. If taxpayers fund certain organizations, salaries, and procurements, it seems appropriate that there be some transparency into how that money is spent and with what effect. New York City learned this lesson in the late 1870s when Boss Tweed perfected a model for using his public office to fill his own bank accounts. One cartoon in *Harper's Weekly* at the time depicts how Tweed even used his post as head of the public schools to replace textbooks used in classrooms with ones that his own printing house produced (Lynch, 2011). That public schools should be accountable to their communities is sensible and fair. Who defines accountability and how they define it is a more complicated matter. The present sense of urgency to hold schools more accountable to the public can be traced back to a federal committee report in 1983 called *A Nation at Risk*. The report, written by a committee of 18 members across private, educational, and governmental sectors, made the formal case that the American school system was falling behind other nations and not doing the fundamental job of schooling its young. The impact of the committee's report remains with us to this day. Diane Ravitch (2013) argues that the Bush Administration's No Child Left Behind (NCLB) legislation and the Obama Administration's Race to the Top (RTTT) program are continuations of the "a false crisis narrative" (p. 9) that American schools are perpetually failing and argues that the premise that schools should be directly accountable for preparing a competitive workforce is wrong. Aspects of one's school experience might directly prove valuable to one's work, but to suggest that a primary accountability metric for schools should be their proven ability to prepare the new workforce is another matter altogether. Some would say that education should focus on students' ability to create and "look at things as if they could be otherwise" (Greene, 1995, p. 22) or that the primary purpose of public education should be to prepare an informed and active citizenry who can grapple with complex political issues and hold elected officials to task (Apple, 1993; Nussbaum, 2010). Regardless of what side of the issue one falls on, it is undeniable that there are different perspectives about what the core purpose of public education should be. At least since 1983, the perspective that views the purpose of education as inseparable from economic prosperity has increased in its dominance. Further, this intertwining of educational and economic ends has increasingly resulted in policy makers embracing the private sector's viewpoints and involvement in educational matters (Picciano & Spring, 2013). It is one thing to invite corporate ideas into dialogue about education. It is quite another thing not only to ask them to inform the creation of learning standards, as was the case with the Common Core Standards, but to also turn to private companies to create schools, partner with districts, and sell products to public educational institutions. As Michael Apple (1996) adroitly observes in his book *Cultural Politics and Education,* "There is a world of difference between taking economic power and structures seriously and reducing everything down to a pale reflection of them" (p. xii). Indeed, one can rightly question whether the private companies so often brought into education reform are themselves held accountable for their effects with the same scrutiny and heated rhetoric that our underfunded districts and schools are, despite the fact that those companies accept public monies. Such is the paleness of the reflection to which Apple refers.

In response to the fiery emergence of cries for accountability during the Bush Administration's No Child Left Behind implementation, Peter Taubman (2009) writes that ". . . accountability [was translated] into teachers' responsibility for their students' learning as measured by performance on tests" (p. 33). As he observes, more recent reforms of both the Bush and Obama Administrations attempt to define accountability not solely institutionally—school buildings, districts, states—but at the individual teacher level and based greatly on test scores created and scored by private companies. The fairness and ethics of holding individual teachers accountable for their students' learning (measured in this way) when much of teachers' school environments as well as the assessments are not in their direct control is highly questionable. By placing such responsibility solely on the backs of educators, Taubman argues, reformers succeed in diverting the public's attention from the more complex—and politically divisive—social, political, economic, and cultural issues like institutionalized racism, sexism, and unequal wages. He notes, "Replacing the substantive focus on the roots of these [socioeconomic] problems, the language of standards and accountability recodes a call to action on a social level as a need for 'highly qualified' teachers" (p. 133). Reformers can fire teachers; they cannot fire poverty.

As Taubman suggests, holding schools and districts accountable requires a logical instrument that can frame expectations and against which they can be measured. It is for this reason that the *Nation at Risk* committee includes categories of recommendations entitled "standards and expectations." The word *standards* can seem to one as neutral, necessary, and commonsensical. Should educators have clearly defined standards for what is taught and even some shared language for how one teaches? The answer appears to be a staunch affirmative. However, as with the definition of accountability above, who defines those standards and how they are implemented is where pale reflections begin to glint. The Common Core Standards offers a rife case in point. The Common Core Standards are said to have emerged from a collective of state governors who enlisted various stakeholders in systematically defining the knowledge and skills necessary for college and career readiness. Covering grades K-12, the standards are organized into math and ELA/literacy documents with the latter covering not only English and language arts, but also the literacy skills necessary in science, history, and technical subjects. States were encouraged or coerced to adopt the Common Core to secure additional and much needed federal funding as well as at the request of philanthropic groups that became more active in education reform during the same time. There emerged three key criticisms of the Common Core Standards, which are applicable to standards more generally. First, critics noted that the authors of the standards overwhelmingly represented private business interests, not public educational ones. Blogger Mercedes Schneider, for example, researched the backgrounds of all listed members of the Common Core authoring team and found "current classroom teachers were intentionally excluded from the CCSS [Common Core] decision-making table—especially elementary school teachers, special education teachers, and teachers of English as a Second Language (ESL). And I have not even touched upon [state governors' organizations] completely ignoring inclusion of teachers currently teaching in varied ethnic, cultural, and socioeconomic regions" (Schneider, 2014). Second, in an effort to align with traditional compartmentalization of grade levels, the standards falsely divide skills that are fluid in practice. Literacy scholar Arthur Applebee notes that one of the key differences between grades 8 and 9–10 writing standards is that students are not explicitly expected to consider their audience when developing a topic until the latter grades. He rightly notes that "it is not unreasonable to expect that we will see curricula that postpone audience considerations until grade 9 for this kind of writing" (Applebee, 2013, p. 29), despite the well-documented scholarship of the importance of audience consideration throughout both reading and writing development at all ages. Third, regardless of what the standards themselves say, the adage that "what gets tested gets taught" is also cause for concern. In the case of the Common Core, as new tests were introduced in New York State, parents from Buffalo to Montauk pulled their children out of school on testing days while reports arose of illogical types of questions and anxiety-producing testing environments. Even comedian Louis C.K., whose daughter attends public school in New York City, took to Twitter to express his anger and indignation. He tweeted, "My kids used to love math. Now it makes them cry. Thanks standardized testing and common core!" Later he added, "The teachers are great. . . . But it's changed in recent years. It's all about these tests. It feels like a dark time" (Mead, 2014). Scholars, critics, and parents agreed that both the standards as documents and their realization in the form of tests were thoroughly problematic to pedagogy.

SACRED DATA

The picture of accountability and standards is incomplete if we do not consider the role that data play in the neoliberal reform movement. One can wish to hold schools accountable (whatever that means) and even have standards in place, but if one does not have instruments to convert the complexity of teaching and learning into quantities that are aligned to those standards the picture will appear incomplete. Enter data. Enthusiasm for data in education reached fever pitch in New York City during the early 2000s when both mayor and schools chancellor injected "data-driven" decision making and instruction into schools and administrative culture. Mayoral presentations about the successes of school reform came equipped with graphs depicting the ups and downs of data trends. As a teacher at the time, I recall vividly the push from my principal for my grade-team colleagues and me to use a common rubric to assess shared writing prompts given to our students, regardless of how inauthentic the prompts were to our curricula or students' lives. At the time, the high-pressure environment included threats to fire school leaders who did not demonstrate annual progress through predetermined quantitative measures. I did not appreciate it then, but at least my principal engaged her teachers in creating the assessments ourselves. Many schools simply procured off-the-shelf products from companies. Both the political climate and the nature of the products tended to treat data in narrow quantitative terms rather than other forms of more socioculturally relevant and responsive data. As Taubman (2009) writes, "Tests provide the equalization of disparate phenomena and render them quantifiable" (p. 27). To underscore, technology is essential to such equalization and rendering. The concept of *rendering* will recur throughout this book to draw attention the ways the complexity of both human and computational worlds are translated for each other. For Taubman, questions abound concerning who writes the tests, how they are administered, and what getting a "correct" answer truly demonstrates about what a student learns or does not learn. Simultaneously, rubrics are a primary instrument used to cull data from teaching and learning. The use of rubrics is especially relevant when considering reforms that target teacher practice, both in teacher preparation programs and for in-service teacher evaluation. We must consider both how data are reaped and what they do (not) represent as well as how data are interpreted and rendered back into sociocultural contexts.

That data are reaped from complex learning environments through the use of tests and rubrics is both so ubiquitous it feels familiar, yet so imperfect that the faith and fever that accompanies the use of such instruments is strange. Some would argue that proponents' faithfulness stems from a historical and cultural belief in the concrete and economic value of the sciences in society. Science, data, technology—they convey to many a sense of systematic certainty (Ely, Vinz, Downing, & Anzul, 2004; Richardson, 1997, 2000) despite the ricketiness of claims to scientific objectivity and fact (Gould, 1996). Regardless of any appearance of firm factuality, both tests and rubrics require that those who develop them engage in a significant amount of forethought and, to a great extent, predetermine the categories from which users of such instruments can select. Both instruments operationalize a process of dividing and conquering pedagogy. Whether it is choosing the "right" answer on a multiple choice problem or deciding if a teacher's lesson belongs categorically in the "effective" or "ineffective" box of a rubric, both the user of the instrument and the person on whom the instrument is being used are confined to someone else's belief system. The possibility that a student taking an exam or a teacher whose craft is evaluated by a supervisor might offer an idea, insight, or technique that is not represented fairly on a test or rubric is, in this setting, systemically unacceptable. For neoliberal reformers, all must be predetermined. Taubman (2009) writes, "Once best practices are agreed on, and their demonstration can be measured, teaching emerges as work that can be chopped up, exported, and . . . digitized" (p. 116). Something similar can be said of testing and learning. Once learning is reduced to selecting the proper answer (which is aligned to standards, of course), what it means to learn can be torn asunder. When working for the city schools I led workshops that walked teachers through the changes in "old" ELA questions and the "new" Common Core ones. It was not uncommon for participants to note that the readings and questions in the Common Core exams were clearly more sophisticated, harder to answer. Harder does not mean better. Such questions are certainly evidence that the test creators are capable of sophistication, but students were still required to merely fill in a bubble. The exams remain inauthentic, decontextualized, and reductive. But they generate numbers that are aligned to standards and purport to represent students' learning—so they do not just live on, they expand like data-driven fire.

When data are generated from different kinds of testing, how those results are interpreted and rendered merits scrutiny. One of my professional interests is using quantitative text analysis to create data visualizations for academic, pedagogical, and public consumption. Anyone working in data visualization learns an early lesson on just how easy it is to misrepresent your data as well as to create a visualization that is too easily misinterpreted. Sometimes, the numbers one has are "dirty," meaning they are not formatted properly or come from too many unknown sources. Sometimes, even if the numbers are sound, how they are organized and exported corrupts their usefulness. Or, sometimes the visual story one tells with the numbers is simply inaccurate. My point here is that even if the data gathered through testing and rubrics were less problematic—systematically and randomly generated, for instance—how they are rendered back into our everyday sociocultural contexts is anything but neutral. Ravitch describes how educational reformers routinely misinterpret the results of NAEP exams to fuel the narrative that schools are in crisis and that teachers are to blame. She notes that there are four levels NAEP exams use to define achievement: advanced, proficient, basic, and below basic. She illustrates how a film director promoting education reform who claims that 70% of 8th grade students do not read at grade level misrepresents the data. Ravitch (2013) explains, "NAEP does not report grade levels. . . . [The filmmaker] assumed that students who were not 'proficient' on the NAEP were 'below grade level.' That is wrong. Actually 76 percent on NAEP are basic or above . . ." (p. 48). Data rendered about teacher performance are also subject to ideological tailwinds, as in the case of a pilot group of New York City teachers whose teacher evaluation scores were published in newspapers along with their names and schools. Or, when the United Federation of Teachers (UFT) negotiated with the city and state to agree on a teacher evaluation system, their public-facing materials made it appear that most of teachers' effectiveness ratings were derived from supervisory observations, but the scale that was created for those observations expanded the possibility for teachers to be rated poorly far more than originally intended. Numbers might not lie, but people who cite numbers lie all the time.

Concern about the lust for data that accompanies the current reforms is not just an academic preoccupation. When policy makers and reformers force educators to think and talk about students in the abstract aggregate that data-filled spreadsheets create, they encourage the dehumanization of our students and the communities from which they come and to which they contribute. Reformers' push for accountability, standards, and data-driven instruction is not a neutral agenda. It represents an ideology, one that seeks to make our students and communities ". . . defined and monitored from afar" (Taubman, 2009, p. 94). This neoliberal agenda attempts to divert public attention from the fact that the human beings in our schools and communities are not quantitative abstractions. They are people with complicated and varied existences. They love and suffer and fear and hope. In creating a professional culture of abstraction, reformers create a state of *blankness* in education, which educational philosopher Maxine Greene (1995) describes thus: "Without some knowledge of connective details, it is extraordinarily difficult to overcome abstraction in dealing with other people. A fearful oversimplification takes over: in blankness, we see only 'Russia,' 'student movement,' 'ethnic minorities.' We are likely to chart things in terms of good/bad, white/black, either/or. We become pawns in a Manichean allegory of good and evil" (p. 95). Of course, even the most hardened reformer knows not to speak in such blatant binaries. It is infinitely less uncouth to speak in terms of reading and math levels (i.e. She's a 2), abstract socioeconomic categories (i.e. He gets free lunch), and other imperfect performance metrics (i.e. I hear you were rated ineffective by the principal). Instruction and decision-making "driven" by data are driven by false dichotomies that fail to grasp the complexity of teaching and learning and unethically ignore the sociocultural and economic issues that affect how students learn and teachers teach.

A TECHNOLOGICAL IMPERATIVE

Reforms that prioritize accountability, standards, and data necessarily rely on different kinds of instruments to translate the complexity of lived experience into data as well as computational assemblages to store, manipulate, feed, and render the vast stores of data generated from large-scale efforts. The "Bush-Obama 'reforms'", as Ravitch calls them (Ravitch, 2013, p. xi), are impossible without technology. Defining the kinds of technology used in education reform requires some unpacking. For present purposes, there are two general types of technologies to consider: analogue and digital.

Analogue technologies refer to the paper-based instruments used in institutions to generate and gather data. Taubman (2009) refers to several kinds of examples as *assemblages* in his discussion of neoliberal reform efforts taking root in his teacher preparation program. He writes, "The loose connections among standards, check sheets, offices that aggregate the data, the technologies that are used, the supervisors and student teachers, the reports generated, the feedback produced by the reports, and the actions taken as a result, all these create assemblages" (p. 123). As referenced above, when principals evaluate teachers with rubrics in the classroom to generate predetermined numbers and language, the technology of the rubric can be said to have converted pedagogy into something abstract and categorical. Or, when students are assessed with even the most fibrous of paper-based tests to select an answer from a list of options, they are in essence being forced to align their minds with faceless and absent exam creators. In both cases, technological instruments are used to extend the natural will of those in positions of power to shape the expression of others. Paleness glimmers, blankness begins.

The second type of technology to consider is perhaps more familiar to us. *Digital technologies* are those technologies that are created with software, hardware, and information systems. I will refer to both digital and *software-powered technologies* interchangeably, although I prefer the latter term. I use "software-powered" to draw attention to issues of power and equity that quickly emerge when one considers software's ubiquitous role in mediating and shaping many aspects of society. Human beings with ideologies and assumptions about the world create software, sometimes in ways that are not in the best interest of users. In its most basic form, we see digital technologies used to make more efficient certain forms of analogue technology. For example, it is not uncommon to see software applications that are used to evaluate teachers using a tablet or video of the teacher's practice. Nor is it uncommon to see students taking computer-based quizzes and exams, an explicit strategic goal of the neoliberal reform movement and Common Core. Digital technologies have become so familiar to many of us that it is sometimes difficult to reflect on just how complex they are and all that they do in ways invisible to the average user. For example, when students take computerized tests for the Common Core, they use devices like tablets or laptops or desktops that are connected to a networking infrastructure. Students navigate the tests by clicking on buttons, menus, and links through what is called a user interface, which despite its graphic appearance actually masks the world of programming languages that would be too confusing for most users to use. Finally, information systems of various sorts talk to each other throughout the process, sending different kinds of data feeds to each other. When Taubman refers to assemblages that are used to operationalize reformers' ideologies, he insightfully identifies analogue components but only hints at the deep role that digital technologies play. As I will discuss at great length throughout this book, it is the relationship between these analogue and digital technologies that merits scrutiny, especially the ontology of what I call *software space*. These technologies are the often seemingly innocuous instruments we encounter everyday and we must clearly see how their ubiquity does not signify their neutrality.

One of the key ways schools have been required to embrace certain technological assemblages is by upgrading analogue filing systems for digital versions integrated with information systems. Schools today are required to have digital systems of storing information locally and are expected to pull from and contribute to district and state systems as well. On the one hand this seems like common sense: in the 21st century, rudimentary operations like data storage and retrieval should be digital. On the other hand, it is one thing to expect schools to keep digital records of their own motivated work, but quite another matter to require schools to quantify teaching and learning in ways they do not choose locally and to share that quantified data with others, which might include the district, state, and third-party companies. It is an often understated consequence of recent reforms that technology companies and consultants have become essential to schools and districts. As Ravitch (2013) observes, "Almost overnight, consultants and vendors offered their services to advise districts and states on how to design teacher evaluation systems, how to train teachers, how to train principals, how to turnaround failing schools, how to use new technologies, how to engage in data-driven decision making, on and on" (p. 15). It is worth noting that whereas Ravitch refers to digital technologies, the kinds of other services she refers to rely heavily on analogue technologies as well. Consider the number of flow charts, standards "cross-walk" documents, rubrics, checklists, and other instruments used when experts and coaches work with schools. Increasingly, these kinds of instruments are mapped to other accountability standards and have digital correlates. For the individual school, analogue and digital technologies are inescapable and it is increasingly impossible to avoid procuring products and services from the education marketplace.

If the technologies marketplace of available educational products was as neutral as some suggest, one might imagine schools to be empowered to make the purchases they need and, over time, the logic of the market could ensure that shoddier educational products would fall away. The marketplace in education is not neutral, nor does it operate as fairly as one might imagine. Instead, it is part of what Picciano and Spring (2013) call an *education-industrial complex,* which they define as revolving around "three main components: ideology, technology, and profit-making. . . . These components interact with one another and are made up of multiple networks and alliances of agencies, organizations, and corporations . . . they overlap in their interests and goals" (p. 2). The neoliberal reform agenda values the application of market-based ideologies to public sectors, including education, in the belief that economic principles like choice, autonomous purchasing power, and the constant use of quantitative metrics to make decisions can improve perceived shortcomings in teachers' effectiveness. Further, technology is regarded as a key lever in operationalizing neoliberal ideologies not only due to technology's inherent structural view of the world and affinity for quantities, but also because embracing technology opens the doors to what *Forbes* magazine called in a headline a "$1 trillion dollar opportunity." The 2012 magazine cover featured Sal Khan, founder of the YouTube channel Khan Academy, which features thousands of video tutorials that Khan created. He was eventually the recipient of private investment from the likes of the Gates Foundation and others. The pedagogical soundness of Khan Academy seems to be of little concern to the editorial board of *Forbes*. Even a pedagogically thin web site that gets millions of daily hits is worth investing in and promoting as an innovation. It is the education-industrial complex made manifest.

The logic of the market neoliberal reformers promote only works, if at all, if there is a level playing field for both small and large companies to participate. In my work, I have organized and participated in many formal and informal meetings of both public and private sector stakeholders in educational technology. A common complaint from smaller companies, some of whom have phenomenally innovative products from which I might imagine teachers benefiting, is that the marketplace is rigged. Venture capitalists and philanthropic groups tend to have eyes only for products that do "safe" work in schools (i.e. creating data dashboards and adult-created "expert" video tutorials) rather than the messier and more complicated work of constructivist pedagogy. Further, when investments are made or certain products are deemed worthy of promotion to schools, it is not uncommon to find that those products are politically connected. When working for the city, I recall one product that I was asked to investigate and review at least three times. Despite my reviews emphasizing that the product was not especially innovative nor was it scalable in a city of tens of thousands of teachers, its promotion persisted. I learned only after the fact that an executive in the company and members of city leadership ran in the same circles.

A reform agenda that promotes accountability through standards and data is a reform agenda that requires both analogue and digital technologies. These technologies are promoted in and required of schools in two interrelated ways. First, they are promoted because in order to gain abstract distance from the sociocultural realities of students, communities, and teachers, reformers must quantify and categorize pedagogy. Technologies are necessary to generate data as well as to store, manipulate, feed, and render them. Second, technologies are promoted because their invocation hearkens economic enthusiasm. Emphasizing technologies is seen as serving economic ends, college and career, preparing workers for the future and creating a new marketplace in the present. Clearly, the assumptions we possess about technology need to be complexified.

TECHNOLOGICAL INADEQUACIES

The eagerness to move K-12 education into software space is part of a wider verve for all things involving technology and concerns me in many ways. My primary concern has to do with the word "technology" as a descriptor. Technology means many things to many people. When I started working as a new professor of education technology, for example, anything that plugged into a wall was considered part of my research agenda and something in which I was interested. As I became more deeply versed in the literature about the role of technology in education, I began to realize that as a field we were missing something really critical about it. In his book *Distrusting Educational Technology*, Neil Selwyn (2014) argues that the role of technology in education is treated in "alarmingly one-dimensional terms" (p. 6). His alarm extends not only to the way policy makers and educators perceive technology, but also to the way educational researchers do as well. There is a "paucity of critique" (p. 11) when it comes to technology, which he argues is part of a broader "orthodoxy of optimism" (p. 13): If there's technology involved, it has to be progressive and good. He concludes, "This tendency for the majority of people to unthinkingly assume educational technology to be inherently beneficial and for a few others to oppose it in generally unconvincing and alarmist terms has limited the quality of debate and scrutiny in the area over the past 30 years or so" (p. 9). Insightfully, Selwyn observes that much of the discourse that comprises the promotion of educational technology—especially when fueled by pedagogues—seems to come from a genuinely positive place. On a certain level, emerging technologies appear to support progressive forms of education that encourage collaboration, inquiry, and critical thinking. He writes, ". . . many people's interest in educational technology is underpinned by a dominant set of values stemming from progressive education ideals and/or social constructivist and sociocultural models of learning—all of which privilege learner-centered and learner-driven forms of education" (p. 32). The collective belief that the use of technology necessitates constructivist and sociocultural models is, however, naive. Buried beneath the surface of the one-dimensional discourse hides the pale reality. Selwyn demonstrates that social media is far less social than we imagine, with a majority of people merely lurking on social media or simply using it to promote their own individualistic work. He also shows how even the utopian world of open-source software development often amounts to rigid hierarchically structured online communities where members are each out for themselves to demonstrate their own talents in hopes of securing future work and professional glory.

Technologies in education can too often effect the opposite of what it is they are boasted to do. That is, the same kind of contradiction Selwyn describes of social media and open-source communities applies more broadly as well. I share Selwyn's concern that reformers situate technologies in ways that deprofessionalize pedagogy. He writes, ". . . these virtual technologies could be seen as placing education firmly in the midst of the immaterial 'new' economy—standardizing and commoditizing education, reducing educational processes and relationships to forms that are easily quantifiable and recorded, distancing educational professionals from the process of educational engagement and thereby deprofessionalizing and deskilling the teaching profession" (p. 62). What emerges is a sad picture, a blankness. Despite the fact that there is justifiable concern about the way technologies are taking root in education, policy makers, educators, and communities too often assume that its use is unstoppable and necessary. Further, when we investigate what educational researchers have to say about technology in schools, we encounter litanies of studies that are swept away in the orthodoxy of optimism. With few critical exceptions (Adams, 2006, 2010; Buckingham, 2008; Jewitt, 2006; Lynch, 2014a, 2014b; Meier, 2005; Selwyn, 2014), it is as if researchers themselves presume the inherent benefits of using technology for teaching and learning. It can be all too challenging to identify, critique, and resist the education-industrial complex. Even the educational research to which one might turn for guidance is all too dim and distracted.

Selwyn argues that unlike other fields in academia, educational technology does not entertain the ideas of those who object to the fundamental assumption that technology is necessarily beneficial to education. Those who disagree, Selwyn (2014) claims, are likely to be labeled Luddites and swiftly dismissed. He writes, "Even in the 2010s, authors advancing a critical or negative analysis are likely to be ignored politely, or else shouted down . . . the academic study of educational technology is perhaps best understood as an essentially 'positive project'" (p. 11). There are many possible reasons for this. First, educational researchers might believe that using technology in educational settings necessarily has the potential to improve pedagogy. One of the obvious hurdles to this belief, of course, is research by colleagues to the contrary. Second, some researchers might realize a pragmatic benefit of taking on the positive project of proving technology's benefits in schools. There is much funding available from public and private sources to prove it. I myself receive at least an email a week suggesting I read a request for proposals or grant opportunity. The operating assumption of funders is that technology in education is clearly good; the assumption of the senders of the emails being that because I am interested in technology in education I would agree with such a positive stance. Still, a simple truth seems to be that there are more funding opportunities to study technology in education than, say, devising more authentic kinds of paper-based writing assessments. Third, some researchers might view the examination of technologies in educational settings as an exciting case on which to test and extend their own research expertise. For example, a composition scholar might wish to study how students' writing processes in online collaborative writing environments differs with their offline processes. In these cases, I caution colleagues to account for the ontological complexity of these technologies and to question the adequacy of their own theoretical and methodological tools. In any case, the result of researchers entering into studies of educational technology without a rigorously critical stance toward the subject results in an "intellectual stance that is evangelical—if not righteous—in its advocacy of this 'truth'" (Selwyn, 2014, p. 12) and, most alarmingly, leads to researchers "[playing] a supporting role in sustaining the hegemony of educational technology by failing to embed its analyses within a wider recognition of the prevailing structures of domination and associated struggles" (p. 160). Educational technology research that fails to critically address the reality of the orthodoxy of optimism and hidden issues of power are, despite an appearance of rigor and validity, offering an incomplete if not misleading representation of the issue.

In response to this picture, Selwyn (2014) offers recommendations to his colleagues. He argues that researchers must ask better questions about the use of educational technology, "to encourage the greater acknowledgement that some things can only ever be discussed and problematized rather than demonstrated and proved" (p. 161). He also makes the valuable suggestion for researchers to acquaint themselves with the history of technology in education as well as other theoretical perspectives that might better inform their inquiries and investigations. The history of technology in education quickly raises to the surface critical questions about the value of using technology in schools. For instance, Larry Cuban's history of technology in schools since the 1920s demonstrates that commercial and political forces have perennially attempted to introduce the latest innovations into schools with recurrent failure. Cuban (1986) examines historical documents that show—over and over—teachers in classrooms as a collective tend to ignore hyped up technologies and, when they do integrate them into instruction, do so to appease administrative pressure. This was the case, Cuban argues, for instructional film, radio, and television. In later works, Cuban (2001) continues his examination of the rise of computers and finds that the same pattern continues. In the case of theory and methodology, there are several other fields that can complexify the way in which researchers approach their work. The primary field of interest for me is software studies, which concerns itself with the ways in which software is quietly and invisibly positioned in our lives. Software studies (Berry, 2011; Fuller, 2008; Kitchin & Dodge, 2011; MacKenzie, 2006; Manovich, 2001, 2013) draw on related fields like code studies and platform studies to offer researchers a rich trove of concepts and methods that expose just how little we tend to know and address about the current educational technologies, most of which are powered by software. Another field that can be of use is multimodal studies. Multimodality (Jewitt, 2006, 2009; Jewitt, Bezemer, Jones, & Kress, 2009; Kress, 2003) draws on research from composition and media studies to present alternative frameworks for examining how modes of communication—other than traditional approaches to writing and reading—impact the kinds of meaning we make of the world. In both cases, researchers who might be approaching educational technology in an overly optimistic or one-dimensional fashion quickly realize that there is much more to technology in education than one might assume. Colleagues' response to such a realization, I hope, is one of thorough excitement.

I wish to emphasize why Selwyn's stance is so vital in case it is not already evident. In the absence of critical research and public intellectualism concerning educational technology, academics are complicit in the misrepresentation and misuses of technology in schools. My own research, in part, deals with examining precisely how technology is positioned in education reform, from state capitals to classrooms. Based on my experiences with state- and district-level leaders, technology companies both large and small, and schools, I can say with confidence that other sources of information about educational technology are filling the gap left by rigorous and readable research. A prime example is the success of a book called *Disrupting Class* (Christensen, Horn, & Johnson, 2008). When I joined the city central offices, I was encouraged to read the book, which positions technology as a key lever for education reform. Former chancellor of city schools, and later Vice President at News Corps' education division, Joel Klein penned a book blurb calling the book a "blueprint" for reform. Over time, I observed it on the shelves of many school leaders and the concepts and lexicon of its pages frequently entered into my conversations with schools. The book is written mostly from a business perspective and attempts to apply one of the authors' concepts called "disruptive innovation" to education as a site of study—a new marketplace. The authors demonstrate little evidence of familiarity with pedagogy and far less with the history and theory of educational technologies. Rather, the book plants its feet in the neoliberal discourse described above and argues that if schools are to prepare students for work in the 21st century they have to be reformed out of the stubborn 19th-century model represented by students sitting in rows. One of the key technologies the authors discuss is the use of online learning in K-12 schools. They predict that schools will be altered dramatically over the next decade and that "by 2019, about 50 percent of high school courses will be delivered online" (p. 98). By "online," the authors discuss a range of models, including tutorial services, student-generated content, and formal online courses. The following paragraph is representative of the level of depth throughout the book when discussing pedagogy:

> The analogous case in education [to health care industries] is that historically, because they haven't known of the existence of remedies for learning problems, students and their families typically put up with poor grades and the low self-esteem spawned by feeling dumb. These user networks will be designed to help students and their families diagnose why they're finding it so difficult to master a subject and then find

their own solution. Just as in health care, students and their families will not wait for their teaching professionals to prescribe a 'therapy.' They will pull the solution out of the user network themselves. (p. 139)

Their naiveté, if it wasn't so influential on policy makers and school leaders, would be laughable. But they write with seriousness and they are read seriously. The authors represent learning as an asocial banking of objective facts and skills, something the educational research and practitioner community has greatly rejected for decades. It is only if learning is viewed so naively and objectively that computerized "user networks" can "prescribe" "remedies for learning problems." What is important to notice here is that the authors believe that technology can diagnose and prescribe learning experiences based on perceived educational "problems." What are the kinds of things technology can diagnose and how does it do so? I will argue that such algorithmic diagnosis and digital prescription writing is only possible if the definition of learning is reduced to one-dimensional blankness.

Whereas Selwyn's (2014) framework provides important and useful concepts for critically engaging with technology, he only alludes to what I view as a crucial paradigm shift needed to advance the field. He writes, "All these technologies—from the most sophisticated immersive simulation to the most expansive virtual world—are predicated upon designer-created hierarchies of 'choice'" (p. 57). Selwyn's words refer to two braided phenomena: the ontology of software and the critical analysis of how human beings produce and promote software's use. Although he does not say *software* by name, the designers to whom he refers who create hierarchies of choice are software companies. I wish to propose that to rigorously examine the role of technology in education, we must advance beyond the word *technology* and begin to discuss software instead.

CONCLUSION

My experiences in New York City are representative of the kinds of education reforms promoted during the Bush and Obama Administrations in the United States between 2000 to 2012. The reform strategy and its associated ideologies existed before that time period and continue after it. Versions of the same agenda can be found in other industries and countries. The qualities are the same: the public-private interplay of data, standards, and accountability through software under the banner of market-driven neoliberalism. The role of software-powered technologies can only be expected to increase in the coming decades, so it is imperative that educators and researchers critically examine what software is and is not. Failure to do so will result in the gradual and inevitable co-opting of public education by those who are least expert to chart its future.

To clarify, I am not opposed to accountability nor am I opposed to standards. I am opposed to waving such words on banners in an effort to authorize the unethical treatment of our children, teachers, and communities. I am also opposed to the failure to hold private companies accountable for the promises, goods, and services they provide schools and districts—often according to wishy-washy industry standards they themselves interpret or feign. It only fuels one's suspicion that private companies avoid accountability themselves because they funnel funding into the campaign accounts of those elected officials who should take companies to task on the public's behalf (Picciano & Spring, 2013; Ravitch, 2010, 2013), not unlike Boss Tweed's corruption over a century ago. If we are to imagine a world in which software-powered technologies are used to truly support administration and pedagogy, we must examine the nature of software so we can identify its misapplications when we see it, articulate what it looks and feels like to misuse software-powered technologies, and pose new possibilities for the research and practice of software in education. I believe this re-imagination is possible, but only if we direct our most solemn and scholastic attention to the nature of software with a keen awareness of the social context in which it is produced and promoted in order to articulate the kinds of pedagogical practices software enables and inhibits. We are fortunate that a field outside education has provided theoretical footholds to begin that work, a field referred to broadly as software studies, to which we now turn.

WORKS CITED

Adams, C. (2006). PowerPoint, habits of mind, and classroom culture. *Journal of Curriculum Studies, 38*(4), 389–411.

Adams, C. (2010). Learning management systems as sites of surveillance, control, and corporatization: A review of the critical literature. In D. Gibson & B. Dodge (Eds.), *Proceedings of society for information technology and teacher education international conference 2010* (pp. 252–257). Chesapeake, VA: AACE.

Apple, M. W. (1993). *Official knowledge: Democratic education in a conservative age*. New York: Routledge.

Apple, M. W. (1996). *Cultural politics and education*. New York: Teachers College Press.

Applebee, A. N. (2013). Common Core state standards: The promise and the peril in a national palimpsest. *English Journal, 103*(1), 25–33.

Berry, D. (2011). *The philosophy of software: Code and mediation in the digital age*. New York: Palgrave Macmillan.

Buckingham, D. (2008). *Beyond technology: Children's learning in the age of digital culture*. Malden, MA: Polity Press.

Christensen, C. M., Horn, M. B., & Johnson, C. W. (2008). *Disrupting class: How disruptive innovation will change the way the world learns*. New York: McGraw Hill.

Cuban, L. (1986). *Teachers and machines: The classroom use of technology since 1920*. New York: Teachers College Press.

Cuban, L. (2001). *Oversold & underused: Computers in the classroom.* Cambridge, MA: Harvard University Press.

Ely, M., Vinz, R., Downing, M., & Anzul, M. (2004). *On writing qualitative research: Living by words.* New York: Routledge Falmer.

Fuller, M. (Ed.). (2008). *Software studies: A lexicon.* Cambridge, MA: MIT Press.

Gonen, Y. (2010, April 7). City schools working on plan to offer online classes. *New York Post.* Retrieved August 11, 2010, from www.nypost.com/p/news/local/city_promotes_online_classes_TykZepBwl7J6sPZNnbIuVI.

Gould, S. J. (1996). *The mismeasure of man.* New York: W. W. Norton and Company.

Greene, M. (1995). *Releasing the imagination: Essays on education, the arts, and social change.* New York: Jossey-Bass.

Jewitt, C. (2006). *Technology, literacy, learning: A multimodal approach.* New York: Routledge.

Jewitt, C. (Ed.). (2009). *The Routledge handbook of multimodal analysis.* New York: Routledge.

Jewitt, C., Bezemer, J., Jones, K., & Kress, G. (2009). Changing English? The impact of technology and policy on a school subject in the 21st century. *English Teaching: Practice and Critique, 8*(3), 8–20.

Kitchin, R., & Dodge, M. (2011). *Code/Space: Software and everyday life.* Cambridge, MA: MIT Press.

Kress, G. (2003). *Literacy in the new media age.* New York: Routledge.

Lynch, T. L. (2011, May). *The Tweed effect: Theorizing the rise of online learning in New York City public schools.* Teachers College, Columbia University, New York, NY.

Lynch, T. L. (2014a). Holy interfaces and the sanctity of software: A critical software analysis of rubrics as vehicles of conservative reform. In M. Tenam-Zemach & J. Flynn (Eds.), *A rubric nation: A reader on the utility and impact of rubrics in education* (pp. 125–141). Charlotte, NC: Information Age Publishing.

Lynch, T. L. (2014b). The imponderable bloom: A multimodal social semiotic study of the role of software in teaching literature in a secondary online English course. *Changing English, 21*(1), 42–52.

MacKenzie, A. (2006). *Cutting code: Software and sociality.* New York: Peter Lang.

Manovich, L. (2001). *The language of new media.* London: MIT Press.

Manovich, L. (2013). *Software takes command.* New York: Bloomsbury Academic.

Mead, R. (2014, April 30). Louis C.K. against the Common Core. *The New Yorker.* Retrieved December 6, 2014, from www.newyorker.com/news/daily-comment/louis-c-k-against-the-common-core.

Meier, E. B. (2005). Situating technology professional development in urban schools. *Journal of Educational Computing Research, 32*(4), 395–407.

Nussbaum, M. C. (2010). *Not for profit: Why democracy needs the humanities.* Princeton, NJ: Princeton University Press.

Phillips, A. (2010, April 14). More schools to experiment with online work, schedule changes. *Gotham Schools.* Retrieved August 11, 2010, from http://gothamschools.org/2010/04/14/more-schools-to-experiment-with-online-work-schedule-changes/.

Picciano, A. G., & Spring, J. (2013). *The great American education-industrial complex: Ideology, technology, and profit.* New York: Routledge.

Ravitch, D. (2010). *The death and life of the great American school system: How testing and choice are undermining education.* New York: Basic Books.

Ravitch, D. (2013). *Reign of error: The hoax of the privatization movement and the danger to America's public schools.* New York: Knopf.

Richardson, L. (1997). *Fields of play: Constructing an academic life.* New Brunswick, NJ: Rutgers University Press.

Richardson, L. (2000). Writing: A method of inquiry. In N.K. Denzin & Y.S. Lincoln (Eds.), *Handbook of qualitative research* (Vol. 2, pp. 923–948). Thousand Oaks, CA: Sage Publications.

Schneider, M. (2014, April 23). Those 24 Common Core 2009 work group members. *deutsch29: Mercedes Schneider's EduBlog.* Retrieved from http://deutsch29.word press.com/2014/04/23/those-24-common-core-2009-work-group-members/.

Selwyn, N. (2014). *Distrusting educational technology: Critical questions for changing times.* New York: Routledge.

Taubman, P.M. (2009). *Teaching by numbers: Deconstructing the discourse of standards and accountability in education.* New York: Routledge.

2 Introducing Software Studies

"Trying to open students to the new and the multiple, we want ourselves to break through some of the crusts of convention, the distortions of fetishism, the sour tastes of narrow faiths."

—Maxine Greene in "Texts and Margins,"
Releasing the Imagination, p. 146

I sat at my desk one early spring afternoon unaware that lines of colleagues were scurrying out of the office and into the halls. When I focused my eyes, I saw lights flashing all around. When I removed my headphones I heard sirens screaming out. It was the fire alarm system. The building that housed the city schools' administrative offices, called Tweed Courthouse, was constructed in the late 19th century but had been given a museum-quality renovation in the late 20th century. Part of that renovation included a state-of-the-art fire alarm that integrated new computer systems and exhaust fans to pull smoke into the building's central rotunda where it was pushed skyward. Somewhere at Tweed that day, a sensor detected something resembling smoke. That detection triggered the lights to flash, a pre-recorded set of instructions to wail, and—unbeknownst to me—the old towering wooden doors of the offices to begin closing automatically.

I grabbed my bag and made it out just in time.

After being reassured there was no fire, I called a colleague, met up outside, and strolled to a nearby coffee house. I bought lunch and a latte, walked back to Tweed, scanned my ID card, took the glass elevator to the third floor, and nibbled my sandwich while returning to the presentation I had been working on.

This experience serves to demonstrate just how integrated software is into our lives. Software powers the fire alarm system at Tweed, the phone on which I called my colleague, the point of sale system at the cafe I relied on to swipe my credit card, the traffic lights and crossing signals I ignored while crossing Chambers Street, the security system that verified my ID card, the elevator system that saved me from climbing stairs, and the presentation application on which I worked. Software is "a layer that permeates all areas of contemporary societies. Therefore, if we want to understand contemporary techniques of control, communication, representation, simulation, analysis, decision making, memory, vision, writing, and interaction, our analysis cannot be complete until we consider this software layer" (italics omitted; Manovich, 2013, p. 15). We will add education to Manovich's list. In what follows, I wish to present an overview of software studies in order to set up an examination of how software is and might be positioned in education. Software studies is the name of a scholarly field that focuses on the nature and effects of software in society. It is related to, but distinct from, other fields like code studies (the close examination of programming languages) and platform studies (the examination of the relationship between software and hardware). Software studies is interested in how software shapes and mediates our lived experiences. As we shall see, such mediation takes many forms from the novel to the eerie.

SOFTWARE IN EDUCATION

There are some explicit and many implicit ways in which software enters into the conversation. In the explicit sense, we hear much said about software in speeches by our leaders who see the inclusion of software engineering education and coding as essential to the prosperity of our economy. In his 2013 State of the Union address, President Obama spoke about an urban school that has a partnership with IBM and educates students for an additional two years in computer science. "Let's also make sure that a high school diploma puts our kids on a path to a good job," the president began. ". . . Now at schools like P-Tech in Brooklyn, a collaboration between New York Public Schools and City University of New York and IBM, students will graduate with a high school diploma and an associate's degree in computers or engineering. We need to give every American student opportunities like this" (Obama, 2013). Applause followed. Days after the president's address, the mayor of New York City delivered his State of the City address. In it, Michael Bloomberg drew the public's attention to two other schools in the city's portfolio explicitly devoted to preparing tomorrow's software engineers. "And since no industry is growing more rapidly than our tech sector," Bloomberg said, "we'll open our second Academy for Software Engineering high school." In addition to these two schools, the mayor added that "With private support, we'll also bring computer science classes to 20 more schools next September" (Bloomberg, 2013). Both public addresses cast a spotlight on the growing importance of software in our lives in the eyes of our policy makers.

In addition to the push for computer science education, there has been a groundswell of support for digital tools and resources. Textbook companies have been grappling with how to make their products digital and interactive in ways that take advantage of the web and the growing prevalence of tablet computers. There is a veritable flood of content available online (i.e. Khan Academy being of the "home-grown" variety; Discovery and History Channels being a corporate type). There are also myriad tools that have become available that make it easier than ever for students and teachers to create and share their own educational content online. These too make up a more explicit promotion of software, even if the word itself isn't used.

Whereas the president and mayor situate the importance of software in terms of an explicit economic imperative one need look no further than one's own daily life to be reminded of its quieter ubiquity. The phones in our pockets have gained in sophistication in the last decade. Whereas they were once for the sole purpose of making phone calls, phones today are fully functional computers. It is software that powers such technologies. Increasingly, software powers our appliances, heating systems, automobiles, communications, social lives, elections processes, and our financial markets (Berry, 2011; Kitchin & Dodge, 2011; Manovich, 2013). When software breaks, we get comical autocorrected text messages (Lynch, 2013), we see mass frustration over health care coverage registration (Kliff, 2013), and we read about space shuttles veering off course or tragically exploding (Fishman, 1996). Sadly, we only seem aware of software's power when it breaks, unleashing a social shout. In April 2013 we witnessed a "flash crash" in which the Dow suddenly dipped 1% and the S&P 500 lost over $120 billion. The disturbing cause of this micro crash was a tweet (Maureen, 2013). The Twitter account of the Associated Press was hacked and the following pseudo-news update went out into the world: "Breaking: Two Explosions in the White House and Barack Obama is injured." Despite the fact that only one news agency broadcasted this news, the markets temporarily (and quickly) spiraled downward. The impact of this tweet was not due to the fact that human stock traders were scanning social media and collectively saw the false tweet at the same time. Rather, it is because software used in trading determines what to sell based on rapid scanning of news headlines. In this case, words that suggest domestic instability—like "explosions" in the "White House"—trigger software to sell. At these times, we sometimes begin to glimpse another aspect of software so easily forgotten. It is created by companies, promoted by interested parties, and requires upkeep and updating that borders on computational coddling. Software is a precarious phenomenon that at best hums along before it arrests our lives with a roar.

In education, the role of software has been growing in recent years. Like the invisible hand of software on Wall Street, software has become a silent partner in education reforms in ways the public and media offer little credence. The rise in common standards for teaching and learning require large-scale testing, which is an undertaking all but impossible without software. As states compete for federal and philanthropic funding for education, they frequently have to agree to share student achievement and teacher performance data. Making databases talk to each other and developing applications that

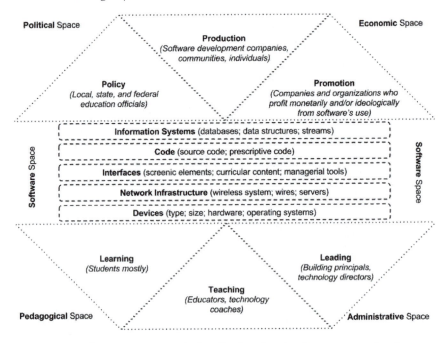

Figure 2.1 Software space map. A visualization showing how computational assemblages comprise software space in education.

allow school officials to analyze and act on that data is work that usually requires states and districts to partner with information systems companies to develop costly software-engineered solutions. As teachers and principals grapple with "instructional technology" questions like using interactive whiteboards and tablets in schools, both policy makers and the private sector are injecting education with "reforms" that make administrators, teachers, and students dependent on software and the companies who produce it. If a certain use of software, however, can lead to roaring social unrest through a tweet, perhaps it is worth better understanding the implicit nature of software and its impact on policy and practice.

MAPPING THE LANDSCAPE

The sample of references to software above are helpful insofar as they demonstrate the ways public figures represent software to others. Such references are also thin and unspecific. I conceptualize *software space* to refer to a complex computational assemblage that includes devices, networking infrastructures, interfaces, code and information systems. Software space is socially situated between 1) political and economic spaces, which includes actors that create policy, produce software, and promote its adoption as well as 2) educational and administrative spaces, which include students, educators, and school leaders (see Figure 2.1). As my evocation of spatiality is intended to suggest, the interplay between the different spaces is fluid and, often, inhumanly fast.

POLITICAL AND ECONOMIC SPACES

Policy

Those who create policy include policy makers at the local, state, and federal levels. In recent years, education policy has been driven by both No Child Left Behind legislation and Race to the Top, both of which include requirements to bolster the generation and use of data (Ravitch, 2013). Data, as a word, seems innocuous and objective. In practice, the word *data* frequently refers to capturing different kinds of measures of student and teacher performance for entry into software-powered information systems. We see this in the case of students who take computerized assessments as well as paper-based tests, the results of which are quickly entered into databases. In the case of teachers, when they are observed and rated in terms of effectiveness we again see how a complex human act—that of teaching—is converted into input for software (Lynch, 2014, 2015a, 2015b). The policies of Race to the Top go further than No Child Left Behind to ensure software's place in education. They require that applicants for Race to the Top funding commit to sharing their teacher and student performance data with their states, who in turn would make that data available to a nationwide syndicate, including private companies. Race to the Top also rewarded districts that articulated their intentions to leverage online learning and other technologies. Its sister program, the U.S. Department of Education's i3 (Investing in Innovation Fund), explicitly funded start-up companies and others in the educational technology field to rapidly prototype and test out new innovations in education. Although the word software is not used, it is precisely what these innovations require.

Production

Those who produce software include software development companies, online communities, and individuals. It has been well documented that contrary to images of lone coders sitting in dorm rooms hacking into government systems, software development is in many ways a collaborative effort (Berry, 2011; MacKenzie, 2006; Rosenberg, 2008). In practice, software is at least partly developed by using blocks of code found in open online communities that have been developed and tested many times before. Computer science students emerge from graduate programs with a foundation in the basics but often rely on their colleagues, communities, and cramming to learn specific programming languages required for certain jobs. Programming languages change, morph, die, and new ones are born. Keeping up to date is necessary to keep one's skills relevant and there are many social ways in which this happens. The challenging process of building a software product is conveyed in *Dreaming in Code* (Rosenberg, 2008), where the author describes following a start-up company's attempt to get its product off the ground. One of the key tropes in the book is that the social interactions between developers was itself a key barrier to successfully producing a software-powered product. In another section of the book, Rosenberg muses that different programming languages reflect "the temperaments and personalities of their creators in some subtle ways" (p. 72). Layers of code written in idiosyncratic programming languages by bevies of individuals run simultaneously and talk to many other systems. That software works at all is incredible.

Promotion

Those who promote software include not only companies who create it, but also those who sell products that rely on software (i.e. computers, mobile phones) as well as those who ideologically believe that the use of software in education is inherently good. Companies whose products rely on software often sell devices of many sorts. For example, a company like Samsung sells a variety of computers and cell phones, all of which include hardware and software supplied by other companies. Without software, their products do nothing. As a result, it is not uncommon to see alliances of software and hardware companies promoting the use of software in education because of mutual benefit (Picciano & Spring, 2013). Other promoters of software in schools have been institutions and individuals who ideologically support the spread of technology in education. The most heavily funded of these groups is the Gates Foundation, who has financially supported "data-driven" instruction initiatives as well as the use of online learning platforms for teacher professional development and the aforementioned inBloom. Influential individuals have also promoted the use of software in the form of online learning platforms used in some blended learning models and virtual schools (Christensen, Horn, & Johnson, 2008), including former Governor Jeb Bush, whose conflict of interests has been the subject of scathing critique (Fang, 2011).

IN SUM

Each of these actors—policy makers, producers of software, and its promoters—have complex social and discursive practices that merit examination and critique. There are pedagogical ramifications to using software in schools in uncritical ways, as we will see below. Policy makers should be asked what of learning is lost and gained when we assess students via software and how it prepares them for an active life in a democracy. Producers of software should be able to explain what the pedagogical and ethical risks of creating a product in one programming language rather than another might be, or how the design of the product's user interface might encourage certain kinds of learning. Companies and philanthropic groups should have to articulate clearly how the software-powered technologies they promote put the goals of pedagogy before those of profit and ideology.

PEDAGOGICAL AND ADMINISTRATIVE SPACES

Students

In discussions of 21st-century learning, it is not uncommon to hear declarations of students' natural abilities to use software-powered technologies. Take coding. There is growing support for students to learn computer programming at an early age. There have emerged in recent years a plethora of organizations both online and offline that seek to help students learn to code. In addition, funding for the creation of learning opportunities for students to learn programming abound. As referred to above, in 2013 New York City opened the second of two high-profile schools dedicated to software engineering. If the largest school district in the country is any indicator, computer programming is becoming part of the modern day trivium. And yet, some commentators have gone as far as to refer to students as "digital natives" (Prensky & Thiagarajan, 2007), despite the insensitive other-ing of our children this term conveys. This representation of students portrays them as having some kind of online omniscience that adults cannot possess. It ignores the fact that students themselves vary widely with regard to computer and mobile phone competency and access, not to mention wide-ranging needs in terms of both online and offline literacies (Leander, 2008; Leander & Zacher, 2007). We might want to think, for instance, that good readers online are good readers offline, but it simply is not the case (Purcell, Buchanan, & Friedrich, 2013). We might want to think that popular software-powered technologies like video games lack pedagogical use, yet there is compelling evidence to the contrary (Gee, 2007). We might want to think that poorer students lack Internet access, but that fails to be so simple as well (Madden, Lenhart, Duggan, Cortesi, & Gasser, 2013). What we do know is that 93% of children between the ages of 12 and 17 report having a computer or access to a computer at home, and 74% of the same population say they access the Internet on cell phones, tablets, and other mobile devices at least occasionally (ibid.). We also know that teachers overwhelmingly report using technologies in their own lives and for finding curricular resources, yet it doesn't translate into instruction with anything near the same frequency (Purcell, Heaps, Buchanan, & Friedrich, 2013).

When considering our students' relationship with software-powered technologies, we must resist the temptation to compartmentalize children's in-school and out-of-school practices. We must also be careful not to conflate the two. Research on students' sense of identity demonstrates that how students perceive and represent themselves online can differ greatly with how they represent themselves offline (boyd, 2006, 2007). Offline, however, does not refer to a singular space: it includes at home, at school, and in social settings (Vasudevan, Schultz, & Bateman, 2010). Some students negotiate the use of software-powered technologies and identity in savvy ways when they create multiple social network accounts, one for friends and one for prospective colleges. Other students demonstrate a lack of common sense and kindness using software-powered technologies like when we read about instances of bullying online.

Educators

Teachers are increasingly required to engage with software. According to Pew Research, 92% of teachers report that the Internet has a "major impact" on their accessing content, resources, and materials for teaching (Purcell, Heaps, et al., 2013). And yet, only 62% of teachers surveyed said their schools do a "good job" supporting efforts to integrate technology into the learning process. The same report shows that teachers of low-income students are more than twice as likely to cite students' lack of access to digital technologies as a "major challenge." As mentioned above, the move toward data-driven instruction has required embedding certain software-powered technologies in educational settings. In terms of basic roster management, it is not uncommon for teachers to use email, digital gradebooks, and networked attendance systems. In addition to managing student information, teachers have also been encouraged to use software-powered technologies in their classrooms, ranging from digital whiteboards to tablets and apps to web-based sites and resources. The list goes on.

Research on teachers' use of software-powered technologies routinely conclude that teachers need immense support in order to use technology well and that pedagogical purpose must drive its use. Studies have demonstrated that the potential benefit of software-powered technologies is contingent on the teacher's ability to integrate them pedagogically (Meier, 2005). Whereas there exist frameworks for supporting teachers in such integration, like SAMR (Puentedura, 2013) and TPACK (Koehler & Mishra, 2009), both lack explicit accounting for the active nature of software raised by software theorists. In addition, even in the case where a teacher is open to using software-powered technologies in the context of a coaching framework, there always exists the danger that the devices and networking infrastructure will fail and relegate the pedagogue to the unproductive role of technician (Sandholtz & Reilly, 2004).

Teachers are also encouraged to turn to software as a way to develop their professional capacity. Online learning has been used for professional development for many years with some success when implemented in authentic contexts and frequent facilitation (Whitehouse, Breit, McCloskey, Ketelhut, & Dede, 2006). Another example is the growing use of video-recording of teacher practice (Vetter & Schieble, 2015). We see this trend in teacher education where new performance assessments require teaching candidates to record themselves teaching and upload the video clip to private and state servers. Further, online repositories of teaching videos have become increasingly available not only from private professional development companies but also openly available on the web.

Leaders

Being a school leader today demands at least some awareness of the role that software-powered technologies play (Lengel, 2012). A school leader has to be familiar if not fluent in various software applications to schedule classes, maintain a budget and make purchases, track student achievement and teacher performance, maintain attendance records, and more. In some schools many of these functionalities are combined into a single application. In other settings, these actions are completed in different systems that do not inter-operate—some new and some legacy—each with its own interface. Importantly, the data that are capture by these systems are often fed to districts and states. In addition, leaders of schools, or their technologists, have to manage backend software that makes the network infrastructure of their school possible. Leaders are responsible for ensuring that server rooms remain cool enough for the equipment to function, that their buildings receive networking upgrades, and that the devices they have are systematically taken care of and updated regularly.

In the last decade, there has also been an increased use of software to compile and disseminate public reports of schools' performance. Under the banner of transparency and data-driven instruction, two hallmarks of the neoliberal reform agenda, school leaders must now use analogue technologies like rubrics to translate the complexity of teaching and learning into data for digital technologies like information systems. Whereas there are merits to using data to inform instruction, the conditions under which such gathering occurs colors the activity. When one of the purposes is for districts and states to publish "report cards" of schools' "performance" we have reason to pause.

IN SUM

Pedagogical and administrative spaces have become software spaces. This should not be surprising as most of society seems touched by software. What it means to teach, to learn, and to lead today necessitates interacting with software-powered technologies. A question remains: What is it that actually happens in software space and how do researchers conceptualize it in order to ask different questions about the role of software in education?

SOFTWARE SPACES

Software spaces refers to a multi-layered assemblage that includes physical devices and hardware, the user interface that we encounter when interacting with devices, various programming languages or code, and information systems and databases. Each of these components have epistemological and pedagogical effects, both individually and when considered in concert.

Devices

We are growing accustomed to negotiating multiple devices as part of our lives and work. The *device* refers to the physical object that we engage with in order to access the digital world. These include tablets, laptops, desktop computers, mobile devices, e-readers, clickers, interactive whiteboards, and others. By devices, I also mean the operating software necessary for a device's basic functioning. When one opens a laptop, for instance, there is pre-installed software that allows the device to boot up. Whereas there are often other applications pre-installed as well, we will treat these as beyond basic and separate. Also included under this category are other physical elements that we must or may use like cameras, microphones, keyboards, track pads and mice, gyroscopic sensors, motorized vibrators, speakers, batteries, and peripherals like headphones.

We should also consider related physical attributes. The durability of a device is of great importance, for instance, when studying their use in schools. So too is the speed with which devices charge and drain. In addition, the size of devices is important. For example, I worked with a new school in New York whose students were overage and under-accredited. Whereas the principal boasted of students each having their own laptops, he neglected to notice that many of the 19-year-olds had hands too big for the small netbooks. Screen size is also relevant as it can be difficult for users to read on screens that are too small or poorly lit. When new requirements for Common Core computerized testing were announced, it was worth noting that the minimum screen size happened to be the standard size of iPads—although one could argue whether students should be taking extended high-stakes exams on new devices that had not been field tested at scale nor that all students would be familiar with. Finally, the weight of devices can impact students' comfort (Musti-Rao, Lynch, & Plati, 2015) as well as the care with which they are handled and used in classrooms.

Network Infrastructure

Increasingly, even basic devices require Internet connectivity to fully function. Connectivity is necessary for devices to hook into school and district information systems. Despite popular perception of a wireless world, the fact is that wireless systems are inherently reliant on wires and associated hardware. When working with schools in iLearnNYC, I was surprised to learn that the quality of a schools' Internet connectivity relied greatly on the very physical cable running under the sidewalk. This telecommunications cable connected to the school building's cables, to servers, to more wires, to splitters, to routers, and to wireless access points. If a wire was sliced, connectivity fizzled. If the server room was too hot, the network slowed to a crawl. Providing wireless connectivity means using a lot of wires and drilling holes all over the place.

In addition to the physicality of the infrastructure itself, the ability of groups of students to connect wirelessly to the network often frustrated educators. The access points used in city schools at the time could comfortably handle about 15 users at once—less than half the number of students, for instance, in many secondary city classrooms. A teacher who didn't know this inherent bandwidth limitation was likely to instruct all students to go online at once, which I often witnessed. Further, all connectivity in a school occurs through the main cable provided by a telecommunications company and which splits off from the street. There is a bandwidth economy that exists in schools about which educators appear to know very little. If some staff members stream videos or music throughout the day, they unknowingly steal bandwidth that could be used for learning. In urban school buildings that house multiple smaller learning communities, negotiating the logistics of bandwidth utilization is often an inelegant and ineffective dance.

Interfaces

Interfaces come in many forms. For our purposes, I will use the term to refer only to graphic *user interfaces* or UIs for short. UIs are the visualizations we see on screens when engaging with software-powered technologies. They are often designed with great intentionality and consist of various elements, including text, images, video, boxes, links, buttons, menus, and more (Murray, 2011). Users submit their selections (their commands for computer systems) through the interface in the form of text entry and clicks. The interface provides coherence, that is, it offers a visual narrative for users to engage with the complexity of software, which in its raw form is indiscernible to human beings and entangled in complex assemblages.

Some have explored how UIs have at least two distinct and related purposes, one of narrative coherence and another of meta-narrative function referred to as an *intraface* (Galloway, 2012). The clearest example is in immersive video games where the primary narrative interface is related to that of, say, a hero's quest while the meta-narrative intraface displays information about the hero and quest like a map for navigation or amount of energy remaining. It should be noted that UIs are under constant development, many prototypes not consisting of a traditional screen or buttons at all. In newer popular interface like touch screens, we have witnessed the move from links, clicks, and scrolling as the main components of interface use to now also include taps, swipes, rotations, and zooms.

Code

Code is an essential part of software-powered technologies and, as a word, can have multiple meanings. As mentioned above, code refers to many kinds of languages. Berry (2011) does a helpful job of categorizing a few different kinds of code for analytical purposes. He refers to source code, prescriptive code, critical code, commentary code, digital data structure, digital streams, and code objects. "Code is processual," Berry writes, "and keeping in mind its execution and agentic form is crucial to understanding the way in which it is able to both structure the world and continue to act upon it" (p. 40). We will draw on such categories and concepts as useful to our purposes, but will always come back to the actions and epistemologies code enables and encumbers in educational settings. Note, however, that Berry's categories of code are not the same thing as the programming languages we might hear about like JavaScript, Python, C, Ruby, and such. Different programming languages can be used to meet different coding needs across categories.

Our discussions will critically address the ontological nature of code, which might be considered intimidating to some readers. To be clear, I myself am not an expert in code. A distinct field referred to as code studies is something I've consulted, but cannot contribute to directly or meaningfully. We can, however, learn enough about the nature of code—what it is, how it behaves, how it is made—to enlighten us about its contribution to the software-powered technologies we see growing rapidly in education. I draw on concepts from my home discipline, English education, which can be helpful to apply to software studies. Code refers to languages, after all. It fundamentally refers to a complex act of writing and reading, to textuality. Compare it to reading poetry. One can learn to read a poem, to be moved by it, and to critically discuss it with a certain kind of support. A linguist would have a valuable expertise to contribute to the reading of the poem, as would a poetics scholar as would a historian. But one does not need to be a historio-linguistic-poetics professor to engage productively with the text.

Information Systems

There has been growing interest in the explicit role of data in schools, including the prevalence of terms like "transparency," "performance," "achievement," and "data-driven instruction." These words all point to the idea that we can measure elements of education quantitatively and can render that measurement to others for both public and private purposes. Less explicit is the role of information systems, which comprise the essential infrastructure that allows data to flow within schools, districts, states, and beyond. Information systems operate according to what Manovich (2001) calls *database logic,* which means they deftly store data for rapid retrieval, algorithmic alteration, and feeding. Along these lines, I have argued that rubrics are increasingly being used not as devices to clarify conversations with students and teachers, but as analogue technologies used to *transcode* the complexity of pedagogy for input into information systems (Lynch, 2014, 2015a, 2015b). Information systems read data input and a transaction occurs that has effects in our world.

Berry (2011) helps us identify another element of information systems, which he refers to as *streams*. As human users continue to engage with software-powered technologies, they generate an immense amount of user data. He adds that software-powered technologies themselves also automatically generate user data about human users. The result is that unprecedented amounts of data are being created, requiring companies and governments to create massive data farms to store all the information. Because software plays such an active role in our lives, in sanctioned and unsanctioned ways, there are now ubiquitous and rhizomatic streams of information about us created constantly. To consider the role of information systems in education, we must be prepared to conceptualize these streams of information software creates, including how information is generated, for what purposes, for whose purposes, and to what effect.

SOFTWARIZATION AND EDUCATION

What does this mapping of the landscape mean for education? for educational research? As software is infused into education for pedagogy, assessment, and administration we run two risks. First, we risk that what it means to teach and learn will be bent toward the kinds of things that software can do well, ontologically. It is well documented that tensions between teaching and technology emerge when software-powered technologies are attempted to be used in classroom settings (Buckingham, 2008; Cuban, 1986, 2001; Koehler & Mishra, 2009; Meier, 2005). Second, we risk that the creation and implementation of technology at a large scale will inherit the assumptions about teaching and learning that those who produce and promote software possess. In short, if politicians and product development teams think teaching means making students consume predetermined content we will see a push toward software-powered technologies that resemble lectures and textbooks. As we do, sadly. The fact is that software space has certain ontological characteristics with which educational researchers should become more familiar. In what follows, I explain some of the characteristics.

Mediation and Shaping

Software is ubiquitous; it "mediates and shapes" (Berry, 2011) lived human experience in both macro and micro ways. One way to consider the ubiquity of software is to identify cases where software malfunctions, thereby revealing its presence. Consider the example of Y2K. When the new millennium approached, the world caught a glimpse of how computational logic works. As *Wired* magazine recalled, the fear "was that older computers still being used for critical functions might break down when the date switched from 99 to 00, since the numeric progression convention, programmed to store data using only the last two digits of any given year, wouldn't recognize the logic of a century change" (Long, 2009). For the months and weeks leading up to the new year, companies as well as individuals scrambled to update software hoping to avoid a digital catastrophe. The idea that computers could not properly process the change from 99 to 00 was something the average person hadn't likely considered. Why would they have? Wall Street has seen its share of software glitches costing companies and stockholders large sums of money. In 1993, trading on the stock market halted for an hour because a squirrel chewed through vital cables that powered NASDAQ. Without power, trading could not proceed. Twenty years later, the Dow plunged 1% for several minutes because of the aforementioned tweet (Maureen, 2013). In 2013, the Obama Administration implemented its healthcare.gov web site, the purpose of which was to help uninsured Americans secure low-cost insurance policies as a result of health care legislation reform. The web site, however, could not handle the number of people visiting and crawled to a stop. The news media's attention to the site only increased traffic, slowing it down even further. Eventually, the president reached out to private sector software expertise to help fix the issues. *Time* magazine reported, "In about a tenth of the time that a crew of usual-suspect, Washington contractors had spent over $300 million building a site that didn't work, this ad hoc team rescued it and, arguably, Obama's chance at a health-reform legacy" (Brill, 2014). The healthcare. gov site relied heavily on sophisticated integrations with myriad insurance companies' information systems. The company contracted to build the site made early (and frequent) errors in their development and like the heel of Achilles brought the reform effort to its knees.

Software also betrays itself in more subtle and mundane ways. The autocorrecting of text messages is something that has sparked a cult following online, with thousands of mobile phone users posting screenshots of the silly and sometimes offensive things their phones' algorithms autocorrect and send (Lynch, 2013). It is also not uncommon today to encounter trouble with one's automobile that requires bringing it to a mechanic who, after looking briefly under the hood, hooks the car's computer up for a diagnostic. I use credit cards for most of my purchases and a plastic mass transit card for the subway—both of which require software to function properly. As do most subways systems, for that matter. Manifold examples are possible to list here, which represent the ubiquity of software. But ubiquity is not the same thing as mediation. How does software mediate and shape lived experiences?

When software mediates experience, it shapes it. Software converts the complexity of the phenomenal world into data for the world of the computer in a process referred to sometimes as softwarization, quantification, or digitalization. Consider what happens when one takes a digital picture. Light sensors capture and convert light waves into digital form, which is represented in both code and via a visual representation presented on a screen to users. The picture is in many ways an illusion insofar as it exists as a file unreadable to human beings. It is this inhuman representation, ironically, that makes the photo so social and shareable. Berry (2011) warns us, however, that "Something of the detail is always lost when moved from the phenomenal world to the discrete world of the computer. Digitalisation is therefore the simplification and standardisation of the external world so that it can be stored and manipulated within code" (p. 54). In the case of taking and sharing pictures, we settle for a two-dimensional visual representation of something that, as lived experience, includes three dimensions and all five senses. Others in software studies might add that it is not just representations of the world that are affected by software, so are our actions as human beings. Kitchin and Dodge (2011) state, "Behavior is therefore necessarily reshaped to make it more amenable to capture in order to fulfill the essential requirements that make a system work" (p. 89). Everyday examples of human behavior bending to the needs of software can easily be observed: we change the way we speak when using speech recognition software, we stop and wait for doors to automatically open for us, we drive dangerously because we want to read text messages, we stare at our phones in unfamiliar cities because the map it depicts seems somehow more believable than the actual city that surrounds us, we rely increasingly on our thumbs to type for us, we follow the life events of friends with a keener eye because it streams before us, we endure lifeless presentations because templates provided by software companies have become a default mode of thinking, we type one perfect letter at a time because most of our writing has to eventually be digitized, and on and on. It is quickly clear *that* software mediates lived experience. What is less evident is *how*.

Software mediates and shapes lived human experience through computational assemblages that comprise what I call *software space*. As Berry (2011) writes, "Software is a tangle, a knot, which ties together the physical and the ephemeral, the material and the ethereal, into a multi-linear ensemble that can be controlled and directed" (p. 3). Untangling software space requires naming its interlocking knots. Software space consists of devices, networking infrastructure, user interfaces, code, and information systems (see Figure 2.1). The relationship between these different layers is not necessarily sequential, although it is often the case that we as users interact with devices that are (eventually) connected to the Internet, using UIs to tell the device and its applications what we want it to do. The UI masks a world of computational gibberish to the average user—like coding languages and information feeds—that are responsible for making the device and applications do what we wish. The movement across software space happens at a rapid pace. Its rapidity, made possible by the fundamental numerical quality that undergirds computer processing, makes software's effects somewhat illusory. In Berry's words, the "quantitative speed of computer processing gives rise to a qualitative experience of computers as miraculous devices" (2011, p. 38). It is this miraculous quality that software studies aims to identify and inspect.

First, software quantifies and categorizes lived experience as data. In his discussion of the use of software in conducting elections, Berry writes, "Translating political rights into digital technical code is not a straightforward process, requiring as it does a set of normative assumptions and practices to be turned into linear flow of binary code that the computer can execute computationally" (ibid., p. 108). This process of translation demands that someone—often programmers and business people—take what is a complex human phenomenon and re-articulate it as discrete behaviors that can then be represented as functions and arguments. As referenced earlier, those "normative assumptions and practices" are not just hidden from users because they are written in unfamiliar and greatly invisible languages, but they are actively masked by the deceptive visual simplicity of user interfaces. Second, software organizes, stores, retrieves, and shares data via information systems. As lived experience is digitized in various ways—taking pictures with cameras, swiping credit cards, posting status updates on social networks—we generate data that get structured, stored, algorithmically manipulated, and fed to other information systems. Our lives are constantly being translated for databases. Manovich (2001) argues that database logic is replacing other ways human beings collectively experience the world. He writes, "The world is reduced to two kinds of software objects that are complementary to each other—data structures and algorithms. . . . Together, data structures and algorithms are two halves of the same ontology of the world according to a computer" (p. 223). Consider, for instance, when you fill out a form online. Each field you complete is predetermined. What you type is stored in digital folders where it can be retrieved as rapidly as needed. Third, software applies algorithms and functions to data and returns data feeds to both users and other information systems. A simple example of this is the widespread use of filters on pictures. When one takes a picture with one's mobile phone, it is not uncommon to be offered a series of filters to apply to the image: sharpen the picture, erase red eyes, or make it look vintage. These filters represent algorithms that can be applied to the digital data stored on your device that represents the picture. Because the digital picture is fundamentally numerical, it is quickly subjectable to mathematical calculations that create certain effects. Or, on the more complex end of the continuum, most of us have experienced commercial web sites that offer uncanny recommendations to us based on previous browsing and purchases. Web sites gather user data on us each time we visit and click around. If analyzed well, the data can be used to automatically customize our future visits. If our interests change and we begin viewing or buying new kinds of products, algorithms are adjusted and the recommendations we see change. I often muse to my wife, for instance, that our streaming video service thinks we are a four-year-old boy because our son prefers watching shows on our computer. Our recommendation queue is lined with cartoons. Finally, software begets software (Berry, 2011). What this means is that as more and more of our world becomes mediated by software, and more data are created that relates to us, it becomes impossible to make sense of such data without new analytical software to do so. Similarly, as we engineer more and more complex software systems that integrate with each other, there develops a need for special software to manage the complexity. It is an often overlooked irony of software in our world: The more it appears to simplify our lives, the more complex software space becomes.

Human-Computer-Human Interfaces

When we examine the ways software renders lived experience it behooves us to acknowledge two interlocking characteristics: the rapidity with which software space functions and the way we experience composite renderings as coherent final products. Berry (2011) raises questions about the speed of software space when he writes, ". . . technology's ability to speed up the exchange of information to such an extent that critical thought itself might become suppressed under the quantity of information" (p. 150). This results in a "fast moving technological culture that privileges data streams over meaning . . ." (p. 167). The significance of the speed at which software operates is something the average user has encountered. We grow impatient when we click on links that don't immediately load. We grunt when attempting to watch an online video and it stalls. Beyond inconvenience, Berry suggests the speed of software affects our ability to think critically, falling victim to data streams. A second characteristic of software space is what Manovich (2001) refers to as *composites*. Manovich has in mind what he calls new media objects, digital products created and disseminated through software like digital art, video, and music. For example, a film we experience in the theater is a composite of myriad different layers, including film, animation, special effects, audio tracks, and so on. Even new media that appear to be monomodal like music recordings are composites. The song we listen to is a composite of various tracks that have been separately recorded, algorithmically manipulated, and rendered in composite form as a single coherent song. In both cases, we must be sensitive to that which software space renders to us. The combination of rapidity and composites can lead users to be dazzled by software-powered technologies. The same combination makes it challenging to slow down and unpack what effect software has on our lives, creating a sleight of hand that we seldom recognize and resist.

Despite its technical appearance, software is flawed and unstable, created by human beings whose ideologies and pedagogies are encoded into it. Kitchin and Dodge (2011) capture software's humanity well: ". . . software needs to be theorized as both a contingent product of the world and a relational producer of the world. Software is written by programmers, individually and in teams, within diverse social, political, and economic contexts. The production of software unfolds—programming is performative and negotiated and code is mutable" (p. 43). A very public example of the flawed nature of software development came to light with the release of healthcare. gov. Within days of its failing to work properly, it quickly came to light that the company that developed the software made myriad errors rendering the site unusable. Such errors are common in software of any kind, but when they go unchecked and fixed they build upon each other and make repair all the more challenging. Unlike other technologies where an error might be more immediately visible—for instance, the wheel on the car that is clearly loose—software errors can exist in multiple places, across different programming languages. What was once a fractured cog in a machine is now a misplaced comma in thousands of lines of code. As the above excerpt suggests, the tenuous nature of programming is compounded by the fact that it is seldom one person doing the work. Software is developed by teams with experts in different languages and parts of the puzzle. Interpersonal errors of communication are as likely as errors in code. What's more, it is common practice for software development teams to rely on libraries of pre-created blocks of code available in online programming communities. Updates to blocks of code, or any other update or tweak, can set off a chain reaction of errors. Berry conducts interesting studies that attempt to uncover the human influence in software development. For instance, he notes that the source code for the voting software mentioned above refers to voters as "he," a clear nod to the gender of the programmer and his assumptions about who is voting. In another analysis, Berry examines software used by Microsoft that was leaked online. The notes programmers left for each other in the millions of lines of code provide a glimpse into just how human software engineering is. For instance, one coder wrote a berating message in the source code demeaning colleagues who, in his or her mind, fail to practice prudent version control and revisions: "If you change tabs to spaces, you will be killed! Doing so f*cks with build process!" (Berry, 2011, p. 69).

Software theorists raise concerns regularly about this human-computer tension. On the one hand, software appears to be objective, neutral, and purely functional. On the other hand, software's ability to perform is directly reliant on users aligning their desires to the predetermined options programmers encode. It is this concern that prompts Berry (2011) to write, "So, when one views the world computationally, one is already comported towards the world in a way that assumes it has already been mapped, classified, digitised" (p. 123). Berry's use of "it has" hides the fact that human beings program computers and it is their view of the world—as individuals and as programmers—to which users are subjugated. Consider times you have navigated a web site or an app and "just wished" the software would provide different options or let you do something from which you are prevented. In these moments, it is not often necessarily a limitation of software but rather of those who design and code it. For example, why can users not see who has viewed their profile in Facebook? This is something many users might want to know. (Those same users might change their minds upon reflection given their own viewing habits.) It is a simple feature, one that many other services enable. Facebook's decision not to make profile views available to users is not the result of a technical limitation. It is a business decision. Keeping with Facebook, many users will recognize the familiar frustration of seeing posts from some "friends" more than others. Despite my own frequent attempts to hide the updates of some connections, I still receive their posts in my stream. With some posts, I am bombarded by memories and feelings associated with people. These feelings are not ones I intentionally sought or requested. My memories are triggered by algorithms that Facebook controls and from which Facebook seeks to profit. It is not in the company's business interest to allow me unfettered control and comfort on their site. The more they can subtly push me to recall old friends and connect with them, the more valuable their data, analytics, and advertising are. Manovich (2001) echoes this sentiment when he writes, ". . . we are asked to follow pre-programmed, objectively existing associations. . . . We are asked to mistake the structure of somebody else's mind for our own" (p. 61). To add to Manovich, it is not simply the structure of someone's mind we are asked to mistake. We are asked to conflate our individual desires with both the ontology of software and the ideologies of the businesses who produce and promote it. In software space, we are surrounded by unforgiving technical standards and guided by the forethought of programmers who are often instructed what to do by business owners. It is true that ". . . behind the freedom on the surface lies standardization on a deeper level" (Manovich, 2001, p. 197). The deeper the standards, the greater the profits.

Control from a Distance

As I have alluded to already, programmers must be able to predict the variables users can input. This is a simple truth of software engineering. Scholars in software studies, as we have seen, are aware and critical of this ontological necessity. There are two main parts to understanding the need for predeterminism. The first is information systems; the second is what Manovich (2001) calls the *logic of selection*. Programmers have to determine in advance the kinds of data they will accept from users and how that data will be stored, retrieved, manipulated, and shared with other systems. Each of these considerations is a field of study on its own. For our purposes, note that the kinds of data users can and cannot enter into a computational assemblage is controlled in order to make software space viable. For example, when New York State began requiring its school districts to feed data to state-level information systems in order to be shared with the third-party company inBloom, the company provided extensive documentation about what kinds of data it would receive and how it would be organized. Whereas we will look at this case in greater detail in the following chapters, a brief sample will illustrate how information systems and the logic of selection work. One of the data domains inBloom provides is called the Discipline Domain. The domain exists to receive and structure data related to disciplinary incidents associated with students. As a student, I might have gotten into a fight in a stairwell that was broken up by school safety officers and which was documented formally by the officers and school administration. In order for information systems to structure and render usable data associated with such incidents, developers have to predetermine what kinds of data it will receive, which they refer to as *entities*. One of these entities is called *DisciplineIncident*. Within DisciplineIncident, there are over 15 attributes like date of event, location, and weapon type used. For each attribute, developers provide a description of the attribute and delineate the kinds of data that are permitted to be associated with the attribute. In the case of the attribute *weapons,* the acceptable data—called *enumerations*—are listed in the order that follows: firearm, illegal knife, non-illegal knife, club, other sharp object, other object, substance used as weapon, knife, unknown, none, and other. There are two important points to take away from this cursory example. First, what is a complex human phenomenon like a fight in school is broken down into discrete elements in order to be entered into an information system. It is driven by database logic, that is, the needs of databases determine the kinds of information gathered and reported. Second, we must consider how data are entered into software space. In the case of a student being disciplined for a fight in school, there is a moment at which a human being reports the incident through an information system. That human being, who is likely an administrator or law enforcement officer, will have to type information into predetermined text boxes and select other information from drop-down menus, lists, or buttons. These features—text boxes, menus, lists, buttons—are how developers control users' actions in favor of the needs of the database.

Software space relies on a logic of selection to ensure that the will of users aligns with the ontology of software. When our safety officer, for instance, enters information about the type of weapon used in a fight, she will not be given the opportunity to enter in the information herself. If, by mistake, she was to misspell the word *knife,* the information system would not be able to process that data easily. Because of software's ontological need for precision and predefinition, we frequently encounter menus, links, lists, and buttons when interacting with software. Our safety officer might be given a drop-down menu from which to select the weapon that was used in an incident. The order in which those options appear is not neutral, however. Whereas an alphabetical list might suggest some objectivity, in the case of weapon types above we see that *firearm* is listed first, *no weapon* is offered near the bottom of the list, and there are three different kinds of *knives* suggested. We will explore the significance of such lists elsewhere, but for the moment it is important to understand that something as seemingly neutral and innocuous as a list provided for a disciplinary report looks the way it does because of a need developers perceive on behalf of software space and how the average user is coaxed to meet that need by interacting with a UI.

Further, buttons are a site of study that has received some analytical attention in software studies. Pold (2008) describes buttons as both emulating the familiar—the act of pressing a button in the physical world—while simultaneously masking the complexity of software space. A button conveys certitude in what is otherwise an ephemeral digital world. When we click a button, we commit ourselves to a decision. Despite the fact that the button is a mere graphic and that the clicking sound it might make a counterfeit sound, users take solace in acting with confidence. It is illusory, but satisfying. Further, the simplicity that the button represents is necessarily false. When, for example, a user clicks a button to purchase a book on a web site, clicking the button masks myriad realities: legal agreements, return policies, the submission of credit card information, metadata about what else the user looked at or previously purchased, and the sharing of the purchase via social media. In some cases, companies use buttons to trick users into purchasing items they may have no desire to buy. Children's tablet applications are a perfect example. My son is fond of apps, especially ones that include his favorite television show characters. It is not uncommon for him to tap an oversized button that redirects him to purchase other products or services. In some apps, a pop-up window appears and contains a small and awkwardly placed button to close it. Much more prevalently placed is the "Buy" button. Fortunately, he does not know how to spell very well nor can he remember my password (yet).

Another example is the default templates provided by popular office software. In her analysis of presentation templates, Adams (2006) argues that the default ways users are encouraged to frame their ideas steers them away from complex narratives and toward pithy summaries and pictures. As a consequence of such templates, she argues, professional cultures that rely on such modes of communication have epistemological blind spots. Adams provides a case in point: "The *Columbia* Shuttle disaster demonstrates the tragic consequences possible here. Critical information presented in a series of PowerPoint slides by NASA engineers to executive decision makers was lost in a sea of significance and, thus, insignificance. Information was broken into points within points of significance through nested bullets" (p. 407). Technically speaking, there is nothing preventing a user from writing complex narrative slides for presentation. Complexity, however, is not what the templates solicit from users. Just a point and a picture, please.

Unoriginal Creativity

There emerges from software space a strange paradox. On the one hand, the ontology of software seems predisposed to limit human beings' original and creative choices. And yet, on the other hand, we use software-powered technologies to create a great deal of creative media. How are we to understand this? Kitchin and Dodge (2011) remark that "While proficiency with software tools may be a requirement in certain creative industries, their use does not mean creativity will happen. Much of the output of even the most sophisticated software is often ordinary and derivative" (p. 121). Manovich (2001) echoes this sentiment, writing ". . . by encoding the operations of selection and combination into the very interfaces of authoring and editing software, new media 'legitimizes' them. Pulling elements from databases and libraries become the default; creating them from scratch becomes the exception" (p. 130). Again, when users create presentations in PowerPoint it is not uncommon to rely on the default templates provided. In fact, companies provide templates not only for where information and images should be placed, but also include "smart art" tools that are intended to make it easier for users to create conceptual visualization. This feature has pre-created flow charts, concentric circle diagrams, and dozens more. Software theorists would argue that these kinds of features, which are ostensibly intended to make creating presentations easy and efficient, actually have the effect of shaping users' thinking and in doing so the kinds of knowledge created both for the person presenting as well as the audience. In other settings like film and television production, there exists a separate industry that creates elements for production companies. These companies might create several different kinds of high definition oceans or swaying wheat field elements. Production companies purchase these elements and manipulate them for their own projects. When the average viewers watch a movie, they seldom realize how what they experience as coherent and seamless is a composite of very separately produced components. The same applies to music recording. As referred to above, it is common practice when recording drums in a studio to put a separate microphone on each drum and cymbal. By isolating each component, whether the digital graphics in a movie or sounds in a musical recording, it is possible to use software to manipulate each element before assembling the whole. These digitizations of lived experience are rendered into code and stored in a computer. They are fundamentally ones and zeros. And yet, they can be rendered back to human beings in a manner with which we relate. I have attended live concerts at which I'm moved by a singer. How is it that I can be also moved by a singer that has been digitized and rendered through software space? In these cases, lived experience travels through software space and is rendered livable again. Film serves as another case in point. When one goes to the movies, one experiences a rendering of software space that took many years, people, software applications, and funding to create. The output is often decisively human. Films evoke sentiment from viewers, moving one to tears, laughter, or outrage. Some films have launched political outcry and action. Somehow, in these cases, software is used so that it transcends the sum of its parts. Any framing of software space would be incomplete without explicitly examining the way in which its ontology relates to the epistemologies it enables.

This raises the question: How does human creativity overcome the ontology of software, which fundamentally demands unoriginality? Music recording serves again as an example. Imagine you have a fantastic song you wrote. When you perform it for others, we can say with some confidence that you are being creative. When you go to the studio to record it, your creativity enters software space. Your sounds are digitized, separated, stored, retrieved, and manipulated by algorithms via the UI of music production applications. In this fragmented digital form, we can say that your creativity has been translated for software or transcoded. If your song remained stored in databases or as a fragmented music file, we might argue that your creativity had been co-opted by software. However, when software space is used not only to digitize but also to reassemble your song in another coherent form that extends its original creative purpose, we can say software has been used to further creativity. Manovich (2013) alludes to the act of rendering in his discussion of the numerical representation as an intermediary. He writes:

> How did we arrive at this new situation where instead of looking at or reading content directly, most of us always experience it through the layer of applications? The seemingly obvious answer is the adoption of numerical code as the new universal intermediary. I call it intermediary because in order to make media accessible to our senses, it has to be analog— a travelling wave of oscillating pressure which we experience as sound, the voltage levels applied to the pixel elements of an LCD which makes them appear as different colors, different amounts of dyes deposited on paper by dye-sublimation printers, and so on. Such conversions from A to D (analog to digital) and D to A (digital to analog) are central for digital media functioning. . . . (p. 153)

For Manovich, to critically consider software space is to question how software renders data (digital) back into sociocultural settings (analogue). It is important to note in the musical example that part of what makes this process successful is the fact that when sensors and software capture and digitize your voice, the loss of quality is perceived as relatively minimal. You record your voice and it sounds like your voice when replayed. If for some reason the recording sounded nothing like the original performance, we would blame software and get rid of it. When we render the complexity of lived experience out of software space, we have to be careful that what software space renders to us furthers our best intentions.

Tracks of Silicon

Software space is a space of paradox: It creates the illusion of freedom by limiting human beings' interactions. Berry (2011) writes, "Computationality tends towards an understanding of the world which, whilst incredibly powerful and potentially emancipatory, cannot but limit the possibilities of thought to those laid within in the code and software which runs on the tracks of silicon that thread their way around technical devices" (p. 169). When engaging with software space, we feel free and marvel at the conveniences made possible through technology. But the freedom and convenience is possible only because we submit to a view of the world that aligns with the ontology of software and predetermined paths of software developers. Further, whereas we might experience software as a uniquely intangible digital phenomenon, it is in fact reliant on touchable chips, wires, and gadgets. Kitchin and Dodge (2011) conceptualize *code/spaces,* which refer to social settings that rely on software to exist. Let us examine some of these spaces to illustrate the paradox described above in action. We'll look at a mass transit system and a ubiquitous feature in web-based searching.

Taking the A Train

Mass transit systems have become coded/spaces: Without software, they cease to perform their purpose. In New York, gone are the days when slipping a token into the turnstile yields admission to the subways. I purchase a plastic transit card once a month. At the subway station, I tap on a computerized machine that guides me to choose the transit card type I want, it accepts my credit card or cash, and issues the transit card. I then walk to the turnstile where I swipe my transit card and, hopefully, am granted entrance. It doesn't always work. One morning, I swiped it multiple times because it didn't read accurately and eventually flashed a message saying I had already used it. When I went to the service booth—many of which have been closed in the name of efficiency—the person behind the glass accused me of using my card to let another rider through the turnstile. Whether because of the look on my face or the tone in my voice, I was eventually permitted to enter through a special gate. When it works, the software-powered transit system is supposed to be more convenient and efficient. When it doesn't work, though, it quickly becomes clear the ways in which software exerts power over me. In the case of purchasing a transit card, the screen presents me with only certain options to purchase. I cannot, for example, buy a card for three days; the increments are set at one day, one week, or one month. There is no technical reason for these options. A group of people I shall never know determined that only those options would be necessary. When I swiped my newly purchased card and it didn't work, I became aware of the ontology of software physically restricting my freedom. Likely the result of uncleaned scanning equipment, software misread my transit card and automatically accused me of something that was simply untrue. The message, which read "Just used at this turnstile," was not accurate. And yet, an unmovable steel bar blocked my entry. Software forced me into a choice: jump the turnstile and risk arrest or appeal to the human being in the booth. In choosing the second option, however, I encountered a person whose understanding of the situation was limited to the way software space rendered me. Still, in this case, if the software used to sell and verify transit cards crashed most riders could step over the turnstile and still get to the platform. This example is a corporeal one in which what software mediates is my ability to physically (and legally) enter the mass transit system. If software crashes at a massive scale, the train themselves would be unable to run. Next, we consider software's effects on sociocultural activity its effects are more subtle.

Searching for Shoulds

On October 19th, 2013, I typed the words "Teachers should" into a Google search box. The company uses a feature that automatically predicts what users are looking for based on what other users previously searched for and clicked on. Below the search box, a dropdown list presented the top searches of other users who typed the same search words on that day. The top three results read: 1) Teachers should be paid more, 2) Teachers should be seen and not heard, and 3) Teachers should be armed. When I conducted the same experiment on April 15th, 2014, the search words yielded different results: 1) Teachers should be paid more, 2) Teachers should be armed, and 3) Teachers should not be armed. What does this change in results suggest about the relationship between software space and society? First, we have to infer the algorithmic logic that makes the results appear. Google tracks what hundreds of millions of people search for throughout each day. Not only does the company provide search results, but they refine their algorithms based on the way different sites are labeled and connected with other sites as well as which links users click on after users have searched for specific terms. Whereas the process seems incredibly objective and mathematical, there are additional factors we should note. For example, Google filters its results to control for pornography. Also, Google "customizes" its results based on users geographic location and previous searches and it is unclear whether search results are, by default, tied to the user's country. In short, what appears to be neutral is not. When I conducted the "Teachers should . . ." experiments, I opened a new browser window in what is called Incognito mode, a method of browsing the Internet in which a user's browser provider does not employ various tools for tracking one's searches. The idea is that by using Incognito mode I would get results from Google that did not reflect all that Google already knows about me.

The results on both days suggest something about the zeitgeist of the English-speaking world, certainly the United States. They suggest that teachers are regarded ambivalently by the computer-using public. On the one hand, teachers appear to be perceived as worthy of better pay. On the other hand, it seems that the public is fixated on a very different kind of debate: whether or not teachers should be allowed to carry guns in schools. Based on my own experience, these results suggest a public interest in two major phenomena in education: the force of education reform that calls teacher pay into question and a tragic list of school-related violence, most notably the Sandy Hook massacre in December 2012. In this example, software space appears to offers individual users free choice to search for whatever they wish. And yet, not only do the eventual search results stem from aggregated data of millions of other users over time, but Google seeks to influence the act of searching itself and gets eerily close to telling users *what they should want* to search before they complete their terms. The individual is forced to consider the populace through the company's algorithmic magic.

SUMMARY

The ubiquity of software means that it increasingly mediates and shapes human experience. It is a concept that is challenging to understand for some, in part because of the speedy, subtle, and invisible ways software operates in our world. Software theorists make it very clear that in order for software to be of use to human beings, it demands that the complexity of lived experience be distilled into simpler data for input and manipulation. To use software is to submit to its ontology. Such a submission is sometimes quite worth it: the convenience of using mobile phones, doors that open automatically, and merchandise that is recommended to us for purchase with increasing relevance. To be clear, those conveniences demand that we submit to software: the sound waves of our voices are captured and digitized, our bodies' movements are captured by sensors, and our every click is being tracked when online. To rely on software—knowingly or unknowingly—is to be rendered readable to software space. Above, I attempt to present software space as a concept, situated within political, economic, pedagogical, and administrative spaces. Most of my examples, however, are intentionally unrelated to education and focused more broadly on general experiences. Education is a complex area of study and merits its own examination, to which we now turn.

WORKS CITED

Adams, C. (2006). PowerPoint, habits of mind, and classroom culture. *Journal of Curriculum Studies, 38*(4), 389–411.

Berry, D. (2011). *The philosophy of software: Code and mediation in the digital age.* New York: Palgrave Macmillan.

Bloomberg, M. (2013, February 14). Mayor Bloomberg delivers 2013 state of the city address. The Official Website of the City of New York. Retrieved January 16, 2014, from www1.nyc.gov/office-of-the-mayor/news/063-13/mayor-bloomberg-delivers-2013-state-the-city-address.

boyd, danah. (2006, February 19). Identity production in a networked culture: Why youth heart MySpace. *American Association for the Advancement of Science,*

St. Louis, MO. Retrieved December 15, 2014, from www.danah.org/papers/talks/AAAS2006.html.

boyd, danah. (2007). Why youth (heart) social network sites: The role of networked publics in teenage social life. In D. Buckingham (Ed.), *Youth, identity, and digital media volume* (pp. 119–142). Cambridge, MA: MIT Press.

Brill, S. (2014, February 27). Obama's trauma team. *Time*. Retrieved December 15, 2014, from http://time.com/10228/obamas-trauma-team/.

Buckingham, D. (2008). *Beyond technology: Children's learning in the age of digital culture*. Maldan, MA: Polity Press.

Christensen, C. M., Horn, M. B., & Johnson, C. W. (2008). *Disrupting class: How disruptive innovation will change the way the world learns*. New York: McGraw Hill.

Cuban, L. (1986). *Teachers and machines: The classroom use of technology since 1920*. New York: Teachers College Press.

Cuban, L. (2001). *Oversold & underused: Computers in the classroom*. Cambridge, MA: Harvard University Press.

Fang, L. (2011, December 5). How online learning companies bought America's schools. *The Nation*. Retrieved December 28, 2012, from www.thenation.com/article/164651/how-online-learning-companies-bought-americas-schools.

Fishman, C. (1996, December 31). They write the right stuff. *Fast Company*. Retrieved January 16, 2014, from www.fastcompany.com/28121/they-write-right-stuff.

Galloway, A. (2012). *The interface effect*. Malden, MA: Polity Press.

Gee, J. P. (2007). *What video games have to teach us about learning and literacy*. New York: Palgrave Macmillan.

Kitchin, R., & Dodge, M. (2011). *Code/Space: Software and everyday life*. Cambridge, MA: MIT Press.

Kliff, S. (2013, October 5). A techie walks us through healthcare.gov's two big problems. *The Washington Post*. Retrieved January 16, 2014, from www.washingtonpost.com/blogs/wonkblog/wp/2013/10/05/a-techie-walks-us-through-healthcare-govs-two-big-problems/.

Koehler, M., & Mishra, P. (2009). What is technological pedagogical content knowledge (TPACK)? *Contemporary Issues in Technology and Teacher Education, 9*(1). Retrieved December 15, 2014, from www.editlib.org/p/29544?nl.

Leander, K. M. (2008). Toward a connective ethnography of online/offline literacy networks. In J. Coiro, M. Knobel, C. Lankshear, & D. J. Leu (Eds.), *Handbook of research on new literacies* (pp. 33–65). New York: Lawrence Erlbaum Associates.

Leander, K. M., & Zacher, J. C. (2007). Literacy, identity, and the changing social spaces of teaching and learning. In L. S. Rush, A. J. Eakle, & A. Berger (Eds.), *Secondary literacy: What research reveals for classroom practice* (pp. 138–164). Urbana, IL: NCTE.

Lengel, J. G. (2012). *Education 3.0: Seven steps to better schools*. New York: Teachers College Press.

Long, T. (2009, December 31). Dec. 31, 1999: Horror or hype? Y2K arrives and world trembles. *Wired*. Retrieved December 6, 2014, from www.wired.com/2009/12/1231-y2k/.

Lynch, T. L. (2013). Pecs Soviet and the Red Underscore: Raising awareness of software's role in our schools. *English Journal, 103*(1), 128–130.

Lynch, T. L. (2014). Holy interfaces and the sanctity of software: A critical software analysis of rubrics as vehicles of conservative reform. In M. Tenam-Zemach & J. Flynn (Eds.), *A rubric nation: A reader on the utility and impact of rubrics in education* (pp. 125–141). Charlotte, NC: Information Age Publishing.

Lynch, T. L. (2015a). Reassessing how we "see" students: The blessing and blight of rubrics (and software) in education. *English Journal, 104*(3).

Lynch, T. L. (2015b). Spreadsheets and sinners: How and why English teachers can claim their rightful place in STEM education. *English Journal, 49*(3).

MacKenzie, A. (2006). *Cutting code: Software and sociality*. New York: Peter Lang.

Madden, M., Lenhart, A., Duggan, M., Cortesi, S., & Gasser, U. (2013). *Teens and technology 2013*. Pew Research Center. Retrieved December 15, 2014, from www. pewinternet.org/Reports/2013/Teens-and-Tech.aspx.

Manovich, L. (2001). *The language of new media*. London: MIT Press.

Manovich, L. (2013). *Software takes command*. New York: Bloomsbury Academic.

Maureen, F. (2013, April 24). Twitter flash crash fueled by high speed trading. *CNN Money*. Retrieved January 16, 2014, from http://money.cnn.com/2013/04/24/investing/twitter-flash-crash/.

Meier, E.B. (2005). Situating technology professional development in urban schools. *Journal of Educational Computing Research, 32*(4), 395–407.

Murray, J.H. (2011). *Inventing the medium: Principles of interaction design as a cultural practice*. Cambridge, MA: MIT Press.

Musti-Rao, S., Lynch, T.L., & Plati, E. (2015). Training for fluency and generalization of math facts using technology. *Intervention in School and Clinic*.

Obama, B. (2013, February 12). Remarks by the president in the state of the union address. The White House. Retrieved January 16, 2014, from www.whitehouse.gov/the-press-office/2013/02/12/remarks-president-state-union-address.

Picciano, A. G., & Spring, J. (2013). *The great American education-industrial complex: Ideology, technology, and profit*. New York: Routledge.

Pold, S. (2008). Button. In M. Fuller (Ed.), *Software studies: A lexicon* (pp. 31–36). Cambridge, MA: MIT Press.

Prensky, M., & Thiagarajan, S. (2007). *Digital game-based learning*. St. Paul, MN: Paragon House.

Puentedura, R. (2013, October 2). SAMR: A brief introduction. *Ruben R. Puentedura's Weblog*. Retrieved January 16, 2014, from www.hippasus.com/rrpweblog/.

Purcell, K., Buchanan, J., & Friedrich, L. (2013). *The impact of digital tools on student writing and how writing is taught in schools*. Pew Research Center. Retrieved December 15, 2014, from www.pewinternet.org/Reports/2013/Teachers-technology-and-writing.aspx.

Purcell, K., Heaps, A., Buchanan, J., & Friedrich, L. (2013). *How teachers are using technology at home and in their classrooms*. Pew Research Center. Retrieved December 15, 2014, from http://pewinternet.org/Reports/2013/Teachers-and-technology.

Ravitch, D. (2013). *Reign of error: The hoax of the privatization movement and the danger to America's public schools*. New York: Knopf.

Rosenberg, S. (2008). *Dreaming in code: Two dozen programmers, three years, 4,732 bugs, and one quest for transcendent software*. New York: Random House.

Sandholtz, J.H., & Reilly, B. (2004). Teachers, not technicians: Rethinking expectations for teachers. *Teachers College Record, 106*(3), 487–512.

Vasudevan, L., Schultz, K., & Bateman, J. (2010). Rethinking composing in a digital age: Authoring literate identities through multimodal storytelling. *Written Communication, 27*(4), 442–468.

Vetter, A., & Schieble, M. (2015). *Observing teacher identities through video analysis*. New York: Routledge.

Whitehouse, P.L., Breit, L.A., McCloskey, E.M., Ketelhut, D.J., & Dede, C. (2006). An overview of current findings from empirical research on online teacher professional development. In C. Dede (Ed.), *Online professional development for teachers: Emerging models and methods* (pp. 13–29). Cambridge, MA: Harvard Education Press.

3 A Critical Imperative for Software Studies in Education

"... there is always a shadow side in American culture—an uncaring, separatist aspect too many associate with freedom—and I believe we must take the shadow into account when we educate and when we think of reform."

—Maxine Greene in "Social Vision and the Dance of Life," *Releasing the Imagination*, p. 67

In spring 2014, my wife and I learned that our son had been accepted into kindergarten. Upon reading the notification email, we breathed a long-awaited sigh of relief. After an intense year of scanning web sites, school visits, and filtering parental gossip, this was no minor feat for any New York City parent. The Bloomberg-Klein administration had restructured New York City public schools in an effort to provide parents with school "choice." The administration undertook the disintegration of large comprehensive schools into smaller ones, multiple schools occupying single school buildings, and creating an elaborate world of selection where the responsibility to provide quality public education was subtly shifted from the city to parents. This labyrinth consists of different types of schools. There are default "zoned schools" that are geographically nearest to families, although not always deemed by parents as safe or adequate. There are "screened schools" scattered around the city, each with idiosyncratic requirements for acceptance: cognitive tests, mock-playdates, music auditions, and so on. There are gifted and talented programs within schools that claim to be for the few and the truly gifted, but seem to ever-expand their offerings to accept the socioeconomically advantaged families who prepare their children for the admissions tests. Schools deemed ineffective are closed as new small schools are opened. Parents considering sending their children to a new school must accept the fact that the school has no record of success to consult. The process for enrolling one's child in city public schools is Odyssean, filled with twists and turns that would drive Odysseus himself to send Telemachus to private school in Troy.

During this time, New York State was in the throes of implementing its education reform agenda. In K-12 settings, this meant increased teacher evaluation and a battery of standardized exams aligned to the Common Core Standards. The morale in schools was low and anxiety was high. School principals my wife and I met attempted to assuage parent worry that their children—who were not yet five years old—would be subjected to mindless test prep. Parental concern grew as news stories aired on public radio about kindergarten students failing exams because they could not understand they shouldn't help classmates who seemed to be struggling with a question.

Software did not create the political conditions of which I speak. But software powers them: computerized exam scoring, kindergarten placement determined by "fair" algorithms that reconcile the "choices" of thousands of families, and various types of software applications foisted upon schools promising to revolutionize education through information systems and "innovations" like online learning. Although the momentum of the early 2000s might be unique, these kinds of education reforms have been examined for many years. In what follows, I explore how education scholars frame their concerns, which some refer to as neoliberal education reform, especially the role that technology plays in it. I add to the conversation concepts from software theorists as a way to suggest the establishment of *critical software studies,* a line of inquiry that inspects the hidden ways issues of ideology, power, and inequity are encoded in educational software spaces.

CRITICAL IMPERATIVES IN EDUCATION

One of the hallmarks of neoliberal education reform is the tethering of social institutions to the logic and well-being of the economy. When implementing its Race to the Top program, the Obama Administration defined the purpose of education in the context of economic recovery. They did not issue a public, explicit definition. Their definition is implied. Funding for Race to the Top comes as part of a bill intended to salvage a crashing economy, the American Recovery and Reinvestment Act of 2009. In fact, President Obama often situates the education section of his State of the Union addresses within economic themes. In 2012, he transitions from discussing job creation to education: "These reforms will help people get jobs that are open today. But to prepare for the jobs of tomorrow, our commitment to skills and education has to start earlier. For less than 1 percent of what our nation spends on education each year, we've convinced nearly every state in the country to raise their standards for teaching and learning—the first time that's happened in a generation" (Obama, 2012, para. 34). In 2013, the president again sets up his education section in response to economic needs: "These initiatives in manufacturing, energy, infrastructure, housing—all these things will help entrepreneurs and small business owners expand and create new jobs. But none of it will matter unless we also equip our citizens with the skills and training to fill those jobs. And that has to start at the earliest possible age. Study after study shows that the sooner a child begins learning, the better he or she does down the road. But today, fewer than 3 in 10 four year-olds are enrolled in a high-quality preschool program" (Obama, 2013, para. 46). For the Obama Administration, the primary purpose of education is to fix and sustain the economy, which includes putting job placement and corporate partnerships at the forefront of their reform strategy. The Common Core Standards are written, we are told, to ensure "college and career readiness." The much-touted P-Tech high school models referred to in the previous chapter require district, university, and corporate partnerships. In addition, the reform agenda places a premium on using data to make educational decisions, partnering with different kinds of software and technology companies to store, retrieve, analyze, and act upon data. I experienced this firsthand as an English teacher in Manhattan when—under the Bush Administration's No Child Left Behind legislation—the city rolled out its $80-million student information system called ARIS, which teachers were expected to use to look up "achievement" data for students and into which teachers were to upload periodic assessment data. The span between a presidential address and the daily life of a Manhattan English teacher felt vast.

And yet, the connection between the two is very real, daily, and personal. Bridging the span requires identifying and examining what Rebecca Rogers (2011) calls the "dialectic between individual agency and social structure" (p. 7) through the narratives or discourses we use. In her introduction to critical discourse studies in education, Rogers describes an analytical approach to discourse that is "problem-oriented" and "recognize[s] that inquiry into meaning making is always also an exploration into power" (p. 1). As I argued last chapter, software mediates and shapes not only our written and spoken modes of communication, but also more computational modes of communication like the use of data. To consider software studies in educational spaces necessitates a critical stance, one that treats seriously the "recursive movement between linguistic and social analysis" (p. 13) and embraces software space as a complex assemblage where human and computational modes of communication converge. A presidential address is not simply bellowed atop tree stumps and mountainsides. The speech is composed, shared, reviewed, and streamed on teleprompters in software space. It is transcoded into video and audio streams for television, online, and radio. Our responses to the speech are tracked and analyzed in real time via sentiment analytics. It is preserved in archival spaces as a digital transcript and video. Policies like Race to the Top that are framed in such speeches are not printed on paper for school officials to read. They are described and hyperlinked to additional resources online. They are talked about on Sunday morning political shows. They require districts to ramp up their use of technologies to create, store, share, and render data. They require schools to purchase hardware to speed up Internet connectivity and devices for all students, despite the fact that there is little evidence for how to effectively implement such technologies in educational settings—despite a naive "orthodoxy of optimism" (Selwyn, 2014, p. 18) that surrounds our public conversations about technology in education and the "paucity of critique" (p. 11) technology receives from the academy.

The Democratic Purpose of Education

If you listen closely to the conversations between educators, administrators, policy makers, and the business community, it is not uncommon to hear different assumptions about the purpose of education. I have conducted exercises at meetings where I ask a table of educators and school officials to write on an index card their two-sentence response to the question: What is the purpose of public education? Upon collecting the anonymous responses, I read each one aloud. The disconnect amongst the definitions nearly always shocks the table. My stance is this: Public education must primarily be concerned with helping create a literate, creative, critical, and civically engaged citizenry. All curricular and instructional decisions must serve this complex single end.

Others articulate the purposes of democratic education better than I and it is with their articulations in mind that I have stated my own. They are concerned not only with democratic education in the abstraction, but also about the ways in which it is compromised to promote short-sighted economic gains. Philosopher Martha Nussbaum (2010) concisely and clearly expresses her concern, writing "the demands of the global market have made everyone focus on scientific and technical proficiencies as *the* key abilities, and the humanities and the arts are increasingly perceived as useless frills that we can prune away to make sure our nations . . . [remain] competitive" (italics original; p. 133). The tension to which Nussbaum draws our attention is between the humanities and sciences, qualitative and quantitative, letters and numbers, the soft and the hard. When a president, for instance, bookends his administration's stance on public education with economic policies he declares to school officials to begin sharpening their shears. When he endorses and forces the adoption of national standards for "college and career" but not other things like community and civic engagement, he sounds the opening bell: let the cutting commence. The result of this narrow privileging Nussbaum describes is dire for democracy. She writes, "Education based mainly on profitability in the global market magnifies these deficiencies, producing a greedy obtuseness and a technically trained docility that threaten the very life of democracy itself, and that certainly impede the creation of a decent world culture" (p. 142). As Nussbaum alludes with her words "obtuseness" and "docility," an essential characteristic of democratic education is the need to teach young people to create meaning by critically engaging with the world around them. One iconic example of this practice is what she calls

Socratic pedagogy. Socratic pedagogy is the practice of systematically and actively engaging all students in the critical examination and construction of knowledge. The deceptively simple ability to speak and listen, write and read with critical acumen and humane empathy for others is one that demands rehearsal often as our children ease into public and global stages. However, as the purpose of education is co-opted by those who believe education is in peril and can only be healed by applying the saving salve of the market-place, we come to place economic ends before our highest educational ones. The sad result, Nussbaum writes, is the lustful implementation of standard-ized tests and "an impatience with pedagogy and content that are not eas-ily assessed in this way" (p. 48). We aspire toward Socrates and accede to standards.

A democratic education must value otherness: other opinions, other gen-ders, other races, other others. This kind of education demands collaboration, community, and safe environments in which one takes risks to understand the complex world of the unfamiliar. Michael Apple (1996) warns that in the name of national interests and reform, we experience something opposite democracy. He writes that reformers succeed in "shift[ing] the blame for unemployment and underemployment, for the loss of economic competitive-ness, and for the supposed breakdown of 'traditional' values and standards in the family, education, and paid and unpaid workplaces, *from* the economic, cultural, and social policies and effects of dominant groups to the school and other public agencies" (italics original; p. 28). His insight is profound. In the name of all things patriotic and good, agents of reform turn their rhetorical and legislative weapons on public institutions themselves in an act of societal self-hate. We will explore this more closely below. What is important to cap-ture here is that the tension Nussbaum (2010) examines between education and economics stems from a comparable tension between public services and private enterprise, democracy and capitalism. The former demands col-laboration and debate, the latter demands individualism and consumption. Capitalistic education privileges a "parade of facts" over "critical thinking and imagination" (p. 89). It is a form of "aggressive nationalism [that] needs to blunt the moral conscience . . . it needs people who do not recognize the individual, who speak group-speak, who behave, and see the world, like docile bureaucrats" (p. 23). The result is that we define the success of our schools by scores of inauthentic and expensive exams rather than students' ability to imagine original questions that improve the lives of themselves and others. As the authors above suggest, to consider democratic education today is necessarily to make explicit the hidden and ubiquitous role of com-mercial influences.

A Neoliberal Economic Crisis Spawns an Education Crisis

One of the most visible critical voices of education reform is Diane Ravitch (2013), education professor and activist who has loudly protested attempts

to "reform" education through economic logic. She writes, "Public education is a basic public responsibility: we must not be persuaded by a false
crisis narrative to privatize it" (p. 9). The crisis to which Ravitch refers
amounts to coordinated discursive efforts by conservative, liberal, and corporate entities to frame schools as unequivocally failing, the country falling
perilously behind economically, and pointing the finger squarely at inadequate curriculum and instruction, an accusation that begs to be remedied
by the development and sale of better products to schools and the disem-
powerment of educators. "Almost overnight," she writes in reference to the
reform movement, "consultants and vendors offered their services to advise
districts and states on how to design teacher evaluation systems, how to
train teachers, how to train principals, how to turnaround failing schools,
how to use new technologies, how to engage in data-driven decision making, on and on" (p. 15). Ravitch's examination focuses on what she calls the
"Bush-Obama reform," adding that "Race to the Top was only marginally
different from No Child Left Behind. In fact, it was worse, because it gave
full-throated Democratic endorsement to the long-standing Republican
agenda of testing, accountability, and choice" (p. 15). The reform narrative
of which Ravitch speaks are told by different people in different positions in
society, from political speeches to newspaper stories to dinner table conversations, that the failure of the American economy is both the fault of schools
and that schools must change to fix their error.

The crisis narrative is comprised of what Peter Taubman (2009) calls ". . .
the drumbeat, the arrogant surety, and the tendentious rhetoric of educational policy" (p. 57). This is not the drumbeat of a single drummer leading
a charge. It is the omnipresent and disorienting thump of a rave. Driven by a
blind faith in commercialism and logic of the market, neoliberal reformers
speak words that betray a "mercenary intent" (p. 5) and offer "the appar-
ent objectivity of quantification" (p. 6) through a battery of standards,
metrics, and assessments. That the standards are created, at least in part,
by commercially minded individuals and implemented through lucrative
partnerships with private companies is difficult for the public to hear. The
drumbeat is too fast, too loud. Taubman refers to the pulsing and numb-
ing effect of what others have called *audit culture,* one in which educators
are offered solace from the drumbeat by accepting the value of standards
and accountability and aligning their craft to the predetermined language
of standards, rubrics, and assessments. He summarizes the effect: "Audit
culture's assumption that if it can't be measured, it doesn't exist, and neoliberalism's assumption that the only good identity is an entrepreneurial
one, lure teachers into sacrificing their autonomy, inner life, and political
engagement for the promise of certainty, professionalism, and local celeb-
rity" (p. 146). The problem with the neoliberal stance in education, Michael
Apple (1993) might add, is that it "assume[s] that by expanding the capital-
ist marketplace to schools, we will somehow compensate for the decades
of economic and educational neglect experienced by the communities in

which these [struggling] schools are found" (p. 19). By linking education so closely to the economic discourse, reformers frame our economic anxiety as the fault of poor schooling and, consequently, rising from the ashes of economic collapse means radically changing the way education looks. One might be quick to point out that despite the clear culpability that banks possess in the economic crisis, they have remained mostly unchanged and unadmonished. Despite their rhetoric, the government has left alone those institutions that actually caused the economy to collapse due to their own dishonesty and recklessness with other people's money. Education, however, has been subjected to aggressive and at times unethical intervention by the government, yet the direct role of educational institutions in the economic collapse is tangential and dubious. If the drumbeat is incessant and sure, the lyrics we hear are not simply lies. Rather, they are ideological and partially true-sounding enough to make for easy listening, relatable to fact. Apple writes, "Ideologies, properly conceived, do not dupe people. To be effective, they must connect to real problems, real experiences" (p. 20). When the stories we see on the news and read in the paper are ones of students performing poorly on tests, of teachers caught in misconduct, and of the relentless efforts of reformers to move schools out of the 19th and into the 21st century, we find ourselves nodding along to the realness of sound bites. When one considers the glaring lack of an organized and popular counterpoint—that is, other than a few exceptions, educators have no loud and public critical response to these discursive attacks—it is unsurprising that the neoliberal cause has been so successful and well funded. Although Apple often repeats the mantra that "reductive analysis comes cheap" (p. xii), it is nevertheless astonishingly profitable. This is especially true when it comes to software-powered technologies, reformers arguing that if our schools are not injected with new technologies they cannot possibly be preparing young people properly, which means readying them for the workforce.

The Cry for Technology

Education reformers position technology as a silicon bullet for fixing schools. There are two main ways technology serves the neoliberal cause. First, if a key theme in the reform discourse is that education is somehow responsible for economic struggle, then it follows to restructure education to be more economically aligned and efficient by ensuring technologies are used to streamline organizational processes and make data available to educators or to replace at least some of educators' work if possible. Second, if technology is seen as pivotal in preparing students for the workforce, then flooding curricula and instruction with technology can be rationalized as benefiting student achievement. If educators are marginalized in the process, neoliberal reformers are at peace with that. Technology, however, is not some purely functional thing. Its complex ontology and epistemological effects escape meditation, not only by reformers but by researchers as well.

Educational technology is commonly referred to in "alarmingly one-dimensional terms" (Selwyn, 2014, p. 6). We are led to believe that solving the perceived problems in education is a simple matter of breaking down firewalls and letting data mingle. Technology is discussed in terms that are deceptively innocuous and matter of fact: We live in a digital age, therefore we need not debate the merits of technology anymore than argue about the benefits of air. Those who do oppose the rise of technology too often do so in "generally unconvincing and alarmist terms" (p. 9) and serious critical scrutiny of technology in education escapes us. The discursive drumbeat carries on undaunted and ". . . what is said about something eventually *becomes* that thing" (italics original; p. 24). This is the case, Selwyn argues, whether we are talking about trends in virtual learning, "open" education movements, video gaming, and social media. The discourse in favor of such initiatives consists of simple-sounding truths that, when left uncritiqued, sow deep roots. In part, the orthodoxy of optimism surrounding technology fits easily in education circles because of the affinity between progressive education and recent technological trends. Selwyn writes: ". . . many people's interest in educational technology is underpinned by a dominant set of values stemming from progressive education ideals and/or social constructivist and sociocultural models of learning—all of which privilege learner-centered and learner-driven forms of education" (p. 32). I found this certainly to be the case working with iLearnNYC. Our materials and pitches were peppered with words like "personalization" and "student-driven" learning. What principal or educator could argue with the need to make students' education more personal? In a fast-paced district with dozens of daily meetings that start late and end early, there was little time to examine the fact that the personalization we could provide was based on watering down curriculum and instruction so students could "'fit' themselves around the coded contours" (p. 86) of online courses and tools designed by software developers and company executives. These technologies that are embraced so broadly and easily "plac[e] education firmly in the midst of the immaterial 'new' economy—standardizing and commoditizing education, reducing educational processes and relationships to forms that are easily quantifiable and recorded, distancing educational professionals from the process of educational engagement and thereby deprofessionalizing and deskilling the teaching profession" (p. 62). It was a sad irony that began to haunt me in my work: Educators embraced the technologies we offered with enthusiastic allusion to Dewey and Freire, unaware that in the name of personalization they were schooling their students in computational compliance.

To tease out the role technology plays in the reform discourse we have to look at the interplay between analogue and digital technologies. That is, we must move beyond the gadgets we see and focus equally on the paper-based devices used to reap data from human experience as well as the information systems and applications used to render data back into the world. Taubman (2009) draws attention to this when he notes that "to realize these [reform] goals a sophisticated data system needs to be put in place" (p.65). He adds that "Once best practices are agreed on, and their demonstration can be measured, teaching emerges as work that can be chopped up, exported, and . . . digitized" (p. 116). As I discussed previously, the drive to collect, store, share, and render data in educational spaces is a defining characteristic of the Bush-Obama reforms. We generate data by chopping up the complex act of teaching and learning into discrete elements that can be quantified and digitized, often using tests and rubrics. We experience this phenomenon via instruments that are implemented in school settings, what Taubman calls assemblages: "The loose connections among standards, check sheets, offices that aggregate the data, the technologies that are used, the supervisors and student teachers, the reports generated, the feedback produced by the reports, and the actions taken as a result, all these creates assemblages" (p. 123). We'll explore more deeply how these analogue instruments function within assemblages. For now, I will briefly highlight the importance of what might appear at first blush a mundane and non-technological point from my experiences with analogue technologies with teacher candidates.

One of my roles in the university is to supervise preservice teachers in classrooms. When I visit a classroom, I sit in the back of the room with a rubric in my hand. As I observe the teacher teaching, I check boxes and scribble notes about what I see. In that act, what I do is not wholly my own nor is it only for my dialogue with the teacher. Rather, I act as an agent of institutional forces. The language of the observation rubric has been mostly predetermined. Not by me. But by others who work for a national organization of which I know very little and whose motives and pedagogical beliefs are not necessarily mine. Still, I check a boxes and circle numbers. The numbers will be entered into a data system—I myself have done the data entry, uncomfortably and soundlessly—and the complex act of teaching and learning is made quantifiable. Once the data have been entered into the system, another assemblage takes over: a computational assemblage that comprises software space. Educational researchers and critics must examine not only the analogue assemblage of which Taubman speaks, but also its digital extensions. Critical software studies aims to do precisely that work.

The Need for Criticism and Bifocality

Before framing critical software studies in greater detail, I wish to return to Rogers's "dialectic between individual agency and social structure" referenced above. The work of the critical scholar must be to examine and make explicit the often hidden ways in which the macro impacts the micro. This has been referred to in different ways by different scholars, for example Gee's (1999) distinction between Discourses and discourses. Another way to frame the dialectic is in terms of *critical bifocality* (Weis & Fine, 2012), which is defined as "a dedicated theoretical and methodological commitment to a bifocal design documenting at once the linkages and capillaries of structural arrangements and the discursive lived-out practices by which privileged and marginalized youth and adults make sense of their circumstances" (p. 176). At its core, critical bifocality addresses the "swelling inequality gaps both within and among nations and aggressive neoliberal inscriptions on public education policy and practice" (p. 173) by exposing the "structural architecture of the problem" (p. 175) and the ways human beings are systematically dispossessed.

Allow me a relevant illustrative example.

Weis and Fine (2012) describe a study Fine conducted in which a large comprehensive high school in New York City was being "phased out" and broken apart into a series of smaller schools as part of neoliberal reforms implemented by Mayor Bloomberg and Chancellor Klein. Fine describes a community meeting where interested and concerned members of the public could learn about the transition plan and ask questions. She writes that "soon the discursive architecture of separate and unequal was flooding the room, being spoken by White and Black prospective parents who seemed to be among the new gentrifiers" (p. 192). As described in the introduction to this chapter, parents wanted to know how children would be offered admission to the new schools. A city representative responded that "any child would be welcome to the school. . . . They will submit attendance, grades, and test scores and the computer will choose those who are eligible" (ibid.). Fine insightfully notes, "As a lottery, the process is fair, but all of the preconditions are coated in relative privilege" (ibid.).

The idea that "the computer will choose" sits at the crux of critical software studies. The computer does not choose. The computer computes based on programs human beings provide for it. Behind such personification lies hidden human actions that perpetuate inequity and promote those already with power. There are two ways I have experienced how this works: as a parent and as a coach in the city. Parents who wish to apply to schools in the city must have the time off of work and a certain level of both cultural and traditional literacy skills to navigate the labyrinth the city has created. As of 2014, parents did not simply provide basic information to a computer and receive a fair and equal assignment. Rather, parents who are able to visit schools for multi-hour school tours are given additional weight in the algorithm the city creates. In addition, schools have parameters set by the district regarding which applicants are privileged in the selection process, including siblings and those who come from specified gerrymandered regions (often made up of parts of several neighborhoods). Finally, when the time comes to enter one's choices into the city's computer system, I was disturbed to see subtle ways the user interface had been designed to trick users into giving additional consideration to their "default" school and to charter schools. Pop-up prompts nudged parents to reconsider their preferences in favor of the ones faceless officials desired.

In addition to personifying the role of the computer, there are other ways officials mislead the public about how truly beneficial and fair the school selection process is. When I left the classroom in 2009 to join iLearn-NYC, I spent six months as an "innovation coach" for three new schools. While at the time the city had over 1,500 schools, it happens that the three new schools with which I worked were in the same building as where Fine conducted her study. It was a common complaint in the schools I worked in that as brand new small schools they were left out of the massive directory of schools the city provided to communities. Many new principals were unable to provide all the necessary data for their school to appear in the main catalog of schools read by parents and students. The result was that the new schools, which were to be symbols of choice and reform, actually became default locations for students and families who did not participate in the selection process at all. In two of the schools I worked at the time, there was a disproportionate number of students with English language learning needs and both formal and informal (dis)abilities. The small schools were not given the resources to support these students.

To consider the role of software-powered technologies in education is necessarily a critical endeavor. It must be bifocal. For all we see and experience knowingly of technology in education, there is much more beneath the surface and its presence and actions are masked by one-dimensional discourses. As we have seen, educational technology is positioned as the handmaiden of economic prosperity: We must teach our students to learn with technology because it is a 21st-century skill and we must inject our education system with administrative technologies so we can recode pedagogy into concrete data that will enable us to measure pedagogy and control it from a digital distance. Examining the role of technology in education means deepening our theoretical and methodological perspectives, turning our critical bifocal gaze to software.

A CALL FOR CRITICAL SOFTWARE STUDIES

It is no surprise that an education reform movement that emphasizes the creation and use of data as a way to better prepare young people for a digital and global economy views as essential the use of software-powered technologies for both administrative and pedagogical purposes. As I conveyed in Chapter 2, software space is positioned ubiquitously as a mediator and shaper across political, economic, pedagogical, and administrative spaces. That is, my focus has been on describing the elements of software space, how they interplay, and some of the critical issues we should be aware of generally. When it comes to educational software spaces, we must examine more closely—and critically—both the structural and the lived effects of software on pedagogy.

There are perhaps multiple ways to go about this work. I do so drawing on the critical voices above. That is, I am interested in how the instruments of which Taubman speaks constitute an institutional assemblage that feeds into computational assemblages in software space. Further, in the spirit of Michael Apple, we must unpack the hidden ideologies and commercial logics that are encoded in software space and, when they do surface, might appear to us as familiar and unsurprising "interactions" with software. Critical software studies must build upon previously articulated theories and methods of critical discourse analysis, braiding traditional language-based discourse analysis with a broadened definition of discourse to include not only software itself but the instruments that are required for its functioning in education as well as the visual ways in which we are presenting software space in the form of user interfaces and renderings. Our challenge in critical software studies is to systematically traverse not just the structural and the lived experiences in education—district policies and linguistic discourses surrounding school choice reform, for instance—but to account for the infrastructural as well, that is, the computational assemblage that is automating neoliberal reforms into the daily fabric of our lives. In what follows, I explore the ways software space mediates and shapes the complexity of teaching and learning.

POLITICS, COMMERCE, AND THE SOFTWARIZATION OF TEACHING

The Push for New Teacher Evaluations

A key reform goal articulated in Race to the Top is to push states to change their policies related to teacher accountability (Gorlewski & Porfilio, 2013; Ravitch, 2013). Specifically, the federal administration calls for "Recruiting, developing, rewarding, and retaining effective teachers and principals, especially where they are needed most" (U.S. Department of Education, 2010, n.p.). Secretary of Education Arne Duncan expresses confidence that if the government can "get rid of firewalls separating student achievement data from teachers" ("'Meet the Press' transcript for Nov. 15, 2009," 2009) they can "reward states that publicly report and link student achievement data to the programs where teachers and principals were credentialed" (U.S. Department of Education, 2010, n.p.), which will lead to better teacher preparation, teaching, and learning—and economic outcomes. The rationale for focusing intently on individual teacher effectiveness lies in the belief that teachers are primarily responsible for whether or not all students learn, graduate from school, and contribute to the economy. For example, the president folds the following lines into his 2012 State of the Union: "We know a good teacher can increase the lifetime income of a classroom by over $250,000. A great teacher can offer an escape from poverty to the child who dreams beyond his circumstance." Despite the political tone of benevolence and common economic sense, there was great resistance to the federal push for states to implement new evaluation systems, putting what some viewed as unfair weight squarely on the shoulders of teachers.

In New York, the state required all districts to choose a teacher evaluation framework and submit an acceptable implementation timeline that aligned with its benchmarks. (It's worth noting in passing that the state's own timeline was glaringly tied to election and funding cycles rather than a patient and realistic sense of the Herculean nature of the task.) New York City's teachers union—the United Federation of Teachers (UFT)—resisted adoption of an evaluation framework to the point that the governor's office had to intervene with a mediator (Cramer, 2012). Eventually, like most other districts in the state, New York chose Charlotte Danielson's framework for effective teaching (Danielson, 2013) as its evaluation schema. As UFT President Mulgrew Miller later admitted publicly, his resistance to the effectiveness framework was less rooted in the actual framework but rather in the ways it would be used politically by those in power. To an auditorium of 3,400 union representatives—out of over 100,000 members—Miller confessed, "It was a strategy decision to gum up the works because we knew what their lawyers were trying to do. . . . That's things I don't get to say in public when I'm doing them, because we knew they had a plan to use the new evaluation system to go after people" (Short, 2014). Similar political battles played out in districts across the country. That is, despite the possibility of using an evaluation framework to support the professional growth of educators, many educators feared the political and ideological motivations behind it would undermine their professionalism.

Measuring Teachers' Performance

Let us look more closely at Danielson's *Framework for Effective Teaching*. The framework was created in 1996 when Danielson, whose background is in economics, worked for Education Testing Services (ETS). She perceived a need for clearer standards of teaching. The resultant framework consists of 4 domains and 22 components, each of which is ranked on a continuum: Ineffective, Developing, Effective, and Highly Effective. When New York City began piloting the framework, it chose specific competencies to focus on in an effort to avoid inundating administrators and educators with too much at once. In the 2012–2013 school year, for instance, schools were encouraged to focus on three components: designing coherent instruction (1e), using questioning and discussion techniques (3b), and using assessment in instruction (3d). In its intended form, the framework appears to focus on relevant aspects of pedagogy and might provide a shared language in professional and supportive conversations.

When the framework was officially assented to by the union following state-intervention, a host of additional issues emerged that betray the neoliberal motives of reformers. First, whereas the original evaluation framework is qualitative in nature, numerical values were assigned the four quality levels. A teacher did not receive an *effective* designation, a teacher received an *effective (3 points)*. Second, politicians and reformers required the use of standardized tests in determining a teacher's effectiveness. Rather than thoroughly relying on a robust (even if imperfect) qualitative framework to determine teachers' effectiveness and professional learning needs, test scores were regarded as a necessary and harder measurement of student "achievement" and, as a result, teachers' efficacy. Tests are the bottom line. Distrust of the commercialized state tests led to the proposal of also including "locally-selected measures." In the end, the 2013 UFT contract evaluated teachers according to three metrics—observational teacher evaluation (60%), state tests (20%), and local measures (20%)—on a continuum from *ineffective (1 point)* through *highly effective (4 points)*.

The math is deceptive.

Whereas it appears that the majority of the evaluation consists of teachers being evaluated by their supervisors, it is not quite so simple. A footnote in UFT materials ("Getting started with the new teacher evaluation and development system," 2013) clarifies that upon official implementation, the ratings for use of the Danielson framework were converted from a 1–4 point scale as mentioned above to a 60-point scale. If this conversion was done evenly, it would have resulted in the following logic: highly effective (46–60), effective (31–45), developing (16–30), and ineffective (1–15). Ineffectiveness, in short, would be limited to 25% of the framework. However, the conversion agreed to in negotiations results in this logic: highly effective (55–60), effective (45–54), developing (39–44), and ineffective (1–38). In reality, then, the UFT agreed to an observation framework that more than doubles the ineffectiveness category, which makes up 63% of the adjusted framework. When simple numerical calculations result in such eyebrow-raising breaches of fairness, we see the power and shamelessness of political math.

Entering Teachers into Software Space

When an evaluation of a teacher is completed, his or her supervisor enters the quantitative and qualitative results into the city's teacher evaluation system. Access to the system is reserved only for authorized users. It is reasonable to assume that the system consists of web pages, links, buttons, drop-down menus, and text boxes through which users interact with software. It is also reasonable to assume that upon logging in, users are shown different kinds of prepopulated information pulled from other city systems. For example, a principal who logs in is likely greeted with her name and can see the online profiles of all teachers who are officially with her school. A teacher who logs in can likely see information like his or her school, the classes taught, and perhaps even student rosters. The principal likely navigates to a designated page where he or she is prompted to enter at least numerical if not narrative information from the observation of the teacher. According to union contracts, this means over 20 components.

In this case, we will focus on the role that information systems play in software space. The system knows who logs in because the user enters in a unique username and password issued by the city. The act of logging in triggers requests for information from other city databases about the user. The parameters of the request are predefined by software developers. In the case of a principal logging in, the system might minimally request her first name, last name, school, and teachers under his or her supervision. What gets returned to the evaluation system might look like this:

1: *firstname; lastname; schoolname; pedagogueID*
2: *sally; leedar; software academy; 1234, 0987, 7890, 2345, 1235, 4444, 2323, 7863*

After navigating to a teacher's profile page, the principal would click on check boxes or buttons based on the teacher evaluation rubric and perhaps enter in some qualitative feedback as well. When he or she submits her observation report into software space, something akin to the following feed might be sent:

1: *pedagogueID; firstname; lastname; schoolname; 1a; 1b; 1c; 1d; 1e; 1f; 2a; 2b; 2c; 2d; 2e; 3a; 3b; 3c; 3d; 3e; 4a; 4b; 4c; 4d; 4e; 4f*
2: *1234; john; dewey; software academy; 3 "Good job John"; 2; 4; 1; 1; 1 "Need to work on this"; 3; 2; 3; 3; 3; 1; 4; 4 "Excellent response to the students"; 4; 4; 1; 1; 2; 2; 2; 2*

The feeds above are extremely streamlined for illustrative purposes, conceptually helpful but I am sure syntactically imprecise. What is important to note in the samples is that while the principal is being fed streams of data and sending streams of data *in* software space, all she experiences *of* software space is a physical device and user interface on the screen consisting of buttons, boxes, and links.

How Teaching Is Rendered Back into Social Contexts

It is always the case that what is entered into software space is rendered back into sociocultural contexts in some form. In its simplest form, the information our principal enters into software space is rendered back as a confirmation message or an automatically generated paper letter for the teacher's file. Or perhaps the teacher receives an email notification that the review was formally submitted and shares it with his mentor or colleague. Data can be rendered back into sociocultural contexts in more extravagant ways as well. In New York State in recent years, for instance, it has become common practice for schools to receive "report cards" from the state based on their test scores and other data. The report cards are posted publicly on the state's web site and make explicit reference to the school's demographic makeup according to race, sex, language status, and learning (dis)abilities. The report cards also feature previous years' achievement metrics and graduation rates as a way to measure growth. They consist of explanatory language written for public consumption, tables of numbers and statistics, and some data visualizations to ease interpretation. New York City had a comparable system for its own schools, with the added input of qualitative metrics and narrative feedback about the school, which is also included in a battery of publicly available reports. The rationale for such report cards is that public schools need to be held accountable to taxpayers and one way of doing so is by measuring their success and reporting it publicly.

Following the same logic, neoliberal reformers encourage districts to issue public reports on individual teachers using the teacher evaluation systems discussed above. In 2012, New York City publicly shared reports of teacher "performance data" using data from 2007–2010 school years. The reports were requested by a number of news outlets under the Freedom of Information Law. Their rationale for the request was "under the belief that parents have a right to the information" (Unknown, 2012). Whereas the city essentially stopped compiling such reports, it did so not because of any ethical discomfort with doing so, but rather because the state was expected to take over that level of reporting in compliance with Race to the Top expectations. The city's reports included 85 categories and were rendered out of software space into news web sites and newspapers not only with teachers' specific school names but also their own first and last names. (See Table 3.1; identifying information changed.) One proponent of the so-called "teacher report cards" opined in a city paper, "Parents, students, taxpayers and policy makers all should expect to see every teacher's report card—just as little Martha and Mario are supposed to present their report cards for inspection" and that forcing such public rendering of teaching will "push the teachers unions' self-serving, anti-student hypocrisy to the shattering point" (Murdock, 2012). Upon release, even high-ranking members of the city schools cautioned that the reports not be taken "in isolation," the chief academic officer insisting "No principal would ever make a decision on this score alone and we would never invite anyone—parents, reporters, principals, teachers—to draw a conclusion based on this score alone" (Santos, 2012, n.p.).

Table 3.1 Listing of teacher reporting data structure categories and sample teacher data.

Data Field	School Input
subject	English Language Arts
grade	7th Grade
dbn	20K259
school_name	J.H.S. 259 William Mckinley
exp_group	More Than 3 Years

(Continued)

Table 3.1 (Continued)

Data Field	School Input
years_of_data	4
teacher_id	
teacher_name_first_1	JANE
teacher_name_last_1	DEWEY
va_pctl_multi	92
va_cat_multi	ABOVE AVERAGE
n_multi	103
va_pctl_0910	85
va_cat_0910	ABOVE AVERAGE
n_0910	30
va_pctl_top3rd	90
va_cat_top3rd	ABOVE AVERAGE
va_pctl_middle3rd	96
va_cat_middle3rd	HIGH
va_pctl_lowest3rd	
va_cat_lowest3rd	
va_pctl_male	91
va_cat_male	ABOVE AVERAGE
va_pctl_female	94
va_cat_female	ABOVE AVERAGE
posttest_multi	0.92
predicted_multi	0.73
va_multi	0.19
va_min_pctl_multi	65
va_max_pctl_multi	98
pretest_0910	0.66
posttest_0910	0.96
predicted_0910	0.8
va_0910	0.15
va_min_pctl_0910	34
va_max_pctl_0910	98
pretest_top3rd	0.93
posttest_top3rd	1.13
predicted_top3rd	0.97

Raising Critical Questions

As we consider the way the ubiquity of software space mediates and shapes education, there are important elements to consider here: the observation instruments used to gather data in schools, the application used to enter observation data into information systems, the kinds of data required as well as how they are structured and validated, and how they are rendered back into social contexts. When we consider the observation instruments, we might ask: How do the rubrics used create false dichotomies and decision points, forcing principals to choose a numerical representation of teaching that is qualitatively inaccurate? Or when using the web application to enter data, how do the menu options, layout of the screen, and forced choices prompted in the system position the principal as a leader, an educator, and a social being? When the data are rendered back to the social world, how are they contextualized by the media and how are the actual data presented? For each of these questions, we must also ask to whose benefit—political, economic, ideological—is it to implement a teacher evaluation system in this way? What other ways can we imagine to rigorously support the professional growth of our teachers? What is lost and what is gained as we trace the complexity of the act of teaching and learning through rubrics, user interfaces, and information systems back into society? Where does the logic of the database assert its needs, its epistemologies? Next, let's explore how student achievement is also mediated and shaped by software.

POLITICS, COMMERCE, AND THE SOFTWARIZATION OF LEARNING

The Push for Common Standards

Teachers were not the sole focus of Race to the Top. Students were also directly affected by neoliberal reforms as their curricula and assessments were shifted to align with the Common Core Standards. In 2011, President Obama framed the Common Core thus: "For less than 1 percent of what we spend on education each year, it [Race to the Top] has led over 40 states to raise their standards for teaching and learning. And these standards were developed, by the way, not by Washington, but by Republican and Democratic governors throughout the country" (Obama, 2011, para. 37). Although he refrains from calling the Common Core by name, the president frames the creation of the standards as a bipartisan state-led effort. New York, required by its Race to the Top award to adopt "common standards," framed the value of the new standards in public hearings and press releases. For example, the education commissioner writes, "We know that moving forward with the Common Core is essential: study after study shows that our students lag behind in the knowledge and skills required for their future. The Common Core standards, designed by teachers and education experts from across the country—and shaped by many New York State educators—will help us do better" (King, 2013). In addition to emphasizing the national nature of the standards, the commissioner adds that teachers and education experts designed the standards. Some commentators criticized who those "teachers and education experts" are (Schneider, 2014). Supporting states in their implementation, David Coleman—one of the lead authors of the literacy standards—presents the value of the standards succinctly in three points: "First, the standards must be college and career ready. . . . The second is that these core standards had to be based on ethics. It was not enough to piously say what we believe all students need to know and be able to do. . . . And third was a level of honesty about time," referring to the perceived inability of teachers to cover and assess all the curricula, which made "assessment a Russian roulette system" (Coleman, 2011). Proponents' language suggests the standards are necessary because states perceived a need to align education standards with the needs of the global marketplace in a manner that was more effectively assessable. Critics argue that not only are the standards themselves "distorting the curriculum" but so is the reckless "evolution of assessments that are being developed to accompany the standards" (Applebee, 2013, p. 30). In the end, the yeas had it.

Measuring Students' Achievement

As literacy researcher Arthur Applebee conveys, we cannot consider the standards alone without also considering the assessments that are developed to evaluate students and schools in meeting them. The federal government provided over $300 million to two test development consortia called the Partnership for Assessment of Readiness in College and Careers (PARCC) and Smarter Balanced Assessment Consortium. Despite claims to the contrary by policy makers, Applebee argues that the impatient implementation of the standards has led to the consortia's rushed assessment development. He writes, "Because of time constraints, both consortia are continuing to make heavy use of multiple-choice (renamed as 'selected response') and short-response formats. Pressures from states concerned about the feasibility and expense of testing have already led to reductions in the time allotted for performance items" (ibid.). In a 9th grade ELA/Literacy assessment sample provided by PARCC, students are asked to read a text entitled "Fields of Fingerprints: DNA Testing for Crops." They are then instructed to answer a series of questions. For example:

Part A Question: What is one question the article answers by explaining the steps required to obtain a DNA fingerprint?

a. How long does it take for scientists to obtain DNA fingerprints?
b. How complicated is the process used to obtain a DNA fingerprint?

   c. Why is it possible that obtaining DNA fingerprints will become more common?

   d. Why is it important to obtain a DNA fingerprint? ("Grade 9 sample items," 2013)

PARCC then provides a rationale for what standards and skills the question is intended to assess. They explain: "The skills of reading carefully, examining key ideas in a text, and applying an understanding of a text are essential for college and career readiness. This item asks students to analyze a scientific text to determine the underlying questions that the text was written to address" (ibid.). With Applebee's critique in mind, we might look at the question and note that it is presented as multiple-choice, not a performance item. Rather than asking students to select from a list of predetermined questions, test creators could have asked students to create their own questions based on the reading. They do not. Despite the fact that allowing students to generate their own questions from the article would likely provide assessors with a more accurate sense of what students know and can do, what we encounter is software-friendly selection items.

Entering Students into Software Space

The reformers' goal is for the new Common Core-aligned assessments to be given on computers (Ravitch, 2013). The implementation of computerized assessments for the new standards, however, slowed down when districts realized the significant infrastructural and logistic demands. Web-based assessments require consistent bandwidth, updated hardware and browsers, new proctoring protocols, and enough devices for all students. In my own conversations with district leaders, I was surprised that the minimum screen size permitted for computerized assessments happened to accord with the best-selling tablet, leading one superintendent I worked with to quip, "We need more actual computers for this. Can you imagine making my kids take high-stakes tests on iPads?" He had a point. Still, in the case that students take high-stakes exams on computers, there are two main ways they enter software space. First, by selecting answers from a predefined menu of options or by entering in original text into text boxes (in the event students are permitted to do so) students are themselves submitting information to software space. Second, the resultant testing data, and other kinds of student information in many districts, are fed to the state where they are housed, manipulated, and reported to the public in different forms like the school report cards discussed above. With Race to the Top, however, there was an additional request. States were encouraged to partner with an organization called inBloom (mentioned above and examined more closely in Chapter 7, this volume). inBloom received commonly structured data feeds from multiple states and then made that data available to commercial groups with products to sell to districts. inBloom emphasized publicly and repeatedly—especially in the face of parent outrage—that the data were encrypted and states or districts had to actively permit companies to access the data.

When inBloom requires student data feeds, it lists a series of required data types. The entity "Student" contains 49 attributes and references. I will include the entire list as it appears in the company's developer documentation, although I will present them more clearly than they appear typically. The name for student gradebook entries, for instance, appears as *student-GradebookEntries*. This form of presentation makes sense if software is the primary reader. For human readers, it is helpful to separate the words to make categories clearer, like *student gradebook entries,* which has the following attributes for students: address, birth data, cohort years, disabilities, displacement status, economic disadvantaged, electronic mail, Hispanic Latino ethnicity, home languages, languages, learning styles, limited English proficiency, login ID, name, old ethnicity, other name, profile thumbnail, program participations, race, school food services eligibility, section 504 disabilities, sex, student characteristics, student identification code, student indicators, student unique state ID, telephone, attendances, cohorts, course transcripts, discipline actions, discipline incidents, grades, parents, post secondary events, programs, report cards, restraint events, schools, sections, student academic records, student assessments, student cohort associations, student discipline incident associations, student gradebook entries, student parent associations, student program associations, student school associations, and student section associations. Each attribute has an associated data type with it, which refers to the kinds of data that can be entered for any given attribute. For example, the attribute *student characteristics* includes another four data attributes: begin date, characteristic, designated by, and end date. When we examine the attributes nested within *characteristic,* we find: displaced homemaker, foster care, homeless, immigrant, migratory, parent in military, pregnant, section 504 handicapped, single parent, unaccompanied youth, unschooled asylee, and unschooled refugee. There are 117 separate entities, each nesting additional data fields. The thousands of data points gathered on individual students, parents, and teachers are collected and stored in district and state databases. They are also fed to other information systems, in which case long strings of data are comprised of discrete data like the simple example in the previous section, each data point usually separated by a comma or semicolon.

How Learning Is Rendered Back into Social Space

In spring 2014, public outcry and concern about both Common Core testing and student and teacher data reporting via inBloom reached its precipice. Parent groups around New York rallied publicly to resist the new tests. On the morning of Common Core ELA exams, parents drew media interest at one Brooklyn elementary school, marching with signs that read "stand up for our kids" and "Brooklyn parents rigorously refuse." One local news outlet reported: "Teachers say they haven't been given the proper guidance or materials to teach the new standards while parents and others say they are more of a pointless ordeal than a true measure of progress. Many at P.S. 321 Friday morning said this week's ELA exam was riddled with baffling questions and content that did not reflect curriculum and classwork" (Unknown, 2014). A month later, comedian Louis C.K., whose children attend public schools in New York City, posted pictures of his children's math homework and expressed his frustration that his children now hated math. In a *New Yorker* article on the comedian's critique, Mead (2014) notes, "It seems likely that if more parents with the wealth and public profile of Louis C.K. showed their support for public education not by funding charter-school initiatives, as many of the city's plutocrats have chosen to do, but by actually enrolling their children in public schools, there would long ago have been a louder outcry against the mind-numbing math sheets and assignments that sap the joy from learning." Whereas the framing of parental outcry might be in terms of "too much testing," I argue that what parents are responding to is a neoliberal agenda that is strategically promoting the softwarization of learning—the needs of software space and information systems for streams of data. The current way we generate such data is through rudimentary testing methods and flawed rubric use. Although software space is arguably capable of managing more sophisticated kinds of data and can manage socioculturally responsive and constructivist processes, those in positions of power are not.

Raising Critical Questions

Translating the complex act of teaching and learning into data for software space is something with which some parents are beginning to express discomfort. Whereas they do not discuss it in terms of technology and software—rather, they talk about their children's stress levels and testing companies—it is the case that software powers these "reforms" and testing efforts. There are critical questions to raise here: Who benefits from common standards? Whereas it might be true that having shared standards allows educators across the country to have a common language with which to discuss pedagogy, it is also the case that common standards means it is easier for companies to align their products (it becomes less necessary to manage each state's unique curricula) and it means that the kinds of data that can be gathered, stored, manipulated, and reported on dramatically increases. It is a neoliberal technocrat's dream: shared standards that are mapped to assessments to gather data and algorithmically recommend purchasable curricular resources to districts. States will buy tests and technology; schools will buy professional development, curricular resources, and software applications to manage the new expectations. It is clear that companies benefit from the softwarization of learning, but how do policy makers? If the political discourse is driven by economic logic and necessity, education provides a chain reaction of benefits. That is, all in the name of creating "college and career-ready" young people, politicians can engage the private sector, like publishers and other technology companies, to solve educational woes while appearing in public to crack down on demonized public sector institutions that waste money and lack accountability. The neoliberal cause profits handsomely even if drawing the ire of a few parents.

WAYS FORWARD

If we are to establish a place for software studies in education, it must be critical in its stance. At its heart, critical software studies regards the use of software-powered technologies in education as inherently laden with issues of power and inequity. It also regards the role that software plays as thickly hidden and unfamiliar to the average person. Not only is it challenging to look beyond the glitz of smooth user interfaces to infer the computational logic behind the functionality on the screen, it can also be difficult to fathom how things like data feeds, for instance, represent teaching and learning. It's much easier, although still not frequent enough, to become irate at one's child's anxiety the night before new exams. If the research community is going to do more to support policy makers and communities in understanding how software space influences the very real and fleshy experiences of human beings, we have to develop and refine methods for examining software space in our everyday lives in education. The previous chapters have first framed the problem, introduced software studies generally, and now suggested the introduction of critical software studies. In the next chapter, I offer a preliminary series of research methods that can be used to systematically collect data in this critical endeavor.

WORKS CITED

Apple, M. W. (1993). *Official knowledge: Democratic education in a conservative age*. New York: Routledge.

Apple, M. W. (1996). *Cultural politics and education*. New York: Teachers College Press.

Applebee, A. N. (2013). Common Core state standards: The promise and the peril in a national palimpsest. *English Journal, 103*(1), 25–33.

Coleman, D. (2011, April 28). *Bringing the Common Core to life*. Talk at the Chancellor's Hall, New York State Department of Education, Albany, NY. Retrieved December 15, 2014, from http://usny.nysed.gov/rttt/resources/bringing-the-common-core-to-life-download.html.

Cramer, P. (2012, March 20). State labor board agrees to appoint mediator in evaluation talks. *Chalkbeat*. Retrieved December 20, 2014, from http://ny.chalkbeat.org/2012/03/20/state-labor-board-agrees-to-appoint-mediator-in-evaluation-talks/#.VJXfBsAk.

Danielson, C. (2013). The framework for teaching evaluation instrument. The Danielson Group. Retrieved December 15, 2014, from www.danielsongroup.org/userfiles/files/downloads/2013EvaluationInstrument.pdf.

Gee, J.P. (1999). *An introduction to discourse analysis: Theory and method.* London: Routledge.

Getting started with the new teacher evaluation and development system. (2013, September). United Federation of Teachers. Retrieved December 15, 2014, from www.uft.org/files/attachments/final-eval-quickstart-guide.pdf.

Gorlewski, J., & Porfilio, B. (Eds.). (2013). *Left behind in the race to the top.* Charlotte, NC: Information Age Publishing.

Grade 9 sample items. (2013, November 12). Partnership for Assessment of Readiness for College and Careers (PARCC). Retrieved December 15, 2014, from http://parcconline.org/sites/parcc/files/Grade9SampleItemSet.pdf.

King, J.B. (2013, December 30). Reflections on the common core. New York State Education Department. Retrieved December 15, 2014, from http://usny.nysed.gov/docs/reflections-on-the-core.pdf.

Mead, R. (2014, April 30). Louis C.K. Against the Common Core. *The New Yorker.* Retrieved December 6, 2014, from http://www.newyorker.com/news/daily-comment/louis-c-k-against-the-common-core.

"Meet the Press" transcript for Nov. 15, 2009. (2009, November 15). *Meet the Press.* Washington, DC: NBC. Retrieved December 15, 2014, from www.msnbc.msn.com/id/33931557/ns/meet_the_press/.

Murdock, D. (2012, February 10). Report cards for NY teachers. *New York Post.* Retrieved December 15, 2014, from http://nypost.com/2012/02/10/report-cards-for-ny-teachers/.

Nussbaum, M.C. (2010). *Not for profit: Why democracy needs the humanities.* Princeton, NJ: Princeton University Press.

Obama, B. (2011, January 25). Remarks by the president in the state of the union address. The White House. Retrieved December 20, 2014, from www.whitehouse.gov/the-press-office/2011/01/25/remarks-president-state-union-address.

Obama, B. (2012, January 24). Remarks by the president in state of the union address. The White House. Retrieved December 20, 2014, from www.whitehouse.gov/the-press-office/2012/01/24/remarks-president-state-union-address.

Obama, B. (2013, February 12). Remarks by the president in the state of the union address. The White House. Retrieved January 16, 2014, from www.whitehouse.gov/the-press-office/2013/02/12/remarks-president-state-union-address.

Ravitch, D. (2013). *Reign of error: The hoax of the privatization movement and the danger to America's public schools.* New York: Knopf.

Rogers, R. (Ed.). (2011). *An introduction to critical discourse analysis in education.* New York: Routledge.

Santos, F. (2012, February 24). City teacher data reports are released. *Schoolbook-WNYC.* Retrieved December 15, 2014, from www.wnyc.org/story/301783-teacher-data-reports-are-released/.

Schneider, M. (2014, April 23). Those 24 Common Core 2009 work group members. *deutsch29: Mercedes Schneider's EduBlog.* Retrieved December 15, 2014, from http://deutsch29.wordpress.com/2014/04/23/those-24-common-core-2009-work-group-members/.

Selwyn, N. (2014). *Distrusting educational technology: Critical questions for changing times.* New York: Routledge.

Short, A. (2014, May 9). Teachers union boss declares war on school reform. *New York Post,* n.p.

Taubman, P.M. (2009). *Teaching by numbers: Deconstructing the discourse of standards and accountability in education.* New York: Routledge.

Unknown. (2012, February 28). Now available: 2007–2010 NYC teacher performance data. *New York 1*. Retrieved December 20, 2014, from www.ny1.com/content/news/156599/now-available—2007-2010-nyc-teacher-performance-data.

Unknown. (2014, April 4). Parents, teachers rally against Common Core tests in Brooklyn. *CBS New York*. Retrieved December 20, 2014, from http://newyork.cbslocal.com/2014/04/04/parents-teachers-rally-against-common-core-tests-in-brooklyn/.

U.S. Department of Education. (2010). *Race to the Top*. Education: U.S. Department of Education. Retrieved December 15, 2014, from www2.ed.gov/programs/racetothetop/index.html.

Weis, L., & Fine, M. (2012). Critical bifocality and circuits of privilege: Expanding critical ethnographic theory and design. *Harvard Educational Review, 82*(2), 173–201.

4   Methods | Texts, Pixels, and Clicks

"There is always a flux in the things and ideas of this world, and there is always the need to catch that flux in networks of meaning."

—Maxine Greene in "Standards, Common Learning, and Diversity," Releasing the Imagination, p. 183

One morning while working with iLearnNYC, I got a call from senior leadership asking for a report. When I asked what kind of report, I was told that they wanted to see metrics for how widely used the online learning environment was so they could speak to the program's return on investment. I said I'd have the report by the end of the day and hung up. As I began clicking through the myriad buttons, links, and data visualizations, I encountered impressive and compelling reporting tools: timelines of user log-ins, heat maps that showed where users performed well and poorly in some courses, and animated charts. Surely, I thought, these will satisfy the request. I compiled a report, sent it along, and an enthusiastic thank you note followed.

But what had I really done?

As I reflected on the kinds of data that had been reported, I became uneasy with my work. Much of what had been reported amounted to clocking the minutes users were logged in to the system clicking on things. It said nothing about whether or not anyone was learning anything. The reports lightly alluded to the fact that the environment and millions of dollars in courses purchased were being used, but not used well necessarily. Was leadership not at all interested in the quality of teaching and learning, or simply the thin activity of users? Could more robust and meaningful reports be compiled? When researchers examine the use of software-powered technologies, do they approach data collection and analysis in a critical manner or do they too become enchanted by the volume and ease of data such technologies can generate? Do we expect too little?

If the leaders of a well-funded, high-profile, and large-scale initiative could be satisfied with paltry reporting, perhaps our collective expectations for software-powered technologies is low. If critical scholars' claims that research of educational technology bends toward shallow optimism and phenomenological thinness (Bromley & Apple, 1998; Selwyn, 2014), perhaps critical software studies can offer methods that capture deeper data. In the sections that follow, I present methods for operationalizing critical software studies in educational research settings. I begin on the periphery of software space with *critical discourse analysis,* focusing on the language that comprises the discourse of education reform with special attention to the ways software is positioned by those in power. Next, I offer two methods that seek to leverage what human users see and experience in sociocultural settings while beginning to scratch the surface of software space. Both *functionality precedent* and *pixel analysis* begin to narrow one's inspection of software space using samples of how it is rendered in the human world, but do not delve deeply into the ontology of software. The next method, *click-commitment protocols,* attempts to straddle the worlds of the computational and human most evenly as it emphasizes how the activity of the one informs the other. Finally, I offer three methods for scrutinizing software space itself: *source viewing, inferred algorithmic logic,* and *data structure analysis.*

When employing these methods, it is important to consider three things. First, these methods are most compellingly used in combinations. In my own work, for instance, I have found using critical discourse analytical techniques with data structure analysis to be a powerful way to connect the words of elected officials with the realities of information systems. Second, all methods are to be used in order to demonstrate how the social is rendered back into the social. The aim of critical software studies is not the creation of knowledge for its own sake, but that the epistemological contributions generated through its undertaking offer insights into social contexts. Third, this list is not exhaustive. One will find that scholars in software studies demonstrate many other techniques, that methods employed in related fields like critical discourse analysis can be adapted for software space, and that methods yet unimagined await. The examples presented here are, I hope, only the beginning of what will become an ever-growing and useful toolkit.

CRITICAL DISCOURSE ANALYSIS

The field of critical discourse analysis (CDA) is well-established with an array of theoretical and methodological branches. One definition of critical discourse analysis states it is "a theoretical approach to studying the role of language in society that originated within linguistics but has found widespread application across the social sciences. The term is also sometimes used to refer only to the methodological framework of CDA that centers on the qualitative linguistic analysis of spoken or written texts" (Given, 2008, p. 145). In the study of CDA in educational settings, Rogers (2011) describes CDA as a "problem-oriented and transdisciplinary set of theories and methods" (p. 1). As it is described above, CDA tends to focus on written and spoken language (the discourse) while attending to the ways language is used by those in positions of power to perpetuate different forms of inequity (the critical). Critical software studies borrows theoretical and methodological tools from CDA but hones in on how written and spoken language, especially of those in positions of power, veils or ignores the very active and ideological work of software in society.

For present purposes, we turn to CDA to help frame 1) the direct dialectical relationship between modes of communication (traditionally linguistic) and social institutions and everyday human experiences; and 2) how complex multimodal forms of communication mask issues of power, including the manifestation of ideologies through software. In his discussion of "hidden power," Fairclough (2001) notes that both the media and standard language are channels through which sociolinguistic power is claimed and wielded. Of media, he writes "through the way it positions readers . . . media discourse is able to exercise a pervasive and powerful influence in social reproduction because of the very scale of the modern mass media and the extremely high level of exposure of whole populations to a relatively homogeneous output" (p. 45). Today, software studies scholars argue that it is software that increasingly mediates human communication: software mediates media. Software is used to not only create but disseminate mass media across a wide array of outlets. If, as some argue, the ontology of software can subtly affect the kinds of things we create with it and even the ways we think through it, it is reasonable to question the degree to which the ubiquity of software is empowering and disempowering the discourses it mediates and shapes. In his discussion of standard language, Fairclough notes that "By coming to be associated with the most salient and powerful institutions—literature, Government and administration, law, religion, education, etc.—standard English began to emerge as the language of political and cultural power, and as the language of the politically and culturally powerful" (p. 47). Again, as has been discussed briefly and will be expanded upon in the following chapters, software space demands standardization of inputs and outputs. Data must be predetermined to a great extent, categorized ahead of time, and fed and ingested by a variety of information systems—all of which are executed through languages, programming languages. If standard English was the language of power and influence in the previous centuries, software either displaces spoken and written language or indiscernibly transcends it. Similar to the way CDA scholars map the interplay between linguistic elements of utterances to socio-political structures of power, in critical software studies we are interested in the way technical elements make manifest the ideological utterances of those in position of power and profit.

In addition to Fairclough's insights regarding language, Gunther Kress (2011) examines the multimodal nature of discourse, which he refers to as multimodal social semiotic analysis, arguing that it "provides a richer perspective on the many means involved in making meaning and learning; on forms and shapes of knowledge, on the many forms of evaluation and assessment; on the social relationship evident in pedagogy; on the (self-) making of identity and, in that, on the means that are central in the recognition of the agency and of the many kinds of semiotic work in learners in learning" (p. 208). For Kress, discursive examinations must account for the multiple modes of communication sign-makers might use to design and create texts. Kress also draws attention to the fact that as sign-makers engage in processes of transduction, that is, "the shift from one mode to another mode" (p. 223), there emerges new epistemological and ontological issues "in the shaping of knowledge" (ibid.).

I highlight these two scholars because they represent two perspectives within CDA that can help researchers critically account for the role of software in education. First, there is a need to unpack the layers of meaning and associated questions of power in the linguistic texts produced by various stakeholders in education, especially policy makers. Fairclough's sensitivity to the dialectical relationship between the linguistic and the social provides us a framework through which we can build. Second, Kress's appreciation for non-linguistic modes of communication like the visual and sound offers a crucial complement to traditional forms of CDA as it opens the doors for researchers to critically and creatively inspect a plethora of communicative devices that make human expression possible in a new media age. In Chapters 6 and 7, I will borrow some principles and methods from Fairclough's toolkit to demonstrate how policy makers message the role of software-powered technologies in educational settings. Such tools are more thoroughly articulated and applicable to our topic. In the case of Kress's multimodal social semiotic approach to CDA, it is necessary to explain how his principles might apply to critical software studies because although Kress thoroughly theorizes and demonstrates his approach to multiple modes of communication, he does not account for the explicit and agentic role that software plays in the creation, dissemination, and response to such multimodal texts. For instance, he might refer to a mode as a "resource for meaning making" (p. 208) or to media as a "means of dissemination" (p. 209), but does not consider the fact that software is used by sign-makers to create their motivated texts. Yet their ability to make is itself subject to the motivations of those who produced the software in use. Words like *resource* and *means* mask the fact that software development is necessarily an ideological endeavor and that the ideologies of those who create it directly affect the kinds of knowledge students and teachers can make when using it.

Kress uses the term *epistemological commitments* to refer to the act of students (and teachers) making decisions about what they know in response to a prompt and asserting that knowledge in a mode of communication. The relationship between signs and knowledge is one of intertwinement: "To *make* a sign is to make knowledge. *Knowledge* is shaped in the use, by a social agent, of distinct representational affordances of specific modes at the point of making of the sign" (italics original; p. 211). The kinds of signs one can make through software appear manifold: written, spoken, drawn, video recorded, sung, and more. However, if software mediates and shapes the process of sign-making, software scholars might argue that software—to some extent—is mediating and shaping the knowledge a student is and is not able to express. There are two main kinds of examples to identify here. The first might be considered creative software like Adobe Illustrator. Although Manovich (2013) has argued that Illustrator and similar software products do in fact affect the kinds of aesthetic expressions artists can make, these kinds of software afford users a great—although not limitless—degree of freedom and choice. The second kind of software in educational settings includes software products that are used for curricular and assessment purposes like online courses. Such software products afford student and teacher users far less freedom of expression, but rather are pre-programmed to narrowly define what users can and cannot do. When working with district leaders, I would refer to this distinction as similar to the difference between a notebook and a textbook. Notebooks are, greatly, content and instructionally agnostic. Textbooks, on the other hand, are quite the opposite: Their contents, purpose, and outcomes are thoroughly predetermined by faceless adults with whom both students and teachers might passionately disagree. Or, to put this distinction differently, some software mediates more than it shapes whereas other software shapes more than it mediates. For example, a student of literature might be asked, "Why might Houseman have chosen to use the word *malt* in his couplet, 'And malt does more than Milton can, // To justify God's ways to man'?" Although the question could be answered in multiple-choice or long answer form, it is much easier in terms of development, useful in terms of analytics, and profitable in terms of the bottom line for a company to choose multiple choice. How does the nature of software and the demands of commerce affect the kinds of technologies and the uses of technologies we see in our schools? The epistemological commitments our students might be able to make are limited only by the kinds of knowledge our teachers and school systems are willing (or allowed) to accept. With better methods of identifying and scrutinizing the ways software acts as a shaper of pedagogy, we might make progress in creating models of software-powered technology use that resembles truly constructivist pedagogies.

FUNCTIONALITY PRECEDENT

One of the key guiding principles of critical software studies is the notion that software does not simply appear out of the ether, but is created by human beings for various purposes. It is important to have a starting point for exposing the humanity behind the technological. *Functionality precedent* seeks to accomplish this by forefronting a relatively simple logic. When one encounters a software-powered technology, it is helpful to question why the product does what it does and not something else. For example, why is the button here rather than there? In addition, one can compare the functionality one encounters in a particular software-powered technology to the kinds of functionalities one sees in other products. The questions one asks narrow in scope. Rather than asking why does a product do this and not that, one asks why does this product not do that thing I know other products can do. The logic is a powerful one for purposes of analysis. Just as CDA scholars develop and employ methods of unpacking what is left unsaid in written and spoken language, functionality precedent asks why the creators of one product choose not to employ a functionality that we know from experience is available in other software-powered technologies. If, from a technical perspective, a particular functionality exists in some products but not others, it suggests that developers might have chosen not to employ it for particular reasons, which might be pragmatic, economic, or ideological. It might take too much time, not yield profits, or conflict with a company's branding or worldview. Below, I offer some examples one might experience in their daily lives in the form of questions users find themselves asking.

Why Can't I Email Pictures My Friend Sent Me via Text Message?

On the first day of school, my wife captured a steady stream of pictures chronicling our son's new kindergarten. Later in the day, she sent a text message to members of our family so grandparents and aunts could celebrate the milestone with us. These pictures now live in my phone, I thought, so I can easily email them to some close friends. When I attempted to do so, however, I could not. Rather, when I clicked the "share" button, I received options to share the photos via social media, but not email. In order to share the way I wished, I had to save copies of the images to a separate place in the phone from which I could email them. I know from my experiences using other technologies that I should be able to simply email photos that exist in my phone already. It is functionality one expects from software. Sending files by email, after all, is one of the most basic kinds of sharing users of software-powered technologies know. If, however, the company that built my phone (as well as its software) chose not to include this functionality, or to have hidden it from my view, it behooves us to ask why? There are many possible reasons, some more likely than others. One possible explanation might be technical: Perhaps the pictures I see on my phone in a text message do not actually live on my phone the way they appear. If this were the case, though, it would not make sense that I be permitted to share the files through other means like popular photo-sharing sites and the company's own cloud service. Another possibility is legal: Perhaps files that are shared via text messages belong to the cellular network providers and there are contractual issues with the maker of the phone's hardware and software simply appropriating such media. This scenario, too, seems unlikely for the same reason as the technical possibility; the phone manufacturer does make sharing the photos an option, just not through email. A third possibility is economic: Perhaps a reason to make it easier for users to share images via social media application than directly through email is because it benefits the company financially if users rely less on email and more on these kinds of services. This possibility gains support when one considers the order in which social media applications appear to users, with the manufacturer's own cloud service appearing first (on the far left) and other companies appearing like runners up. The purpose of this example is not to demonstrate that the company in question is guilty of depriving users of functionality they might prefer in favor of options that serve their economic ends. It is to demonstrate how one can unpack one's experience as a user of a software-powered technology to raise questions about how the ideologies of the creators of software and hardware are subtly imposed on users. My response to being unable to share photos by email must not be, "Oh well, my phone can't do that." Rather, my response must be, "Wait, why can't I do this and to whose benefit is it that I share photos this other way?"

Why Can't I Highlight a Passage on My E-Reader and Copy It?

The use of e-readers is increasing in popularity in school. The benefits of using e-readers range from building students' "digital literacy" skills to saving schools money historically spent on the purchase of textbooks. While working on a project using e-readers, I was surprised to learn that there was no simple way for me to highlight and copy text from the book I was reading and paste it into a word processing document I was using to write an article. I could, however, highlight a passage in the text and copy it to a clipboard that exists in the e-reader itself or I could share a highlighted passage via social media. The ability to copy and paste basic text is a ubiquitous functionality we use everyday. For what reason might I be unable to copy a passage and paste it wherever I want? One main reason might be related to copyright: Perhaps the material is doggedly protected through digital rights management protocols that demand users cannot copy a text and do whatever they want with it. What, one might argue, would prevent a user from copying an entire work and sharing it with the world? This rationale makes sense when applied to the entirety of a book, but not to phrases, sentences, or even paragraphs. What's more, the e-reader manufacturer seems to not object to users sharing these smaller excerpts from the text via social media. Another reason, again, might be related to economics. Perhaps the reason to restrict users' ability to copy and share the text is because it benefits the companies involved if users must limit their engagement with the e-texts to the company's own devices and environments—with an exception made for strategic social media partners. The hope might be that if a critical mass of users is sharing excerpts from books through e-readers then these users become essentially micro-advertisers for the e-reader manufacturer and e-books industry. Perhaps there are untapped revenue streams that can be generated if users begin sharing their readings with the world through a shortlist of the big social media outlets. As this case suggests, the rationale behind companies' actions might be a combination of motivators.

Why Can't I Play Music Bought from One Company on Another Company's Device?

In the cases above, I do not refer to any specific companies by name. In this example, naming the companies offers greater clarity of the issues at hand. My brother-in-law has had a cellular phone for many years; the hardware is made by Samsung and the software that powers the phone's operating system is made by Google. After touring my sister's new iPhone (made by Apple), he decided to switch phones. He had also recently received a tablet made by Amazon and was newly excited by the idea of having access to his media libraries more conveniently. When it came time to make the switch, my brother-in-law realized that the transition was anything but seamless. To start, his choice to switch phones required that he negotiate with his cellular network provider, who claimed he could not "upgrade" his phone at a low cost until his current contract expired. What's more, when he was able to use my sister's iPhone for his new phone number, which was not technically an upgrade, he could not easily move his applications and media from his old phone (made by Samsung, run on Google) to his new one (made by Apple). The result was that after his switch of phones, his applications and media lived in a number of different places. Some lived with Apple, others with Amazon, and still others with Google. What made it especially frustrating for him was that these different companies did not make it possible or easy for users to purchase media from another company and simply play it on a different company's device. There is no technical reason this should be the case. Unless restricted by the company, file types can be accessed across a range of devices and applications. In this case, however, the companies above tethered their hardware, software, and media together so users were coerced to remain in the companies' respective ecosystems and marketplaces. It would be like cassette tapes would only play on a Walkman if the tapes were produced by Sony and that albums distributed by Atlantic Records required a different device. The reasons companies might restrict users to limited devices and software seems clearly to be motivated by the prospect of commercial gain. It does not benefit the user to be unable to view content she purchased on certain devices and not others when the functionality of those devices is nearly identical. Still, the effect is precisely what companies want: Many users will not consider purchasing media from anywhere other than the company that powers their device because the inconvenience is too great a cost.

PIXEL ANALYSIS

In multimodal studies, there are different methods for systematically analyzing visual texts like advertisement, pictures, and television advertisements.
These methods might, identify categorical patterns in a visual text in order
to bring to the surface how a designer's decisions impacts a reader's reaction. For instance, Gunther Kress (2003) demonstrates how to read images
in terms of the difference between screens and pages. He writes, ". . . in
screens the point of entry is a problematic issue, whereas for the traditional
page it was not. The 'point of entry' for the page is so much of conventions
that it has ceased to be visible" (p. 136). Kress's point is that when users
encounter a web page, there are multiple ways they can "enter" the reading
of the page. Some users might begin by reading the images at the center of
the page whereas others might find themselves drawn to more text-based
headlines. When it comes to reading on the screen, conventions have yet
to be determined. Traditional pages are not the same. When turning to a
traditional page, it is very clear where one should begin conventionally:
the upper leftmost word in a sentence. Not so with screens. Kress uses the
concept of *blocks* as a way to analyze how screens are composed and how
meaning can be made from them. Blocks of content on a screen, Kress
argues, have "a uniform function (and structural meaning) across occasions
and sites, irrespective of its content" (ibid.). He then goes on to use these
blocks as units of analysis, making a case that the way blocks are "bal-
anced" on the page gives spatial and semiotic emphasis to some content
more than others.

I propose that researchers can build upon Kress's analytical method by
using basic web development tools to quantify the very blocks of which he
speaks while also analyzing the content of such blocks not only for their
semiotic effect but also for their critical significance. I refer to this process
as *pixel analysis*. Kress's method is mostly concerned with what happens
between the surface-level materiality of the sign—images presented on a
screen, for instance—and how the sign-maker used the affordances of the
sign to convey meaning to others. I would add that when we are examining
the use of multimodal signs created with and conveyed through software
space, we can also analyze the ways in which sign-makers' decisions were
informed by the ontology of software as well as how users' experiences of
those signs is shaped by software space. Pixel analysis helps us delimit a
set area of a screenic element and extend Kress's multimodal analysis into
software space.

To begin, pixel analysis requires that researchers use a web development
tool that allows them to measure different areas on the screen. These tools
can be found by searching for *pixel measurement tool* or *pixel ruler* and can
either stand alone as distinct applications or can be used as an extension of
one's web browser. For purposes of example, I visited the *New York Times*
web page on September 10th, 2014. The viewable page (without scrolling

down) measured 1422 x 744 (all measurements in pixels). The main block that houses the content of the screen measures 973 x 735. Written news text comprises two main smaller blocks: a story about the president being ready to authorize airstrikes (173 x 272) and some op-ed titles and overviews (380 x 221). A photograph and caption for a story about the 9/11 memorial comprises a block measuring 379 x 284. The main banner and navigation buttons to different sections of the site measures 976 x 138. A large advertisement for a car company sits beneath the header measuring 969 x 253, although it shrunk into a smaller band during my measurements, thereby revealing more of the page content. There are also two smaller advertisements by the same car company on either side of the *Times* banner, each measuring 185 x 95. Four additional buttons sit atop the site for navigation by section (75 x 15), searching (75 x 15), subscription options (110 x 35), and logging in (55 x 30).

When analyzing these numbers, it is important to remember that the total screen measurement is determined or at least affected by the size of the monitor one uses. More helpful is the measurement for the total area of the main content block, the ratios of which give a more accurate and useful metric. For the *Times,* the total area of the main content block is 715,155 px. The total screen space allotted to content is 47,056 (text; airstrikes content), 83,980 (text; op-ed content), and 107,636 (image; 9/11 content), meaning approximately 33% of the screen that users are presented with consists of actual textual and visual news content. The advertisement for the car company receives 39% of the screenic space, with the remainder devoted to the *Times*'s own branding and navigation features. Also, recall that the advertisement actually shrunk while I was collecting measurements. Such movement is of modal significance because it draws users' attention.

As Kress (2003) notes, the move from the page to the screen represents a larger cultural move from writing to images, a transition which newly available software-powered technologies have accelerated. With traditional media, the cost of images was prohibitive. Today, Kress notes, "there is little or no cost to the user in choosing a path of realization towards image rather than towards word" (p. 5). Pixel analysis provides researchers with harder data with which to capture and analyze such realizations. The fact that so much of the *Times* web site consists of images, to say nothing of the way in which text itself is arranged in blocks, suggests that the path has been chosen. A question this raises, however, is why. Why is so much of the web site image-based when so much of what one would expect from a news outlet might be linguistic? The answer to this seems straight forward for the reasons Kress discusses: Our culture is moving toward more visual means of communication, especially in popular discourses, so it is fitting that a major news outlet relies more heavily on images on its web site. This explanation would be compelling if it was not for the categorization we did of the kinds of texts and images that appear on the screen, which reveals that two-thirds of the web page is non-news content. This fact suggests that while our culture (broadly speaking) might be moving toward more visual modes of communication, it is still worth unpacking *who* in our culture is communicating with whom and for what purpose. Nearly 40% of what appears on one of the world's most reputable newspapers' web site is provided by a car company targeting the kinds of people marketers think read the *Times*. The multimodal tension, then, represents more than a turn in literacy practices. It suggests a socio-political line of questioning that is, in this case, as much about commercial influence in society as it is about the role that the software that powers such web sites and advertisements play in our world.

The advantage of using pixel analysis is that it builds upon a previous qualitative method—Kress's use of blocks as units of analysis when examining multimodal texts like web pages—and offers a way to add a quantitative dimension to data collection and analysis. It would be one thing to observe that advertisements comprise many blocks on a web site. It is more precise and compelling to say that advertisement comprises 39% and to trouble what that number means and how it fluctuates over time and across sites. Without a quantitative measure, such observations are limited in their application. The amount of space any sign-maker chooses to give to different kinds of signs reveals something about his or her priorities, values, and ideologies. The fact that a newspaper offers over a third of its digital front page to an advertisement says something about how its executives view both the digital product and its readership. One would not be likely to see an issue of the paper version of the *Times* with a front page covered in so colorful and prominent a sponsorship. Pixel analysis offers tools to capture such phenomena quantitatively and to dive more deeply into their potential significance.

CLICK-COMMITMENT PROTOCOL

The *click-commitment protocol* derives from two complementary theories, one in software studies and one in multimodal studies. First, Pold (2008) writes about the nature of buttons in software space, arguing that "The [digital] computer interface does away with the analog mechanical functionality, but the function of buttons here is to signify the same stable denotation, even though its material basis is gone. That is, interface buttons disguise the symbolic arbitrariness of the digital mediation" (p. 32). Buttons are paradoxical: They are both immaterial pixels on a screen and they are essential for users to make very material decisions and take action in the world. Consider the way one purchases goods from an online retailer. On the one hand, the screen with which one interacts is intangible and illusory. Digital visual representations create the appearance of concrete goods and even human-like recommendations of what to buy. When one clicks a series of buttons to execute a purchase, however, the result is that an actual item arrives in the mail sometime later. The precipice between the digital world of computation and the fleshy world of human beings is often marked by a button. The button circumscribes an area of pixels that, when clicked, triggers information feeds that signal to very real machines and human beings to act. Let us not, however, confuse what the button enacts as a *choice* as is so often the case in education. Let us instead call it *selection*. The possibilities for what the button digitally realizes are predetermined by the creators of the software space of which it is a part. Choice suggests freedom; selection conveys preordination.

Second, Kress (2003) posits the idea that students make epistemological commitments when they attempt to express what they know in educational settings. He describes in the context of a study of students' work in a secondary science classroom that different modes of communication enable students to commit to what they know in different ways. When learning about the circulation of the blood, students created two different texts produced in two genres: 1) diary entries from the perspective of a red blood cell and 2) a concept map showing how blood circulates. The former genre appears much more effective, Kress (2003) argues, for demonstrating the content knowledge in this case. The sequential nature of diary entries—that is, that the genre demands they are entered in a linear manner—reinforces the sequentiality of how blood travels throughout the body. Concept maps do not support the content as well. He writes, "In the concept map . . . movement is indicated in a much sparser, less diverse, more abstracted way, as vectors with directionality or direction, that is, through arrows pointing from one 'place' to another" (p. 54). The concept map, in this case, was not drawn to emphasize the order of things but rather the relationship amongst different parts of the blood circulation process. Because of the mode chosen, students were prepositioned to commit to one kind of knowledge more than another.

Combining these two concepts, I suggest that because software-powered technologies are frequently navigated by users through different kinds of clicks (of menus, of buttons, of links), and because teaching and learning is increasingly mediated and shaped by software-powered technologies, it is essential that we regard clicking as not merely a functional act but as a commitment to knowing and learning. There are two main forms of clicking: 1) for purposes of navigation and 2) for purposes of epistemological commitment. A look at both of these uses will help clarify how they are distinct as well as how they can become conflated.

Clicking for Navigation

When users click in software space, it is through a user interface representing visual signs that mask the actual code. Code comes in many forms. For example, when I roll my mouse over the "Technology" button on the *New York Times* web site, what I see is a simple word that is part of a horizontal menu toward the top of the screen that, when my mouse arrow overlaps with the button, turns from an arrow to an icon of a hand. I click the button and the screen changes from one web page to another one. Although it is not easy to see, the button I encountered represents a URL: http://www.nytimes.com/pages/technology/index.html. Rather than requiring me to type in this web address, I click on a simpler button. Importantly, I also encounter links and arrows that are not visually presented as buttons but which serve a similar purpose. I click on images to see larger versions of them. I click on play buttons to activate embedded videos. I click on article titles and am taken to fuller versions of stories. When I click in this way, I am doing so primarily as a form of navigation, perhaps reading or viewing content momentarily or perhaps ignoring the content because I am trying to find my way to a specific destination on the site. Every click I make is viewable to those who control the web site. By interacting with the user interface through clicks, I render some part of myself knowable to others.

Clicking for Epistemological Commitments

Clicking for purposes of commitment is ontologically different from navigation, even if it appears to be the same gesture from afar. When one clicks on a button to make an epistemological commitment, one's purpose is not primarily navigation but rather knowledge. To click in this case is to commit to knowing something. For example, when signing up for new services or making purchases online, users are often prompted to "agree" to terms and conditions. These terms and conditions are often very lengthy and written in a contractual form that renders them indecipherable to most of us. It is also not usually necessary to read the entire document, as the "I agree" button is clickable at any moment. When one clicks, however, one commits to having read and understood the contract. The simplicity of the button reduces the complexity of the contract to a mere rectangle on the screen and in so doing induces the user to simply click. These kinds of uses of buttons, it is worth noting, blur the line between navigation and epistemological uses of buttons. In the case of the terms and conditions button, it appears to me when I have already expressed a desire to do something (i.e. purchase a song), which suggests that I am clicking to navigate. However, in order to continue my navigation, I must falsify an epistemological commitment the materiality of which could be enforced to the fullest extent of the law.

In educational settings, we see epistemological uses of buttons appear in other ways. The most prevalent is perhaps the use of buttons when assessing students' learning. This use is an extension of analogue assessment mechanisms like multiple-choice questions. When a student clicks on a multiple-choice selection button in an online course, for example, that student commits to knowing some kind of academic content. In these cases, like the example of online purchases, the role of the button is one of illusion or "symbolic arbitrariness" as Pold (2008) calls it. The button in such cases represents both predetermined knowledge of the test writers (who are often faceless adults who might or might not be teachers) and also cryptic information streams that are fed into databases. One could argue that the student in such cases is not, in fact, making an epistemological commitment at all. Rather, we might call it epistemological *compliance*. There is no opportunity for the student to genuinely commit to his or her own knowledge. Instead, the student is asked to comply with the epistemological commitments of others and is rewarded for desirable compliance. Students comply rather than commit, select rather than choose.

Another example one encounters in educational settings is the use of text boxes in which students appear to have the true freedom to write an open response to a prompt. Upon writing their answer, say in the form of a paragraph, students often click on a button in order to submit it. In the case of one vendor used in iLearnNYC, students who filled out their text boxes were promised immediate assessment. They clicked "submit" and were presented feedback immediately. The feedback was not what students expected. Whereas students might have expected that their thoughtful and original responses to an open prompt would be responded to with thoughtfulness and originality, instead they found that regardless of what they typed into the textbox, software had been programmed to return the same feedback, something to the effect of, "If you wrote that the poet uses metaphor well, you're right. If you didn't write that, go back to module two." The tension of the button betrays itself again. In this case, the button reduces the originality of a student's written response to blankness, while returning back to the student feedback that is insultingly generic in both the assessment itself and in its patronizingly chummy tone.

The examples I offer above focus on the role of buttons as sites of epistemological commitments for students. There is a revealing example worth mentioning from an administrative perspective as well. Two of the common reasons administrators express wanting to use online and blended courses with their students relate to data and reporting. Administrators believe—or are led to believe by sales pitches from vendors—that by making students learn in online environments they will be better able to track students' learning and engagement, advancing students to more challenging content or intervening sooner if students struggle. The key to this "personalization" is the online environment's reporting functionality. Whether the reports are compiled and read manually or if the reporting data are used to reveal or withhold content from students algorithmically (a feature often known as "adaptive release"), administrators can become enchanted by the idea that technology could help give each child what he or she needed when they are ready. The problem with this enchantment is that it is blind to its epistemological fallacy. What is it that the online environment used to determine what students know or don't know? Clicks of buttons and links. Some learning environments would accompany such data with reports about how much time students are logged into the system. In these cases, however, the definition of learning is splintered into a series of fairly effortless clicks, not authentic expressions of knowing anything. It would be like crouching down at a student's desk while she completes a worksheet, counting the number of times her pencil taps the paper, measuring the length of her strokes, and assigning greater credit to the frequency of taps and lastingness of her lines. One could fill spreadsheets with such numbers and render them in complex data visualizations that would impress parades of bureaucrats and neoliberal reformers. It means essentially nothing, amounting only to a pricy digital distraction.

SOURCE VIEWING

Using source code to conduct analyses is a method I first encountered in David Berry's *The Philosophy of Software* (2011). Berry examines the potential of critical code analysis in the context of electronic voting programs. In this digital age, the use of software-powered technologies to make certain social functions more efficient and speedy through software space is something we have seen in health care with the digitization of health records and the launch of a health insurance marketplace as well as in education with the rise of "data-driven" administration and promotion of digital resources in the classroom. The process of public voting has also received attention from policy makers and technologists. It seems from afar that the use of software to facilitate voting makes clear sense: There is an element of repetition, simplicity, and scale to the functional act of voting that makes it a sound candidate for software. However, as Berry points out, the active mediating quality of software means that the will of voters could be affected by the will of software developers and programmers. In his brief but illuminating analysis of one voting application's source code, Berry shows how assumptions about gender reveal themselves. When programmers document source code, they leave notes to other programmers clarifying why they have written the code the way they have. In the case of the voting application in question, Berry points out that the voter is referred to in the source code as a "user," a "voter", and as "he" (pp. 115–116). These words signify ideological tensions present in the software development process in which the very real human beings who are actively participating in the democratic process are identified in ways that are technical, functional, and gendered. While I do think that some of the same issues exist in analogue voting processes (I am often befuddled by the voting operations in my own district), the method he suggests is rife with possibility for educational researchers.

Viewing Web Page Source Code

In educational settings, viewing the web page source can offer researchers insights into how organizations function. In most browsers, right clicking anywhere on a web page will provide the option to "view page source."

In addition, there are hosts of web development tools available in browsers that can offer us insight. Viewing the page source alone can yield useful data. For example, when visiting the web site for Success Academy, a charter school organization founded by Eva Moskowitz, I observed that in addition to using Google Analytics in order to track users, they employ a company that specializes in real-time analytics. That is, it is not uncommon for companies to track the number of users who visit their sites, as well as some geographic information, browser type, and Internet service provider. One can see the following code in most web sites today, which identifies the use of Google Analytics:

```
<script type="text/javascript">
        var _gaq = _gaq || [];
        _gaq.push(['_setAccount', 'UA-8528348-2']);
        _gaq.push(['_trackPageview']);
        (function() {
                var ga = document.createElement('script'); ga.type = 'text/
                javascript'; ga.async = true;
                    ga.src = ('https:' == document.location.protocol ? 'https://ssl':
                    'http://www') + '.google-analytics.com/ga.js';
                    var s = document.getElementsByTagName('script')[0];
                    s.parentNode.insertBefore(ga, s);
            })();
</script>
```

In this case, Success Academy pays a company for more advanced analytic information, including deeper reporting of user information, real-time graphs of activity, and heat maps of how users navigate the page. We know this because a search of the word "click" in the page source code reveals the following block of code.

```
<script type="text/javascript">
var clicky_site_ids = clicky_site_ids || [];
clicky_site_ids.push(100686535);
(function() {
        var s = document.createElement('script');
        s.type = 'text/javascript';
        s.async = true;
        s.src = '//static.getclicky.com/js';
        (document.getElementsByTagName('head')[0] ||
document.getElementsByTagName('body')[0]).appendChild(s);
})();
</script>
```

A visit to getclicky.com—the web site named in the page source code—reroutes users to a company called Clicky, which boasts that their service "lets you see every visitor and every action they take on your web site, with the option to attach custom data to visitors, such as usernames or email addresses. Analyze each visitor individually and see their full history" (n.d.). How does this kind of analytics compare with typical programs used by districts and schools? How is this kind of data used by the organization, which is known to heavily recruit (and some would say exclude) children from some communities and not others? A frequent criticism of charter school organizations is that they knowingly exclude students and families who they determine will not "succeed" in their schools, which is unethical (if not illegal) and not an option for public schools. Should oversight entities have access to such analytic data in order to ensure that Success Academy acts on all data fairly? These questions are valid ones to raise and emerge by simply viewing the source.

Proprietary Barriers to Analysis

One of the main challenges to employing source viewing more frequently is that the code one might wish to examine is often inaccessible because it is protected by the companies or individuals who create it. Berry describes the unique analytical opportunity that emerged when a copy of Microsoft's source code was leaked online, revealing to the world the human side of software engineering as the company's developers traded sardonic notes to each other throughout. The leaked source code was by far an outlier. Much of the software that researchers would have access to is not full application source code, the exception being the kinds of open-source products like the voting software mentioned above.

I do not wish to suggest that because source code is protected researchers should simply walk away. On the contrary, there is an argument to be made for certain kinds of software-powered technologies being used in public schools to be *required* to be subject to analytical scrutiny as a form of oversight not unlike conflicts of interest protocols at public agencies. For example, while working for New York City, I was required to complete a long document that asked for the names of relatives who might have ties to the city, share detailed information about the kinds of money and assets I possessed and the companies with which I might have had business dealings. It took several hours to complete and over one hundred dollars of my own money to process. It also took two years for someone to look at it and call me in due to a red flag analysts observed. At the time, I was a doctoral student at a private graduate school in the city and taught classes in their English education program. The graduate school also had a contract with the city schools. For a half hour, I tried to explain to the agent (who worked out of an official city police department building) that while the graduate school name might be the same, it is a massive school and the degree-granting program for which I taught did not itself have a contract. In the end, it was easier to apologize and say it will never happen again.

My point in sharing this anecdote is that public agencies have a responsibility to ensure that the public good is not being compromised by corruption. Although I loathed taking time out of my day to sit through a grilling about my meager income from teaching graduate courses at night, I understood and respected the spirit of the process. As software continues to mediate education, researchers and policy makers must become more sensitive to the fact that the private interests·of the organizations and companies who are increasingly invited into our schools and teach our children might very well be shaping the educative services and products they provide. The corruption scandals of the 19th century that resulted in conflict of interests boards today (like Boss Tweed's Ring in New York), might have their correlate in software space today. Exposing such conflicts begin by viewing the source code of an application or web page.

INFERRED ALGORITHMIC LOGIC

The discussion of source viewing raises an important challenge in critical software studies: How do researchers critically examine the role of software when so much of software space is invisible or digitally walled off? My suggestion that educational technology companies should have to open their software to critical examination is a serious one. It is also likely to remain merely an academician's suggestion for some time due to a lack of political support it would require to make implementable. Still, we are not lost. There is a way to systematically hypothesize and analyze the work of software even when we cannot "peek under the hood" of applications. I refer to *inferred algorithmic logic* as a case in point. This method uses as an entry point of analysis that which we can observe as users. It requires that researchers collect observations of specific behaviors that emerge out of software space and into our own worlds. Then, we ask ourselves: What is the implied algorithmic logic that makes what I am experiencing through software space possible? By focusing on the algorithm, which Manovich (2001) calls one half of the world according to software (the other half is databases, which we will consider in the next section), we strategically hone in on an ontological element of software space that is at the heart of the tension between the user and the producers of software. Whereas pixel analysis focuses on the interface for a similar reason—as a site of tension—and functionality precedent compares what a specific application does and compares it to other similar functionalities, the algorithm is what is enabled and rendered through the interface and manifests itself in various functionalities.

Two Examples

Inferred algorithmic logic offers an informed and detailed description of what functionality and algorithmic logic is in place to effect that which the user experiences. It requires the researcher to think like a computer and tease out how the actions of software have been designed in order to fulfill its creators' goals. To examine algorithmic actions, then, is inherently dialectical. It is insufficient to focus solely on mathematical formula, but rather it is about how the logic that drives the algorithm affects users' experiences. For example, when I visit a popular online marketplace, I am greeted by dozens of images and deals that appear to be tailored to my interests. I see recommendations to buy books on data visualization and literacy research, vacuum cleaners, and a specific line of children's toys. When, however, I go to the same web site on a different computer I have never used, I do not see these same suggestions. Why? The activity of software in this case is powered by algorithms that use records about my previous browsing and purchases to make "suggestions." Algorithmically, I am likely to buy more children's toys because I have a history of doing so on the site. As a researcher, I am often pleasantly surprised by the book recommendations that the site suggests. I have read several books that I might not otherwise have discovered if they hadn't appeared on my screen. When I use a different computer and browser, however, the algorithms that the company uses do not have access to the same kind of data about me. As a result, I am offered very different kinds of products to purchase because, computationally speaking, I am a different person. Much of this functionality, it is worth noting, is made possible by increasingly powerful web browsers, which sync to multiple devices, integrate with a range of products and services, and whose default mode is to remember a great deal about its users. An algorithm's best friend.

In the previous example, the products recommended to me when visiting the web site are based, at least in part, on an algorithm that takes into account what I myself have purchased or viewed previously. When watching movies and television shows via a streaming video service, a similar logic appears to be at play. Based on user behavior and refined by accounting for the types of videos viewed, an algorithm makes "personalized" recommendations for "me." I use scare quotes for both *personalized* and *me* because there is something inherently impersonal about it. What the algorithm works with is not personal information, but rather an unrecognizable and categorical version of me. I am, to an algorithm, a collection of categories. For example, if I were to watch *Animal House* using this streaming video service, my person-hood is algorithmically tied to categories like comedy, frat humor, Jim Belushi, and such. The next day, I might see recommendations for me to watch movies that share some or all of the same categories, like *Blues Brothers*. What the designers of the algorithm are aiming for is a use of its video catalog's metadata (the kinds of invisible data that are linked to a media file or object) in order to target market me. When my son uses the same video streaming account to watch children's shows, the categorical metadata associated with those shows are added to a user profile that owns the account. The next day, he might be recommended not only Dr. Seuss shows, but also the raunchy *American Pie* movies. What this example demonstrates is that to the designers of software space and algorithms, media like streaming movies and television shows are simply files (or "objects" in some circles) that possess metadata. I am not a person to them, I am a profile. Unbeknownst to them, the profile associated with the single video streaming account belongs to three individuals—me, my wife, and our son—and we each prefer very different kinds of entertainment.

When researching software space, researchers must always be sensitive to the fact that for many actions that software makes, there are algorithms behind the scenes making it computationally possible. Such algorithms are created by human beings using mathematical formula and functions that treat metadata as variables. The variables and the formula can be tweaked over time, automatically and manually. The first step researchers should take when examining such phenomena is to isolate the occurrence. Second, offer an informed conjecture about what action software seems to be making and what information it is using to do so automatically. It can help to think in terms of computational relationships like if/then and while/during as a way to see the world from software's perspective. Third, ask why the designers of the software—including the algorithm—might have created their product to act in the way you observe. What goals does it achieve? How does it suggest the way the designers of software perceive the user? Finally, scrutinize the effect the phenomenon has on the user. Does it force the user to click or view or listen to something he or she might not want? Does it delay the user's ability to use the technology to accomplish what he or she wishes? Might it expose user information in unclear ways? These are some questions that might guide one's research and many more await creation.

The Categorical Imperative in Education

Above, I list commercial examples of how algorithms work in our world. My discussion is somewhat thin and others do it much more thoroughly (Berry, 2011; Fuller, 2003, 2008; Kitchin & Dodge, 2011; MacKenzie, 2006; Manovich, 2001, 2013). My purpose is to make clearer to educational researchers the notion that algorithms work behind the scenes to make software space act the way we experience it, that human beings design algorithms certain ways for certain reasons, and that those ways and reasons have direct effects on users' lives. This is no small claim in educational settings. The idea that a mathematical formula or code might be the conveyor of an educational philosophy with which students, teachers, and parents disagree or abhor is not one we as a research community have historically taken up. While we do have bodies of work that look critically at the tension between neoliberal reform agendas and democratic education, we have seldom deeply conceptualized the role that software—not "technology" broadly speaking—plays. The closest example might be critical work done on the problem of textbooks in schools (Christian-Smith & Apple, 1991;

Luke, 1988), which examines closely their content and production processes. With software-powered technologies, we can see how it is no longer just the content in books and the producers of such materials, but with software it is also a matter of how the values of its producers operationalize their agenda in the form of software, which acts so quickly and "smartly" that we hardly remember that software itself is a human creation. Both the quickness and the smarts we witness are due, in part, to the role that algorithms play. They are fundamentally the result of dual processes: categorization and quantification. As Taubman (2009) points out, this act of distancing ourselves from the fleshy realities of pedagogy—whether through a rubric or through algorithmic formula and metadata—has the same problematic end, which both Taubman and Selwyn note. Taubman (2009) refers to "control from a distance" (p. 40) and Selwyn (2014) calls it ". . . standardizing and commoditizing education, reducing educational processes and relationships to forms that are easily quantifiable and recorded" (p. 62). In both cases, when referring to software-powered technologies, the distance these scholars refer to is one of algorithmic altitude. Such altitude is only possible if the metadata provided has complex structural value, which is why analyzing data structures is of equal value and import.

DATA STRUCTURE ANALYSIS

Data structure hardly sounds like an area of study for educational researchers. Rather, it sounds as if its study rests squarely in the domain of computer and information science. However, as discussed above, the fact that standards and categories are being used throughout education to "reform" schools to address issues that are as social, economic, and cultural as they are academic suggests that any sense of objective quantitative distance is phantasmal. Data are samples of complex phenomena. For those who hold data up on a pedagogical pedestal, there is the belief that with enough kinds of data it should be possible to improve the ways teachers teach, students learn, and districts spend their money. Data are as ideological as they are informational. It is necessary to move beyond theorizing the role of data and to unpack the way data actually function in software space.

Data are generated to be stored, retrieved, and manipulated through databases. Manovich (2001) defines the database as "a structured collection of data. The data stored in a database is organized for fast search and retrieval by a computer and therefore, it is anything but a simple collection of items" (p. 218). Databases come in different types—hierarchical, network, relational, and object-oriented—each of which approaches the organization of data differently. In a database, each object is potentially equal to any other object. That is, when I search a library database for books by "Milton," it does not matter how large or small the individual books are nor when they were created. A basic database treats information associated with the books—metadata like titles, authors and years of publication as well as text files that might contain the entire works—equally. It is this equal treatment of individual objects that makes speedy retrieval of information possible. The way such data and metadata are structured increase or decrease searchability.

Data can be generated many ways. As Taubman (2009) notes, one way is via the use of analogue technologies to sample measurements of complex human experiences. Rubrics are one example, where predetermined qualitative language and quantities are used to represent phenomena. Data can also be generated by users themselves in both explicit and implicit ways. Explicitly, users can knowingly submit information to software space, say, by filling out a form online. In these cases, the fields on the form are provided and act as categories; the user only has to add her or his specific information. Implicitly, users provide data to software space without fully realizing it. As web browsers become increasingly sophisticated, they gather vast amounts of data about their users: search history, frequently visited sites, personal information like mailing address and credit card numbers, previous purchases, and more. Whether or not users know it, they are generating what Berry calls "streams" of data that intensify over time. Once data are generated they are stored and subject to algorithmic manipulation. A simple example of this is when we take digital pictures and are given the option to immediately alter the pictures' appearance by applying filters. Each filter is an algorithm that mathematically adjusts the quantities associated with pixels to produce aesthetic effects. There are numberless ways to gather, store, manipulate, and render data. Rendering data, however, is of particular interest as it is where an individual's interpretation of data can directly influence others. It is not uncommon, for instance, to see oppositional political parties using the same data to publish very different reports and visualizations, which are intended to encourage the public to interpret the data and their associated political agendas. I will examine the use of visualizations in some greater detail in the chapters that follow. For the current section, it is important to unpack how the structures of data can serve as a site of study for researchers.

Feeding Congress: An Example of Data Structures

One of the ways information flows across the Internet is through data feeds. *Data feeds* refers broadly to the sharing of defined sets of data between specified entities. A common way to share data in specified ways both widely on the Web and between designated systems is called an application programming interface or API. The *New York Times* offers a series of APIs for developers of software products to use. One such API is called The Congress API, which allows developers to be fed data automatically about roll-call votes, members of Congress, vote data, and biographical information. In order to receive or send the Congress API, a developer has to organize her data systems in a structure specified by the *Times*. The developer can then send requests to the Congress API for information, which will be returned to and stored in the developer's system. For example, if a developer wanted information about members' biographies and their roles, she could send the following request to the Congress API:

http://api.nytimes.com/svc/politics/{version}/us/legislative/congress/
members/{member-id}[.response-format]?api-key={your-API-key}

In this case, we have a URL (a web address) that is sent to "api.nytimes. com/svc/politics." The developer specifies what version of the API she is requesting and includes specific information like the member ID for the congressperson, the file type the developer wants to receive the information in, and their unique API certification key. Although what is sent looks a lot like a typical URL, what is returned is a very specific set of data in a specified structure. There are dozens of different kinds of data that a developer can request, but they must be requested according to the parameters the *Times* sets. For example, where there is a placeholder for 'response-format' in the API above, the *Times* specifies that it must be either XML or JSON formats. That is, if a developer was to want the data in a format for Excel (.xls), the *Times* would return an error message because the response format does not match the options provided. When requesting data about votes by type, a developer has to choose from predetermined categories of vote types determined by the *Times*'s own development team, which includes *missed_votes, party_votes, loneno* (which indicates the times a member was the only no vote), and *perfect* (which returns data about the members who voted yes or no on every vote for which she was eligible). It is important to recognize that these data structures are predetermined and complied by developers whose primary purpose is to elegantly and efficiently structure and share information. Such sharing requires mutually agreed upon data structures and ways of working. When we are examining the role of software space in education, data structures are an incredibly important area of study because they reveal how teaching and learning is abstracted, categorized, and structured for communication and manipulation in software space.

Data have inherent ontological and epistemological limitations, which directly impact how they can be discussed by policy makers and companies as well as how they are interpreted and rendered in the public discourse. When human phenomena are abstracted as data, they are transcoded from their original experiential forms and become categorical and numerical values. These values are structured in certain ways, which must make sense to both computer systems and to the human beings whose ideologies and agendas the abstraction and sharing of such data benefit. Because all data are necessarily removed from their original sources, their values are a distant representation and the nature of such a representation dances to the tune of two fiddlers: one informational and the other ideological. When data being represented are phenomenologically simple, the use of data can be convenient, efficient, and useful. For example, knowing whether or not a specific senator voted for a specific bill. However, data cannot easily capture phenomenological complexity like why a senator chose not to vote for a specific bill, which perhaps has something to do with the nuance of the bill's language and how it might affect her constituents. Some suggest that despite such phenomenological distance, if we gather enough data on enough phenomena we have the computational capacity to draw exciting insights. This might be true, or it might be false and overeager. When dealing with complex phenomena like teaching and learning, our data are nearly always abstracted categories and numbers the values of which are determined by policy makers and companies rather than by schools and communities. The categorical inaccuracy of the data we collect and use in education makes amassing more of it an exercise in profitable futility, like the captain of a ship who navigates by routinely rounding up her coordinates. We will arrive somewhere eventually, but it will doubtless be very far off course.

IN SUM

By bringing to the research community's attention these methods of analysis, I believe that we can intervene earlier in educational reform efforts and software development to chart newer and truer courses forward. If we continue to research the role of technology in education—from policy to practice—without accounting for the agentic and ideological qualities of software space, we will be asking the wrong questions, gathering the wrong data, and conducting our analyses without the theoretical footing that might get us closer to understanding a complex and mostly invisible phenomenon. The methods outlined above are demonstrations of how we might capture software in the act, so to speak. I am particularly interested in what colleagues from other fields might add to this slender list. Multimodality scholars doubtless have other methods that might translate naturally to critical software studies. For example, how might multimodal transcription tools be modified to account for software? Might we simply add a column to such transcription tools that say "software activity"? These are the kinds of questions I hope we begin asking and the kinds of techniques I hope we prototype.

As incomplete and imperfect as it is, the above methods are a beginning. In the next chapter, I apply a critical software studies conceptual framework and research methods to a series of studies in order to demonstrate how a focus on critical software studies can extend and deepen our approach to examining the role of software in education. Raising our collective awareness of how software mediates and shapes what it means to teach and learn is a first step in making critical software studies a ubiquitous, even if subtle, component of our output as a field.

WORKS CITED

Berry, D. (2011). *The philosophy of software: Code and mediation in the digital age.* New York: Palgrave Macmillan.

Bromley, H., & Apple, M. W. (Eds.). (1998). *Education/Technology/Power: Educational computing as a social practice.* Albany, NY: SUNY.

Christian-Smith, L. K., & Apple, M. W. (1991). *The politics of the textbook.* New York: Routledge.

Fairclough, N. (2001). *Language and power.* New York: Longman.

Fuller, M. (2003). *Behind the blip: essays on the culture of software.* Brooklyn, NY: Autonomedia.

Fuller, M. (Ed.). (2008). *Software studies: A lexicon.* Cambridge, MA: MIT Press.

Given, L. M. (Ed.). (2008). *The Sage encyclopedia of qualitative research methods* (Vols. 1 & 2). Los Angeles: Sage Publications.

Kitchin, R., & Dodge, M. (2011). *Code/Space: Software and everyday life.* Cambridge, MA: MIT Press.

Kress, G. (2003). *Literacy in the new media age.* New York: Routledge.

Kress, G. (2011). Discourse analysis and education: A multimodal social semiotic approach. In R. Rogers (Ed.), *An introduction to critical discourse analysis in education* (2nd edition). New York: Routledge.

Luke, A. (1988). *Literacy, textbooks, and ideology: Postwar literacy instruction and the mythology of Dick and Jane.* New York: Falmer Press.

MacKenzie, A. (2006). *Cutting code: Software and sociality.* New York: Peter Lang.

Manovich, L. (2001). *The language of new media.* London: MIT Press.

Manovich, L. (2013). *Software takes command.* New York: Bloomsbury Academic.

Pold, S. (2008). Button. In M. Fuller (Ed.), *Software studies: A lexicon* (pp. 31–36). Cambridge, MA: MIT Press.

Rogers, R. (Ed.). (2011). *An introduction to critical discourse analysis in education.* New York: Routledge.

Selwyn, N. (2014). *Distrusting educational technology: Critical questions for changing times.* New York: Routledge.

Taubman, P. M. (2009). *Teaching by numbers: Deconstructing the discourse of standards and accountability in education.* New York: Routledge.

Unknown. (n.d.). Clicky. Retrieved November 4, 2014, from http://clicky.com/.

5   Reimagined Research

"For all his scientific intentions with respect to the effects of light on appearances, without imagination Monet could not conceivably have seen the façade of Rouen Cathedral in so many ways: as a stern embodiment of a dark faith, as a dancing radiant screen of promise, as a delicate lacy veil."

—Maxine Greene in "Texts and Margins,"
Releasing the Imagination, p. 140

In a small room in Queens, New York, about 50 people gathered to hear from a group of vendors offering different products to schools: online Advanced Placement courses, educational videos, game-based history courses, and so on. After hearing one pitch from a vendor they all start to sound the same. Their respective products are claimed to be designed by teachers (although one can seldom find the names of those teachers), tested and updated regularly, contain multimedia to engage students, and are said to be of the highest quality. There is one phrase, though, that when uttered, causes the eyes of attendees to look up. *Research says.* With those words, pens begin to jot down notes, heads nod. On one occasion, I decided to interject mid-sales pitch.

"Can you tell us more about the research you are referring to?"

"Let me see," the salesperson replied as she sifted through her notes. "I don't appear to have it here but if you leave me your contact information I'll send it to you."

"Was the research study conducted on your product alone? And if so, did your company pay for the study?"

"Again, I'll have to ask back at the office—"

"The word *research* suggests objective and thorough evaluation, but the fact is that there are a lot of ways it can look and some 'research' that is cited by companies like yours is often not what it appears to be."

At this point, others appeared to stop listening to me so I took the social cues and halted my inquisition. A few days later, the salesperson emailed me a link to the company's web site on which a whitepaper by an "independent research group" was posted. The best I could tell, the research group consisted of members of the company and some doctoral students like me. On the one hand, I felt perfectly at peace with my indignation in response to the salesperson's reference to research. At the same time, I was all too aware that the research we produce as scholars seldom makes its way to schools and companies, and when it does it can appear to different audiences that researchers are merely writing for themselves in both the content and form of their studies.

When it comes to research about educational technology, I confess to having been frustrated at times. I agree with Selwyn (2014) that too many researchers have allowed themselves to be blindly optimistic when it comes to technology. One way to extend and deepen our gaze, I believe, is to move beyond technology and critically examine the nature of software. In what follows, I apply the theoretical and methodological framework developed in the preceding chapters to several educational studies. I have chosen studies that have impacted my thinking about education, technology, and literacy by scholars whom I admire immensely. This is an incomplete list, of course, but it represents various kinds of qualitative educational research studies that might take a slight or drastic turn if concepts and methods from critical software studies were part of the research design. The lengths of the studies range from article- to book-length. To be clear, I do not mean to suggest that the researchers *should* have done anything differently than they did. Rather, it is to demonstrate what is already immediately possible in the field if we consider the ways software mediates and shapes our experiences. For each study, I provide a summary (albeit, imperfect) and then locate one or two elements on which to apply a critical software studies perspective, concluding with a discussion how this perspective could have resulted in new inquiries, insights, and knowledge.

TEACHING BY NUMBERS | TAUBMAN

In previous chapters, I have referred to the critical educational research of Peter Taubman (2009), specifically his book *Teaching by Numbers: Deconstructing the Discourse of Standards and Accountability in Education*. Taubman's book creates an invaluable theoretical foundation for researchers interested in the interplay between the discourse of reform and its realities, both historical and current. Published as President Obama takes office, the book stops as the Bush administration exits, leaving No Child Left Behind intact legally though bruised and battered from implementation challenges at the state level and widespread criticism. When Taubman refers to "numbers" in his title, he means reformers' attempts to translate the complexity of teaching, learning, and living into data for analysis and action. Testing is a primary way such numbers are conjured. Once generated, data must be entered into software space through information systems. In a reference to New York City's student information system, ARIS, he writes, "Tests will provide the data, which ARIS will then aggregate, disaggregate, and turn into information that will be used to hold teachers accountable" (p. 21). As Taubman suggests, it is highly contestable to suggest data represent much about how teachers teach or what students learn. For instance, testing data do not represent what students have learned, but represent a representation of what students have learned as mediated through test questions. Taubman analyzes a series of examples, prompting him to reflect on precisely what is lost in batteries of such questions. "As one reads through these tests, tracking the various questions, a view of knowledge emerges that equates understanding or creativity or erudition with information retrieval, the ability to concentrate for long periods of time on a meaningless task, alacrity in making decisions, and compliance with directives that have no relevance to one's own interests, desires, abilities, knowledge, or understanding" (p. 26). Despite the inhumanity and invalidity of such tests, neoliberal reformers called for numbers generated from tests (sold by companies) aligned to standards (developed greatly by companies) that could be used to hold schools and educators accountable (so companies could manage schools while rapidly repairing/preparing teachers). And so they did.

Despite his astuteness and passion, Taubman mostly avoids the implicit and explicit role software-powered technologies play in these reforms. And yet, without analogue and digital technologies, the reforms to which he refers cannot scale. He hints at the technicity of the neoliberal agenda when he writes about the way neoliberal reforms affected his teacher education program. I cited his reference in an earlier chapter, but it is useful to reprint in this context: "The loose connections among standards, check sheets, offices that aggregate the data, the technologies that are used, the supervisors and student teachers, the reports generated, the feedback produced by the reports, and the actions taken as a result, all these creates assemblages" (p. 123). The assemblages to which Taubman refers constitutes software space. He lists analogue technologies like standards and check sheets, which are used to transcode the complexity of learning to teach into data. When he refers to "the technologies that are used," he alludes to the software applications, user interfaces, databases, data feeds, and reports that comprise an assemblage mostly hidden from public view. What the assemblage renders to the public is a headline about the ineffectiveness of teachers accompanied by a chart with numbers.

Critical software studies could add greater depth to Taubman's scholarship. One area that could be analyzed is the relationship between the classroom observation of a teacher by a supervisor, the rubric that is used to transcode the complexity of the phenomenon into values (categories and numbers), and the software application used by the university to enter that data into information systems. As Taubman puts it, ". . . instruments that are part of various educational assemblages, requires teaching, curriculum, and what happens on a given day in a given classroom to be recoded or translated into measures that can be quantified" (p. 122). At each juncture, one can ask: What do we sacrifice of the complexity of pedagogy and what does software space gain? I will use my own university's process to evaluate teaching candidates as an example. In our program, teaching candidates complete their student teaching experience in accordance with state regulations for certification. They spend more than 100 hours in their school, observing a mentor's instruction and taking over the responsibility for teaching several sections of a course. Five times a semester, a supervisor from the university comes to review the candidate's practice. That supervisor uses a rubric provided to him by the university, which frames several categories for observation. In New York State, these supervisory rubrics are increasingly made to align with the categories and language of the Danielson Framework. After observing the candidate's instruction, the supervisor sits with the candidate and discusses his observations using the language of the rubric. When the observation is complete, the supervisor is asked to submit his numerical and qualitative evaluation to a data tracking system the university purchased, which holds a digital version of the same rubric used in the classroom observation. As all supervisors use the same mechanism, administrators at the university can see an itemized breakdown of their students' scores and feedback, which is then used—in theory—to refine the program and to meet requirements set forth by national accreditation agencies.

In this example, software space begins with the establishment and forced adoption of evaluation standards. The language and numbers of the standards serve as a filter through which the supervisor's observations are fed. It is no longer about the supervisor's own language and values. The supervisor's role is to align the way he communicates with someone else's language and conceptual framing. A rubric is the instrument through which this occurs. It serves as an intermediary instrument between human and software space. When the supervisor enters such data into the university's information system, the complex act of teaching and learning is fully transcoded for software space. These two instruments—the rubric and the information system—work tightly together. In both cases, the supervisor is forced to conform with both the standards and the language of others. The rubric has predefined categories and boxes that are greatly prepopulated with the language of standards. The information system has a user interface that only permits the supervisor to enter predetermined information. If the supervisor notices something that is not part of the standards, there is no easy way to account for it.

It is also worth considering the degree to which the standards and instruments serve software space at the expense of the teaching candidate. Someone who has not been teaching very long might find the breadth of the teaching standards intimidating and be distracted from focusing on his or her interaction with students. The standards, in software space, are treated as representative of quality teaching yet they are inherently incomplete and quite a distance from human interaction. In addition, a supervisor might find that the use of the rubric for observations and conversations becomes a distraction from being fully and critically present while observing the candidate's teaching. These are, of course, debatable and discussable points I raise. In the end, however, one's ability to research the kind of phenomena Taubman draws our attention to is strengthened by unpacking the role that software space plays because it takes our attention through the phenomenal into the computational.

DISTRUSTING EDUCATIONAL TECHNOLOGY | SELWYN

In Chapter 1, I refer to the work of Neil Selwyn as a way to critically frame our examination of software-powered technologies. Whereas I refer briefly at times or allude to the fact that Selwyn's arguments would benefit from a more thorough accounting for software, I do not elaborate. In what follows, I wish to make clearer how critical software studies could strengthen and broaden the scope of Selwyn's work. Selwyn (2014) discusses an "orthodoxy of optimism" (p. 13) that surrounds research about technology in education. He argues that "any account of technology use in education needs to be framed in explicit terms of societal conflict over the distribution of power" (p. 19). He later adds, "we need to explore the idea that the digital technologies used increasingly throughout education are also best understood as ideological in character and form—that is, shaped by dominant sets of values and interests, and then acting (however subtly) to perpetuate the dominance of those values and interests" (p. 31). Selwyn explores the subtle sway of technology by looking at four sites of study: virtual technologies, open technologies, games, and social technologies. I will limit my analysis to his writing on virtual technologies.

In his discussion of virtual schools, by which he means both synchronous and asynchronous applications of digital technologies, Selwyn argues they tend to "replicate the familiar spaces of the school, college, and university" (p. 48) despite claims to innovation and newness. The "most significant" form of virtual environments are learning management systems or LMSs, which have been popular in higher education for many years and are gaining in popularity in K-12 settings, as in the case of iLearnNYC. Whereas on the one hand, LMSs seem uniquely structured to make virtual learning possible, it is also the case that they excel at administrative oversight. That is, they "have been integrated increasingly with digital technologies designed to support the routine processes of data collection, record keeping, monitoring and assessment, creation and distribution of learning resources, and coordination of students, teachers, parents, school leaders, and administrators" (p. 50). Whereas LMSs are positioned often in a discourse of emancipation and choice, Selwyn concludes that such illusions are achieved by reducing education to a series of compartmentalized components like abstract knowledge and skills. He writes, "A significant element of this reduction of education to its core constituent elements is the recasting of 'virtual' education along more business-oriented 'data-drive' lines" (p. 58). He concludes that the promotion and adoption of virtual technologies like LMSs are "placing education firmly in the midst of the immaterial 'new' economy—standardizing and commoditizing education, reducing educational processes and relationships to forms that are easily quantifiable and recorded, distancing educational professionals from the process of educational engagements and thereby deprofessionalizing and deskilling the teaching profession" (p. 62). Selwyn's critique is one with which I find much agreement. It also remains mostly theoretical, with some anecdotal examples used to pull theory toward the ground but, in the end, not applied to more empirical evidence. What kinds of evidence might one use to extend Selwyn's theories and what methods might be used to examine such evidence?

Consider the example of group discussions, which are a popular teaching method in both face-to-face and online classes. In a physical setting, students might be asked to move their desks together and to share their responses to a reading given for homework. As students discuss, they might pull ideas from annotations they made or they might skim the reading because they didn't read the assignment for class. As members of the group speak, others might interrupt, gesture, or make eye contact with the speaker to signal that they wish to add something. During the activity, the teacher might circulate around the room and listen in, perhaps taking notes of what she is hearing or interjecting when a group is struggling. After the small groups discuss, the teacher might ask for a member of each group to report and take notes on the board in order to arrive at some kind of collective reading of the text. In a virtual environment like an LMS, group discussions are also a very popular method. In an online course, for instance, a teacher might create random groups where several students have access to a message board visible only to the instructor and the members of the group. Students might read the same reading, but then each compose a written response and post it to the message board. Depending on the assignment, the other members of the group might be required to respond to each of their peers' responses. The instructor can read all the responses as they come in and also review reports about student activity that will tell him who has contributed responses, what the average length was of the responses, and which students have responded to each other most. If the instructor wishes for all students to talk (asynchronously) as a whole class, he would have to create a separate area in the message boards where all could debrief outside of their small groups.

What is lost and what is gained in these two scenarios? How might software (however subtly) be affecting pedagogy?

There are two main ways we might consider the way software affects pedagogy in the scenario above. The first is more positive in nature. By using online message boards, all students are required to contribute to the discussion of a text or question and are held accountable for such contributions. That is, whereas in a physical classroom it might be possible for some students to "hide" and avoid speaking, an online message board makes it impossible to do so. Not only might the instructor manually check that each student wrote and posted responses, but an instructor can often also use the LMS's reporting dashboard to see at a glance which students contributed and some quantitative information about those posts. The second way to consider software's effect is one of multimodal loss. When sitting in a physical environment with each other, students and teachers can draw upon multiple modes of communication in order to make meaning together. Members of a small group discussing a text, for instance, speak to each other (oral mode), use hands and facial expressions when communicating (gestural), and might draw quick sketches to explain something (visual). These multimodal resources are available not only to the students in communicating their ideas, but also to the teacher in assessing students' focus and quality of discussion. Even a relatively new instructor might be comfortable assessing and interjecting in a group discussion as a way to shape students' thinking. In an online environment using message boards, such intervention is only possible later in the process. Students, in short, draft their responses in one mode before communicating their ideas in the same single mode. The instructor has far less to work with in terms of assessing students' learning process, but far more in terms of ensuring individual accountability for learning products, albeit monomodal.

From a pedagogical perspective, the difference between online or face-to-face discussions might be simply a matter of preference once the limits and affordances are weighed and considered. From an administrative perspective, however, software space offers much more insofar as its transcoding of all student and teacher interaction into data means that control from a distance is much more possible. An administrator who is being held accountable for producing data and evidence of student learning that aligns to certain standards can hardly be blamed for having a preference for teaching and learning in an LMS. The reports come easily.

MULTILITERACIES | NEW LONDON GROUP

The New London Group (Cazden et al., 1996)—comprised of 11 of the world's leading literacy researchers—wrote a seminal article that provides a theoretical case for conceptualizing literacy research and practice in terms of multiliteracies in response to the rapidly changing social environments brought on by globalization and the rise of technology. The outcome, the authors state, is twofold: "creating access to the evolving language of work, power, and community and fostering the critical engagement necessary for [students] to design their social futures and achieve success through fulfilling employment" (p. 60). As human beings' work-, public-, and private lives are impacted by the intermingling of cultures and infused with ever-evolving technologies, the authors argue that schools should begin to create learning experiences for students based on "a metalanguage of multiliteracies based on the concept of 'design'" (p. 73), which includes the semiotic resources at students' disposal for making meaning of the world. In addition to traditional linguistic modes of meaning making, the authors argue for conceptualizing other modes as well, referring to visual, audio, gestural, spatial, and multimodal meanings. They write: "In a profound sense, all meaning-making is multimodal. All written text is also visually designed. Desktop publishing puts a new premium on visual design and spreads responsibility for the visual much more broadly than was the case when writing and page layout were separate trades. So, a school project can and should properly be evaluated on the basis of visual as well as linguistic design and their multimodal relationship" (p. 81).

In addition, the authors are keen to critique the role that corporations increasingly play in education. Whereas businesses both fuel cross-cultural interactions through globalization and increase the drive behind developments in technology, the authors caution: "But fast capitalism is also a nightmare. Corporate cultures and their discourse of familiarity are more subtly and more rigorously exclusive than the most nasty—honestly nasty—of hierarchies" (p. 66). The corporate culture the authors describe is one that demands "assimilation to mainstream norms" (ibid.) and restricts the growth of those who do not assimilate. Further, such fast capitalism "is also a vicious world driven by the barely restrained market . . . we need to be aware of the danger that our words become co-opted by economically and market-driven discourses, no matter how contemporary and 'post-capitalist' these may appear" (p. 67). In the authors' view, language(s) is power—in our personal, professional, and public experiences—and as the media and modes of communication shift with advances in technology and culture, so too does the way in which power is granted and denied.

The definition of multiliteracies put forth in the theoretical treatise, however, does not explicitly acknowledge the role that software plays in mediating and shaping human experience. One exception is a brief section where the authors note the pivotal semiotic role graphics play in the user interfaces we encounter. They write, "With a new worklife comes a new language. A good deal of this change is the result of new technologies, such as the iconographic, text, and screen-based modes of interacting with automated machinery: 'user-friendly' interfaces operate with more subtle levels of cultural embeddedness than interfaces base on abstract commands" (p. 66). Note, however, that whereas the authors explicitly reference user interfaces, it is not with an expressed awareness of software but rather of the multimodal quality of the signs expressed. In short, their attention is semiotic and exists just above the surface of software.

What might critical software studies add to the authors' ideas?

There are two main additions I would suggest. First, the definition of design the authors discuss focuses on the affordances of different semiotic systems, "the grammars of languages, and the grammars of other semiotic systems such as film, photography, or gesture" (p. 74). The do not, however, account for the way design and designers of software space enable and inhibit one's semiotic resources. As I have referred to previously, autocorrect is a helpful example (Lynch, 2013). A person might have fluency in linguistic modes of meaning making. She might be able to deliver ideas using clear vocabulary and compelling metaphors, for instance. However, if the person is communicating via a device with autocorrect enabled, she might find that the design of software space intrudes upon her linguistic design when her words automatically change before her eyes. Or, consider a person's fluency with visual design. Imagine a student who can deftly create sophisticated concept maps in chemistry class using colored pencils and paper. When asked to recreate those maps using "innovative" visualization software, the student might find that he lacks familiarity with the user interface (which is designed by software development teams and graphic designers) or that learning how scalable vector graphics work in software space is surprisingly difficult to implement. In these cases, software space chafes against human beings' lived experiences and modes of meaning making. Software space designers impose their logic—their grammar—upon designers across modes.

Second, the ubiquity of software space, coupled with its economically driven nature, means that the languages and logics that comprise its discourse and grammar are becoming a language of power. We see this in education where policy makers and companies gain public support for efforts to reform schools by holding teachers and students to higher standards and make them publicly accountable. The operationalization of these reform principles, however, translates into standards and taxonomies that are used to organize abstracted data by various means and structure such data in databases so they can be manipulated algorithmically. The public hears only "standards" and "accountability." Once it becomes evident that pedagogy is being falsely categorized and quantified, the public becomes less accepting. Recall the uproar of parents in New York State as the realities of Common Core testing became evident. There were protests outside schools across the state. I argue that what parents responded to in that instance was the language and grammar of software space, which was being used for political gain. The more one knows about how software space functions, the more empowered one is to resist and wrangle it for more collective and noble ends. Software is the meta-mode of communication that is increasingly enabling and inhibiting all other modes of communication we have come to rely upon to design our social futures.

REIGN OF ERROR | RAVITCH

One of the most outspoken opponents of neoliberal education reforms is educational historian Diane Ravitch. In a popular and comprehensive critique, Ravitch (2013) frames the problem of corporate-friendly reform and offers a series of solution steps. Similar to other critical education scholars referred to above, Ravitch argues that public education is being systematically outsourced to the private sector via a series of discursive and legislatives moves that promote achievement (measured via testing), accountability (testing and publicly reporting data), "choice," and commercial partnerships. Underlying Ravitch's stance is an awareness of the inherent contradiction of accountability-based reforms that rely on commercial partnerships. She writes, "The transfer of public funds to private management and the creation of thousands of deregulated, unsupervised, and unaccountable schools have opened the public coffers to profiteering, fraud, and exploitation by large and small entrepreneurs" (p. 4). In the name of public accountability for schools, reformers have enlisted the aid of private companies who are themselves accountable to no one.

One kind of such companies are educational technology companies. Ravitch writes about how, under the banner of Race to the Top, technology companies were positioned to insert themselves in at least two places in education: administration and instruction. For example, she writes about how the federal government's emphasis on data led to the Gates Foundation underwriting "the creation of a large database project to collect confidential student data with Wireless Generation, a subsidiary of Rupert Murdoch's News Corporation" (pp. 23–24). The name of this initiative is inBloom and will be examined more closely in Chapter 7. Ravitch also demonstrates how even non-technological reform principles translate directly to empowering technology companies. Reformers' assertion that public funding should follow children—the same logic that drives the use of school voucher programs—is a deceptive tactic to pry public funding from public schools and divert it to private companies, including online learning companies. She warns, "As public money is dispersed, so is public oversight and accountability for the spending of public money" (p. 21). In a chapter devoted to virtual learning, Ravitch analyzes the discursive deception in how policy makers and companies talk about the merits of K-12 online learning. "Surely every student should learn to use computers and the Internet in school. The possibilities for imaginative teaching and learning and research are boundless. But," Ravitch writes, "that is quite different from inviting the private sector to make money by enrolling students in virtual academies" (p. 196).

Whereas her convictions are strong and her logic compelling, Ravitch's claims about the deleterious uses of technology in schools would be bolstered with deeper attention to the software-powered technologies that undergird the topic at hand. Some of the use of technology in the examples she discusses in the book like virtual schools, computerized testing, and entrepreneurial technologies developed to support the Common Core Standards implementation are explicit and clear. Less obvious, however, are the ways in which the accountability movement creates a veritable industry devoted to transcoding the complexity of teaching and learning for software space. Under the banner of accountability, teachers are forced to comply with teaching standards that are used by administrators—via rubrics—to translate the fleshy realities of classroom practice into data. Rubrics in such cases serve as a qualitative waiting area before numerical data are generated and entered into information systems. Such teaching standards are used not only by educators and school principals; they are used by companies as a taxonomy for organizing, searching, recommending, and hawking products. Consider the case of an individual teacher whose principal determines she needs to improve her lesson planning. What does the human conversation between the two professionals about the teacher's practice contain that gets lost when translated to a qualitative rubric? What of the qualitative rubric is lost in the simplicity of a number? And, perhaps most insidious, by what logic are companies that sell to teachers aligning their products to standards and with what effect? These questions must be asked because there is a rapidly growing industry of companies who believe that if they can just get their hands on detailed teacher evaluation data, they can sell targeted resources to teachers based on the algorithmic magic that occurs when one mixes standards, numbers, and metadata.

CRITICAL BIFOCALITY | WEIS AND FINE

In their ethnographic studies of the relationship between communities and schools, Weis and Fine (2012) make explicit attempts to account for the intertwined nature of both macro- and micro-level "structural dynamics," the way policy affects the daily lives of human beings, specifically with regard to "aggressive neoliberal inscriptions on public education policy and practice" (p. 173). They describe eloquently a "commitment to bifocals—dedicated theoretical and empirical attention to structures *and* lives—[that] can be adjusted to varied contexts, historic moments, and accompanying institutional arrangements" (p. 174). They refer to this concept as *critical bifocality*. For Weis and Fine, the work of researchers must, to some degree, identify the complexity of injustice and thoroughly examine both large-scale and daily ways such injustices are perpetuated. Fine applies the concept of bifocality to her research on how education reforms intended to close the "achievement gap" perpetuate those individuals' and communities' dispossession. She writes about a school in New York City in which public meetings were held to discuss the city's intention to close the old comprehensive high school that served mostly communities of color and open multiple smaller schools in the building in its place, which would provide an opening for families in the school's affluent neighborhood to also apply. Parents from different communities raised questions about who would benefit from the new schools, what kinds of students would be allowed to apply, and whether the metal detectors currently used in the school would remain. Having attended similar meetings, I appreciated Fine's observation that "the discursive architecture of separate and unequal was flooding the room, being spoken by White and Black prospective parents who seemed to be among the new gentrifiers" (p. 192). She then discusses a city representative who spoke about how children would be admitted to the school, saying, "any child would be welcome to the school. . . . They will submit attendance, grades, and test scores and the computer will choose those who are eligible. Then we'll interview" (ibid.). Fine notes, "As a lottery, the process is fair, but all of the preconditions are coated in relative privilege" (ibid.). She then goes on to discuss how social, economic, and cultural inequalities ensure that students in families with the means would be cared for and those without become part of "the searing capillaries through which systemic miseducation of children of color stains our national history" (p. 194). Fine's observation that the lottery is fair and that the preconditions are unjust is astute. The fairness of the process is predicated on the assumption that all students have received equal educational and familial support and that all families are equally prepared to navigate a thickly bureaucratic process of applying for a new school. (Some of the documents used by the city resemble tax forms.) Fine's examination would also benefit from extended critical analysis through software space.

The city official's claim that the "computer will choose those who are eligible" is utterly false in two ways. The first is the falsehood that Fine notes above, which is that the preconditions drip with inequity. The second is this: The choice of who is eligible is made through software space, which means that there are human beings who determine the logic through which software identifies (let's not call what the computer enacts a "choice") the students who are eligible. What is the implied algorithmic logic at play here? Based on what the official stated, the city has compiled data about students' attendance records, their grades, and their test scores. Those data are structured in specific ways that are determined by either school officials or by consultants. In this case, the "student" to which we refer is likely identified in software space via a nine-digit identification number. The humanity of the student is likely rendered in software space as a comma separated variable (CSV) that lists the categories being reported on the first line and then assigns specific data to those positions in the sequence in the lines that follow:

StudentID;AbsenceTotalDays;SchoolID;ELATranscript_FinalGrades;
MathTranscript_FinalGrades; ELATestScore; MathTestScore
123456789; 14; 02M987; 93; 78; 82; 65

The data structure draws attention to the dramatic categorical and numerical representation of students in "the computer." The idiosyncrasies, passions, and struggles of an individual student are rendered as simple variables in software space. The possibility that the student is working very hard in math, improving each week, and cannot attend after school because both parents work and she is needed home is not represented. Software space can treat all input equally, with sameness. It cannot account for equity and fairness—unless one believes that equity and fairness is simply a matter of tweaking an algorithm based on socioeconomic status, gender, ethnicity, and free lunch status. In such a case, and it is a popular stance with state- and national-level officials, providing all students with a quality education is just a matter of getting the algorithm right. In any case, it is not the computer that "chooses." Human beings tell computers what to do with either great intentionality or greater ignorance. Wearing critical bifocals when researching these kinds of phenomena might well include not only accounting for the macro-level of policy and the micro-level of daily experiences. It might also demand a third nano-focality: that of software space.

SINGLE STORIES | BEHIZADEH

In her meta-analysis of large-scale writing assessment, Behizadeh (2014) writes that "Writing instruction that fails to connect to students' funds of knowledge is not only conceptually unsound but pedagogical impotent" (p. 9). The author argues that the kind of high-stakes writing assessment in wide use today, called direct writing assessment in which students respond "cold" to a prompt in a timed environment, impact the ways writing is taught in schools. She claims that a "mechanical view" (p. 2) of writing persists, where educators and administrators define writing instruction as the drilling of compartmentalized skills despite the fact that composition theory has evolved far beyond such a limited definition. Rather, today writing is regarded by many researchers as sociocultural, meaning it "considers varied contexts and defines writing as a contextual process" (p. 2). Socioculturally responsive writing models value the individuality of students' contexts and cultures, their languages, and the many modes and genres of composition beyond traditional writing. One of the more promising models for sociocultural writing practices has been attempts to implement large-scale portfolio assessments, which allow students to receive feedback from multiple stakeholders throughout the writing process and for students to choose what to write based on their passions and interests. Behizadeh argues that large-scale portfolio assessments would be of high consequential validity, unlike direct writing assessments that encourage students to write inauthentically and teachers to teach poorly: "when only one way of writing is tested, and when that test has high stakes for teachers and students, instruction will focus on this one form of writing and the recognition of multiliteracies will be less likely to occur" (p. 7).

In Behizadeh's article, she seldom refers to software or to technology save for a brief mention of the rise of automated essay scoring products. Whereas, in some of the other discussions of research studies above, the role of technology is implied or even mentioned, this study serves as a case in point of how critical software studies can add an additional trajectory for inquiry and examination. Specifically, although unstated, whenever Behizadeh refers to the notion of "large-scale" she is necessarily talking about analogue and digital technologies. The use of rubrics aligned to standards, as we have seen, is a common flag marking the presence of analogue technologies. And where analogue technologies are found, software soon follows. In the case of large-scale writing assessment in New York State, students might take state exams that consist of both multiple-choice and written answers, including direct writing assessments. When students have completed their exams, teams of teachers divide up the examinations and score them according to an answer key and essay assessment guide, which includes explanations of the rubrics, scoring protocols, and annotated sample essays. Teachers then determine a numerical score for the essay ranging from 0 to 6. When the exams are completely assessed, they are handed off to administrators and staff who enter the scores into a state reporting information system. It takes both analogue and digital technologies to execute large-scale assessment and, in the end, state officials require defined numbers that can be used as a metric for evaluating the quality of schools and teachers. A barrier for large-scale portfolio assessment, in addition to the misperception that it is inherently unreliable, is technological. How does one scale an assessment mechanism that consists of multiple drafts, genres, topics, and assessors? It sounds unwieldy and costly.

In fact, software-powered technologies can be used to facilitate the portfolio assessment process very well. Higher educational institutions have used portfolio assessments at scale for some time. In theory, even basic document management systems like those used by editorial boards for academic journals can be used for students to submit multiple samples of their writing and for such samples to be assessed by multiple people according to a shared framework. The final score that a student receives could be a combination of an assessment from multiple assessors and a student's own self-assessment. The two different assessment systems, direct writing assessment and writing portfolios, serve as a case in point for how software space can be used. In the first instance, software space is used to narrow the categories and languages human beings use to talk about students' writing. The rubrics and protocols are tightly controlled by administrators and companies, leaving teachers who assess students' writings very little wiggle room. The role of the teacher is one of compliance, to generate data. When data are created, they are entered into an information system where they can be aggregated and disaggregated, manipulated, and reported. The primary purpose of analogue and digital technologies is one of data generation and reporting. In the second example, however, the primary role of software is to facilitate authentic human interaction. That is, software space is used to manage the sharing, assessment, and communication of student writing. Whereas, in the end, a number might well be generated, there are two major differences. First, the kinds of things students can write about and the process for teaching writing is radically different in its sociocultural sensitivity and soundness. Second, the process of assessment allows for multiple stakeholders, including family and community members, to offer feedback in a complex and nuanced way. The role of software is to intensify, rather than eliminate, the very social and human qualities that comprise literacy and assessment practices.

Large-scale nearly always requires the use of software-powered technologies, but it does not have to mean those technologies are used in dodgy ways. There are two reasons why poor uses of technology persist, which Behizadeh and others in composition studies might be interested in pursuing. First, direct writing assessments persist because they are perceived by those in positions of power as reliable metrics of students' writing abilities. Second, and I think more compelling to administrators, direct writing assessments are already thoroughly supported by private companies who can design tests questions and even score the essays if needed. There is an industry intact and altering the way large-scale assessment is done would rattle that industry. Technically speaking, it is completely possible to establish regionally controlled large-scale writing portfolio assessment systems that are more pedagogically sound and authentic to student's lives. Politically, such a near and achievable system might well remain out of the question.

ONLINE PROFESSIONAL LEARNING | DEDE

The use of online learning to extend and deepen opportunities for the professional development of teachers is something that has been explored for decades. One of the leading researchers of the use of online environments for such purposes is Chris Dede at the Harvard Graduate School of Education. Despite policy makers' and administrators' enthusiasm for the use of online technologies for professional development, Dede (2006) notes that such programs are often "not of high quality, offering 'fragmented, intellectually superficial' seminars" (p. 1). In one literature review, Whitehouse, Breit, McCloskey, Ketelhut, and Dede (2006) examine the kind of research that, at the time, had been conducted on the use of online learning for professional development. After reviewing nearly 400 articles on topics related to online professional development for teachers, the team narrowed their final sample down to 40 studies that met their standard for high-quality empirical research. The articles tend to address five areas: 1) design of professional development, 2) effectiveness of professional development, 3) technology to support professional development, 4) online communication and professional development, and 5) research methods. The authors, focusing their conceptualization on how professional development examined in the literature was designed and implemented, found that most online professional development research reflected social constructivist and communities of practice perspectives. In the end, they encouraged other researchers to consider not only the design and implementation of online professional development, but also to look distinctly at evidence of participants' engagement and formal evaluation of their experience. In sum, the meta-analysis revealed that there was a gap in the literature: data associated with participants' actual experiences in online professional development were being ignored in favor of instructional design and execution.

I would argue that when examining participants' engagement in online environments, researchers must be sensitive to the very active and stealthy role that software plays. When designing an online professional development course for a school district about bridging the Common Core Standards and the Danielson Framework, I emailed a district leader for more information about how she would like to frame assessment questions throughout the course. She shared a series of questions, including something like the following: "How does the Danielson Framework describe effective classroom discussion?" The intention was for teachers answering the question to type in their own response. The district leader felt strongly, and I agreed, that listing multiple-choice questions might generate quick reports for administrators but would only convey cheap reductionism to teachers.

Then the emails flew between us. I emailed her to ask how she imagined the short answer questions would be assessed. She said that she expected the "computer" to do it because she and her team did not have time. I replied then that if she wanted the questions to be automatically assessed, I would need to know what acceptable answers were. She replied by copying the language from Danielson's rubric saying that "something like this" would suffice. I replied that we could program the system to look for key words and use the ones within the rubric to serve as a dictionary. For instance, the word *student-driven*. She replied that using those words would be great. I replied asking if she and her team wanted to include similar terms like *student-generated* or *kid-created*. She replied that those would be accurate and acceptable. I then replied asking if she would accept misspellings like *stduent-driven* as well. She called me at my desk and asked me if I was joking.

I was serious.

When setting up automated assessment mechanisms, someone has to determine what all the acceptable variables are, which includes reasonable misspellings. The district leader thought that "some algorithm would catch all that." The truth, though, is that programming languages can only work when they are told precisely what to do under predetermined situations and conditions. There is a distinction between processual uses of technology and epistemological uses. In the former, software-powered technologies might be used to support a social human activity. For example, I use video conferencing to have regular meetings with colleagues in other parts of the country. In this simple case, the role of software is limited to the transcoding of sensory phenomena into digital code: the sound waves of my voice and the light waves that bounce off my face captured by my computer's microphone and video camera. These data are transmitted to a colleague's machine via a vast networking infrastructure and reassembled, say, in Georgia. The result simulates face-to-face communication, which allows us to work together. In the processual case, the information systems, databases, and algorithms that are in use still demand categorical predetermination but the data that are being categorized are transcoded sensory data like sound waves. The kinds of categories and algorithms used are limited to efficiently converting, sending, and receiving packets of relatively few data types. Whereas my colleague and I might create knowledge together as part of our conversation, we are not using technology for the knowledge construction but rather to facilitate our communication. We create knowledge; software processes waves and data. However, when software is used to do epistemological work we quickly see how it necessarily fails to live up to potential. That is, if a company intends for software to create or verify knowledge—as in the case of automatically assessing short answer quizzes—the types of data that need to be categorized and transcoded are epistemological. They are not simply sound or light waves. The fact is that software cannot do epistemological work well. Rigging it up to appear to do such work results in human beings having to program software for all possible inputs, which includes misspellings of words. In short, when software appears to be doing epistemological work, it is only because many human beings have worked together to create a compelling computational illusion. When examining the use of online learning in professional development, accounting for the subtle ways software space shapes the kinds of experiences that are and are not possible should be a common step.

DIGITAL HUMANITIES | MORETTI AND RAMSAY

There are different definitions for the *digital humanities*. For present purposes, I will define the term as the use of software-powered technologies to examine sites of study associated with humanitarian areas like literature and historical artifacts. One of the most oft-quoted figures in the expansion of the digital humanities in the study of literature is Franco Moretti. Moretti's concept *distant reading* is a helpful one to use as a way to tease out how critical software studies can deepen and extend research in the digital humanities. In his book *Graphs, Maps, and Trees: Abstract Models for Literary History,* Moretti (2007) reviews what he means by reading from a distance as "a process of deliberate reduction and abstraction . . . where distance is however not an obstacle, but *a specific form of knowledge*: fewer elements, hence a sharper sense of their overall interconnection. Shapes, relations, structures. Forms. Models" (italics original; p. 1). As an example, Moretti argues that the study of literature is necessarily limited by the fact that of the myriad books that have been published over the last three centuries, only a fraction of them have been read and analyzed. The literary canon is filled with books the authors of which might be uniquely gifted, but they are also lucky that their works survived the stampede of other authors' books vying for readers' and critics' attention. As a literary historian, Moretti wanted to challenge this narrow reality and get a better sense of the "hidden tempo" (p. 29) of the rise and fall of literary works across time and sociocultural settings. One analysis demonstrates that despite the fact that the novel as an artistic form launches in popularity at different times in history, the pattern of its rise is eerily similar whether in 18th-century Britain or 20th-century Nigeria. Such knowledge creation is only possible when the data of literary study moves beyond "close readings" on pages of individual works and treats as data large corpora of texts, book sales ledgers, and other big literary data sets.

Another approach to the digital humanities is the use of computational software to study the linguistic elements of smaller samples of literary works. In these cases, scholars might use natural language programs to create tree-like visualizations of how sentences or lines are structured. Or, one might take the entirety of a single literary work and use software to parse out words, tally their frequency, and project patterns of usage. We might refer to such approaches as quantitative literary analysis or computational text analysis. Ramsay (2011) refers to this method as *algorithmic criticism*. He writes, "Neither the critic nor the editor (to say nothing of the theorist or the teacher) seeks a definitive answer to the questions posed by the apparently simple matter of where scenes begin and end, because criticism is concerned not with determining the facts of the text, but with the implications of the text in its potentialized form. The computer, if it is to participate at all, can only serve to broaden that potentiality" (p. 67). In an example of his method, he shows how another researcher was able to use a popular computational text analysis application to calculate the most frequently used words in both Homer and Shakespeare, quickly demonstrating quantitatively that words associated with the themes of masculinity and love topped both authors' lists. Ramsay's purpose in this example was simply to demonstrate how speedily and concretely software can be used to do what would have taken a researcher months to do by hand. If Moretti believes the value of software in literary analysis is one of distant reading, Ramsay shows how software can be used for close reading as well.

From a critical software studies perspective, one might examine the ways in which such approaches can be used to position students of English in relation to texts. I would argue that both approaches—distant and close—abstract readers from the texts insofar as software works in both cases to transcode words into categories and values. Both create a distance. Whereas Taubman compellingly demonstrates the problems of turning the complex act of teaching and learning into abstracted data, I believe it is quite possible to leverage software in the study of literature and use its distancing quality to deepen students' appreciation for texts. Though some of the examples that both Moretti and Ramsay conduct are sophisticated and complex, there are more basic versions of such methods that are not only replicable in secondary settings but could provide students with new entry points into literary exploration. A simple example will help here. In *Moby Dick*, the word *Ahab* is used with great frequency after he perishes whereas the word *whale* dips in usage during the same time in the book. Using an open-source web-based text analysis application, this quantitative fact is easily observable. Software provides student-readers with distance from the words in context and pulls them back to a categorical level where one "reads" through software's lens: categories, values, tallies. These kinds of readings are, in my view, more distant than they are close, yet they position students to critically respond to software's reading very closely. This serves as a unique case in point of how software can be positioned to deepen pedagogy rather than cheapen it. We are not using software to automatically assess the quality of literary works nor are we trying to automatically grade students' interpretations. The purpose of learning to read literature is one of meaning making, of negotiation. Hardly software's forte.

THE READER, THE TEXT, THE POEM | ROSENBLATT

Nearly 70 years ago, literary scholar Louise Rosenblatt (1938) published her seminal work *Literature as Exploration*. Written at a time when positivistic approaches to literary interpretation were dominating education, Rosenblatt's work argued that readers' experiences were an essential element for interpreting literature. The meaning of the text was not embedded in the words on the page alone, nor in the author's life and times. The meaning of the text required the uniqueness of the reader. The book had great influence on literacy researchers as well as other fields. Rosenblatt (1978) later added to her theory with what she called *transaction theory*. Using the word *transaction* as opposed to *interaction*—a distinction the scholar borrows from John Dewey—Rosenblatt framed a theory of reading literature that posits a reader, a text, and a poem. The poetic experience is that which is created during the transactions of the reading event. A human subject reading a written text in a specific place and time generates a unique poetic effect, which might change even if rereading moments later. "A person becomes a reader by virtue of his activity in relationship to a text, which he organizes as a set of verbal symbols. A physical text, a set of marks on a page, becomes the text of a poem or of a scientific formula by virtue of its relationship with a reader who can thus interpret it and reach through it to the world of the work" (pp. 18–19). In addition to this triad—reader, text, poem—Rosenblatt also posits a continuum for kinds of reading ranging from *efferent* to *aesthetic*. Efferent readings are associated with informational, factual, and scientific texts in which the purpose of reading is the collecting of information for some specific purpose. Aesthetic readings are usually associated with fictional and literary texts in which the purpose of reading is to have some kind of artistic experience. For example, "The analyst is not reading a text in order to create a work of art; he is reading it efferently in order to make a systematic classification of elements" (p. 89). One of the ways we might consider the effects of critical software studies on transaction theory is 1) to briefly consider how software "reads" the world according to Rosenblatt's framework, and 2) to explore how using software to read literature can affect the meaning making process for students and teachers.

What does it mean to consider software as a reader? At first, this question seems quick and simple to answer. Software does not "read" per se, it does something else that is not what is meant by "reading" in educational circles. I would suggest, however, that software does indeed read and that if we allow ourselves to theorize so, we can arrive at new ways of integrating software-powered technologies into our schools. Software, I submit, conducts extremely efferent readings of texts. Upon execution, software processes a digital text word by word albeit very quickly. At the most basic level, software treats language in a text as values: categories and numbers. Software conducts a purely informational reading of the text, retrieving the text as data and parsing it according to programmers' commands. At the other extremity, a human reader who is engaging in a literary reading purely for aesthetic fulfillment might read the same text and be emotionally stirred by the beauty of the language. Whereas software as reader retrieves data, the human reader remembers past experiences triggered by the reading. Software reads a text as a predetermined dataset; the human reader actively creates a reading event in response to her own experiences and the words on the page.

Rosenblatt might say that software's reading, if we are to call it a reading, is thoroughly efferent in nature. It is a readerless reading, perhaps, and readerless readings have clear transactional consequences. "When the transaction between [human] reader and text is thus ignored, the formal aspects of the text come to be viewed as essentially static. Rhetorical and critical terms becomes mainly classificatory and anatomizing, a naming of static components" (p. 89). As has been explored throughout this book, software space demands classification and anatomization, or what Taubman refers to as abstraction and control from a distance. Software's thoroughly efferent approach to texts that software possesses can be an asset to the teaching of literature if software's reading is presented as one kind of reading to which students can respond and resist. Software space is incapable of rendering an aesthetic reading, but this is not to say that a reader's ability to have an aesthetic experience when reading a text cannot be supported by software. In Chapter 8, I will present examples of how the quantification of a literary text and visualization of the resultant data can create not only a visual interpretation of the text but add to students' opportunities to create aesthetic responses.

A question remains: If one uses software's reading of a text in order to create meaning, how does its use affect the theoretical triad upon which transaction theory rests: reader, text, and poem? It seems like it is contestable, yet defensible, to say that software reads a text. Such a reading, however, is extremely efferent. If students engage with such quantitative literary analyses, and such analyses affect their abilities to appreciate a written text as aesthetic, how are we to understand software's role? Moretti's concept of *distant reading* might provide some use. One might be tempted to say that when using software in the way described, the reader's experience of the text is temporarily abstracted or made distant. There is, in a sense, an efferent filter layered over the reading event as the reader's transaction is mediated through software. But does such mediation make aesthetic experiences impossible? I would argue that in the immediate transactional event in which software mediates, yes. A reading of a text that is rerouted through software is incapable of direct aesthetic effects. However, successive transactions contain the reader's history with software's reading and might well make new efferent *and* aesthetic experiences possible. For instance, in the example above I described the simple example of how Melville's use of the word *Ahab* increases after the character's death whereas the use of *whale* decreases. This quantitative reading becomes part of my experience and when I reread the novel my attention to Ahab's name is increased, thereby changing my transaction and resultant poetic effect. For students who struggle with traditional readings of literature, this kind of efferent detour might be a welcomed and appropriate support mechanism that enables their future aesthetic experiences.

The implications of applying transactional theory to critical software studies are more than pedagogical. They are also political. Rosenblatt suggests so when discussing the danger of not teaching students to understand the differences between efferent and aesthetic readings: "Small wonder," she writes, "that graduates of our schools (and colleges) often read poems and novels efferently or respond to political statements and advertisements with an aesthetic stance" (Rosenblatt, 1994, p. 29). When we confuse these two kinds of readings, rather than teaching students to recognize the ways they intertwine during complex transactions with texts, we position our young people to be dulled and duped. The current education reforms are a case in point. The public is told that education reform is simply a matter of high standards, accountability, and achievement—all noble-sounding aspirations that merit the nodding of heads. Such discursive moves please us to hear. At the same time, reformers implement the Common Core Standards, which places a premium on efferent readings of literary works. A lead author for the Common Core literacy standards, David Coleman, went as far as saying to a group of New York State school officials that when it comes to students' feelings, "people really don't give a shit about what [students] feel or think" (Coleman, 2011). Given the successes of the neoliberal reform movement, widespread enthusiasm for science, technology, engineering, and mathematics (STEM) education, and the precarious state of reading and writing in our country, it is high time for English educators to account for the uniqueness of software-powered technologies in their discipline and respond with readerly vengeance.

IN SUM

The above sections attempt to demonstrate how critical software studies might inform educational researchers' conceptual and methodological work. Each offers only a cursory exploration, but it is, I hope, something upon which others can build. The fact is that education will continue to be mediated by software. Software, scholars argue, shapes all that it mediates. It has been demonstrated already during this century that the subtle and sometimes deleterious impact of software on pedagogy will not be attended to by policy makers or the private sector who mistake digitization for progress and newness for innovation. Rather, scholars must rigorously explicate the ways software space can empower and also devour our highest hopes for teaching and learning. It will take an impressive and diverse body of scholarly work to turn back the effects of years of stump speeches and sales pitches that have convinced even seasoned educators that software-powered technologies signify progress and we should all go along with it. No, we should not. And we'll have the research to prove it in a decade or so.

WORKS CITED

Behizadeh, N. (2014). Mitigating the dangers of a single story: Creating large-scale writing assessments aligned with sociocultural theory. *Educational Researcher, 43*(3), 125–136.

Cazden, C., Cope, B., Fairclough, N., Gee, J., Kalantzis, M., Kress, G., . . . Nakata, M. (1996). A pedagogy of multiliteracies: Designing social futures. *Harvard Educational Review, 66*(1), 60–92.

Coleman, D. (2011, April 28). *Bringing the common core to life.* Talk at the Chancellor's Hall, New York State Department of Education, Albany, NY. Retrieved December 15, 2014, from http://usny.nysed.gov/rttt/resources/bringing-the-common-core-to-life-download.html.

Dede, C. (Ed.). (2006). *Online professional development for teachers: Emerging models and methods.* Cambridge, MA: Harvard Education Press.

Lynch, T.L. (2013). Pecs Soviet and the Red Underscore: Raising awareness of software's role in our schools. *English Journal, 103*(1), 128–130.

Moretti, F. (2007). *Graphs, maps, and trees: Abstract models for a literary history*. New York: Verso.

Ramsay, S. (2011). *Reading machines: Toward an algorithmic criticism*. Urbana, IL: University of Illinois Press.

Ravitch, D. (2013). *Reign of error: The hoax of the privatization movement and the danger to America's public schools*. New York: Knopf.

Rosenblatt, L. M. (1938). *Literature as exploration*. New York: Modern Language Association.

Rosenblatt, L. M. (1978). *The reader, the text, the poem: The transactional theory of the literary work*. Carbondale, IL: Southern Illinois Press.

Rosenblatt, L. M. (1994). The transactional theory of reading and writing. In R. Ruddell, M. R. Rudell, & H. Singer (Eds.), *Theoretical models and processes of reading* (Vol. 4, pp. 1057–1092). Newark, DE: International Reading Association.

Selwyn, N. (2014). *Distrusting educational technology: Critical questions for changing times*. New York: Routledge.

Taubman, P. M. (2009). *Teaching by numbers: Deconstructing the discourse of standards and accountability in education*. New York: Routledge.

Weis, L., & Fine, M. (2012). Critical bifocality and circuits of privilege: Expanding critical ethnographic theory and design. *Harvard Educational Review, 82*(2), 173–201.

Whitehouse, P. L., Breit, L. A., McCloskey, E. M., Ketelhut, D. J., & Dede, C. (2006). An overview of current findings from empirical research on online teacher professional development. In C. Dede (Ed.), *Online professional development for teachers: Emerging models and methods* (pp. 13–29). Cambridge, MA: Harvard Education Press.

6 Politicians' Text Messages

"Literacy in more than one medium will be required if people are to deal critically and intelligently with demagogues, call-in shows, mystifying ads, and news programs blended with varying degrees of entertainment."

—Maxine Greene in "Texts and Margins,"
Releasing the Imagination, p. 13

As I ran to the farewell party for Chancellor Joel Klein, I wondered which of the rumors would be true. Some said there would be celebrities in attendance. One colleague swore she heard Jay-Z would perform. The mayor, said another, was sure to show. When I arrived at Tweed Courthouse, party-goers from throughout the system mingled. School officials, standout principals, and administrative staff glided from conversation to conversation amidst the sounds of one of the city's high school jazz bands. (The Jay-Z rumor proved false.) At one point, someone quietly circulated lyric sheets and the building's rotunda echoed with a tribute song called "Sweet Chancellor Klein," replacing the chancellor's name for Caroline's. After some time, the hundreds of attendees were called to attention. Klein's deputy of innovation, John White, who left the city shortly thereafter to be head of schools in Louisiana, addressed the crowd and lauded his boss's accomplishments. Then, Mayor Mike Bloomberg arrived. Swarming with security detail, the mayor delivered his prepared laudatory remarks, including a joke in the form of a multiple choice exam question.

"Which of the following text messages would the chancellor least want to receive in the middle of the night?" he inquired.

"A) OMG." Chuckles rolled around the room.
"B) WTF." The chuckles swelled.
"C) UFT." The room erupted with laughter.

I remember standing in the crowd that afternoon watching the mayor exit. Something about it didn't sit well with me, even amidst the smiling colleagues and swirling songs. In retrospect, the mayor's joke proves indicative of something bigger than a public jibe at organized labor. It represents a great deal about the education reforms that overcame our schools with the Bush Administration's No Child Left Behind legislation in 2001 and the Obama Administration's Race to the Top competition in 2009. Erasing the traditional divide between Republicans and Democrats, both sides of the aisle shared a neoliberal perspective on how to "fix" schools. Both initiatives feature politicians aggressively using software-powered technologies to implement reform. As discussed above, testing is one major way software is put to political use. Another way is the requirement for ubiquitous information systems to collect, analyze, and report on student and teacher data.

BUY THE NUMBERS

Again, I turn to Peter Taubman's *Teaching by the Numbers* to examine more deeply and critically the discourse of policy makers as they push for software-powered technologies to realize their reform agenda, what Taubman describes as a discursive "drumbeat, [an] arrogant surety" (2009, p. 57) of the neoliberal reform movement. He summarizes the reformers' discourse as demanding "consistent standards aligned with performance objectives, for accountability measured by data produced by tests, for scientifically based practices modeled on medicine, and for education that prepares students for the global economy . . . [as well as] providing students with twenty-first century skills, on ensuring all students learn, and on touting the teacher as responsible for that learning" (p. 76). One of the key levers used to make the reform discourse stick, Taubman argues, is large-scale testing. Testing offers a kind of certainty and finitude in response to the otherwise messy work of teaching and learning. He writes of the danger of relying on high-stakes testing this way, that it "abstracts us from the specificity of our situations, turning us into a portable number, and locates us with a much greater universe of numerical numbers: we are one number among many" (p. 53). For decades, the chorus of voices of those who wish to reform our education system through abstraction has increased in volume. Not only in their loudness, but also in their control of the dominant discourse that comprises education in the country. Reformers did so through No Child Left Behind by legally requiring districts and states to report on yearly progress of students in literacy and numeracy as measured by prescribed assessments as well as through the multi-billion dollar coercion of state education departments in Race to the Top. The result affects not only K-12 schools, Taubman writes, but also teacher education where the same apparatus has made schools of education comply with external oversight agencies.

The success of this trifecta—standards, accountability, and data-generating tests—lies in the fact that using them together results in distilling the slippery and amorphous act of pedagogy into concrete numbers aligned with pre-defined linguistic categories and mathematical correlates. Taubman writes that a ramification of large-scale, high-stakes testing is a popular and politicized epistemological stance that "equates understanding or creativity or erudition with information retrieval, the ability to concentrate for long periods of time on a meaningless task, alacrity in making decisions, and compliance with directives that have no relevance to one's own interests, desires, abilities, knowledge, or understanding" (p. 26). It is also a lucrative endeavor with companies lining up to sell schools the products they need to quantify pedagogy, not only in the case of formal testing, but also the use of rubrics and forms as tools neoliberal reformers use to control and convert the complexity of teaching and learning into concrete numerical metrics. This is the case, for example, in teacher education where national accreditation agencies demand schools use systems of gathering "data" on teaching candidates' learning experiences. What counts as data is limited to broad linguistic categories and, eventually, numbers. In what follows, I shall use Taubman's conceptual framework above to analyze the "discursive transformation" (p. 56) that occurred during the implementation of the Obama Administration's Race to the Top program via "phrases, rhetorical moves, and logics" (p. 59). In order to foreground the hidden role of software throughout the discourse, I organize the following analysis according to the social spaces described previously: political, economic, pedagogical, and administrative.

POLITICAL AND ECONOMIC SPACES

The Federal Framing of Reform

On July 24th, 2009, the president and Secretary of Education Arne Duncan announced the start of their education reform program. In his speech, President Obama said:

> Because improving education is central to rebuilding our economy, we set aside over $4 billion in the Recovery Act to promote improvements in schools. This is one of the largest investments in education reform in American history. And rather than divvying it up and handing it out, we are letting states and school districts compete for it. That's how we can incentivize excellence and spur reform and launch a race to the top in America's public schools. That race starts today. (U.S. Department of Education, 2009)

The president implies this large sum of money is available because legislators believe that the country's economic woes are related to—if not caused by, in part—the country's school system. He also suggests that distributing the funding equally to all school districts would somehow not yield the results he seeks. In the spirit of unbridled capitalism, he dangles a very large carrot in front of fiscally famished states and districts. School districts interested in the president's announcement visited the U.S. Department of Education's web site where they found pages of information framing the Race to the Top competition. The following bullet points, which articulate four key commitments the government expects from applicants, were posted on the site's main page. Applicants were committing to:

- Adopting standards and assessments that prepare students to succeed in college and the workplace and to compete in the global economy;
- Building data systems that measure student growth and success, and inform teachers and principals about how they can improve instruction;
- Recruiting, developing, rewarding, and retaining effective teachers and principals, especially where they are needed most; and
- Turning around our lowest-achieving schools (U.S. Department of Education, 2010).

Many states began changing regulations and even legislation to accord with the above Race to the Top criteria, believing that doing so would increase their chances of award (Robelen, 2010). Whereas technology is not explicitly mentioned very prominently, we shall see below that it is essential.

One Sunday morning four months later, the secretary alluded to this phenomenon while on *Meet the Press* ("'Meet the Press' transcript for Nov. 15, 2009," 2009), where he appeared with conservative icon Newt Gingrich and civil rights activist Rev. Al Sharpton. The show's host, David Gregory, introduced his guests who were invited to talk about education in America. The discussion begins with Secretary Duncan who describes his Race to the Top program:

> We want to reward those states, those districts, those nonprofits that are willing to challenge the status quo and get dramatically better, close the achievement gap and raise the bar for everybody. And what's been so encouraging is before we've spent a dollar, a dime of Race to the Top money, we've seen forty-eight states come together to raise the bar, higher standards for everyone (to stop lying to children). We've seen states remove barriers to creating new innovative charter schools. We've seen folks get rid of firewalls separating student achievement data from teachers'. There's been the extraordinary movement in the country before we've spent one dollar.

The secretary's premise remained steadfast and on point with the president's: Our schools are not preparing students for the new economic needs we face and we have to radically force change. The show's host echoed the belief that the "problem" in education is a matter of "results."

In another setting, this one to an audience of conservative business and political leaders, Duncan frames the need to reform education thus:

> Our K-12 system largely still adheres to the century-old, industrial-age factory model of education. . . . Technology can play a huge role in increasing educational productivity, but not just as an add-on or for a high-tech reproduction of current practice. Again, we need to change the underlying processes to leverage the capabilities of technology. The military calls it a force multiplier. Better use of online learning, virtual schools, and other smart uses of technology is not so much about replacing educational roles as it is about giving each person the tools they need to be more successful—reducing wasted time, energy, and money. (Duncan, 2010, para. 29)

Here again, the secretary promotes the idea that our schools are failing because they operate in an old model of teaching and learning. Technology can help break this model, he claims.

The administration's campaign did not limit its reach to the K-12 system. It had direct implications for higher education as well, especially schools of education. In another example, Secretary Duncan gives a speech on teacher education at Teachers College, Columbia University. In his own words:

> The draft Race to the Top criteria would also reward states that publicly report and link student achievement data to the programs where teachers and principals were credentialed. And the federal government has funded a large expansion of teacher residency programs in high-need districts and schools, including one to be run out of the Teachers College. (Duncan, 2009, para. 42)

For purposes of analysis, I will focus on a core notion that Taubman (2009) articulates and which subsumes the themes he outlines, namely that neoliberal reformers seeks "control from a distance" (p. 40) over schools by mandating the generation and use of data to determine student and teacher performance. As we will see, this motif is driven by a forceful free-market logic that views the private sector as a partner in education, often signified with words like *innovation, choice, transparency, personalization,* and *data-driven* practices.

In order to achieve the distant control of which Taubman speaks, neoliberal reformers execute a five-part strategy which "consists of condemning the schools, manufacturing a crisis, starving public schools of resources, standardizing curriculum and teaching methods, and opening up education to for-profit companies" (p. 104). We see evidence of each component of the strategy in the excerpts above. In addition to the president's implication that poor education caused the economic collapse, the secretary creates a sense of crisis that results from shoddy schooling. He refers to a "status quo" that must be challenged, perpetuated by people who must "stop lying to children." He prefaces his call for more technology by stating our schools are stuck in a "century-old, industrial-age factory model." Interestingly, whereas the Race to the Top criteria refer to systems of standardization in order to "measure" students and "inform" teachers, when the Common Core or teacher evaluation standards are alluded to it is seldom by name and often framed as coming from states.

One could argue that having common standards could be a valuable addition to the professional community of educators if the primary purpose of such standards were to strengthen communication and the ongoing refinement of one's pedagogy. In the context created by the neoliberal reform movement, however, that is not the primary purpose of such standards. Rather, having standards in place allows two interlocking maneuvers. First, standards enable companies to create products and services for schools without having to attend to state-by-state differences in curriculum and instruction. This is especially relevant for companies who create and sell tests, which are the primary means by which schools will be held "accountable." With the widespread acceptance of testing as a measure of learning, "the way is opened for the packaging and selling of strategies, methods, and techniques" (p. 45). Second, academic standards make it possible for data gathered to be structured, analyzed, and shared according to more sophisticated technical standards. The former is clear enough to articulate; the latter is more opaque.

What do academic standards have to do with data structures and information systems? Neoliberal reformers leverage standards in order to position software and information systems in education in ways that put pressure on educators and allow companies to profit. Consider this illustration, ignoring momentarily the myriad issues associated with testing culture. If one thousand students take the same American literature examination and what we know about their collective performance is each student's grade, we might be able to see which students are in most need of drastic attention. That's about it. But, when we align each test question to a standard—like a Common Core standard—it becomes possible to analyze each student's performance in a more granular way because we can say that the student struggles with specific knowledge and skills as articulated in the standards. If the marketplace conditions are right, a teacher could log into a web-based portal, fetch a standards-based report on each student's academic needs, and purchase "personalized" lessons or activities for each student. This scenario is precisely what Race to the Top attempts to realize and is as aggressive in its implementation as it is ignorant of pedagogy. For Taubman, he is correct in his assessment that No Child Left Behind created a political climate in which the aggregation of numerical data became a primary goal to "measure" educational success—a climate to which Race to the Top seamlessly contributed.

As data reign in Race to the Top, companies reap the benefits. The "standards and assessments" referred to in the guidelines were developed with input from the business community and shepherded into reality through the development of various semi-education/semi-business organizations like Achieve Inc. (which Taubman discusses). The tests that measure student learning were developed by groups whose mission appears to be noble and new like the Partnership for Assessment of Readiness for College and Career (PARCC). Further, publishing companies received much advisement on how to quickly align their inventories of textbooks and curricular resources with the Common Core. Further, standards and data benefit not only publishers, but information technology companies as well. "Building data systems," which require tight structural schemas for organizing, aggregating, and analyzing students and teacher data is not something districts themselves can likely do. The more data that are generated and required to be fed to the state—as is the case with Race to the Top—the more districts must rely on outside vendors to bolster or provide their information infrastructure as well as provide new software applications to help analyze and make sense of data. The emphasis on standards and accountability measures—while seemingly innocuous or even noble to many listeners—has the effect, Taubman argues and I agree, of rendering abstract the very human elements of teaching and learning, including students' and teachers' ethnicity, gender, socioeconomic status, and individuality. And public monies flow to companies unencumbered.

Taubman conveys an awareness of the central role technology plays in the neoliberal reform agenda. He calls attention to the lustful drive for numerical data and the mechanisms that are institutionalized in order to generate such data like rubrics, forms, and other tools to control schools from a distance. Let us turn our attention to how one district—New York City—responded to Race to the Top via the discursive moves evidenced in the state's Race to the Top application, public relations materials, and words of its leaders.

How a District Raced and Won

New York State applied twice for Race to the Top and won in their second attempt. When the state sent representatives from the Board of Regents to Washington, DC, to present their revised application, they brought along some additional support, including New York City Chancellor Joel Klein. There are noticeable differences between the first round and second round application, including enhancing plans to "measure student growth" and "improve instruction," to "close the achievement gap," and to emphasize some of the state's innovations, like creating teaching evaluation systems and expanding online learning programs (Quillen, 2010).

Two of the city's programs, School of One and the Innovation Zone, seemed tailored to the emphases put forth by the Obama Administration. School of One focuses on 6th grade math. Students begin the year by taking a series of baseline assessments that evaluate both the number of content students have "mastered" as well as the kinds of learning modalities they seem to respond best to. One day, a student might come in and work in a small group led by a resident teacher; the next day that same student might sit at the computer and work independently on problems provided by various online companies. Everyday, students take pre- and post-tests to assess the extent to which they have sufficiently covered the material. Over time, an algorithm automatically (although tweaked by human beings) creates a "playlist" of both content and mode of learning for each individual student. It's this kind of "personalized" approach that led *Time* magazine (Unknown, 2009) to name School of One in their Top 50 Innovations of 2009. Despite such laudations, questions linger about the School of One. For instance, with such close attention paid to how individual students "learn" best, it seems less likely students are going to be challenged to learn in ways unfamiliar to them, thereby failing to push students out of their comfort zones because the algorithm didn't say to. Still, it is the School of One's perceived success that prompted the city to venture further into online learning with its iZone.

The iZone's press release describes it thus: "Schools in the iZone will adopt new approaches to instruction, using online courses, adaptive technologies, and real-time data to help teachers create more targeted lessons" (NYCDOE, 2010). The *New York Post* reported early on that "City education officials are planning a boom in online learning that could see as many as 80 public schools delivering a large chunk of their instruction via the Internet in the coming school year" (Gonen, 2010). The popular educational blog, *Gotham Schools*, ran a piece about iZone in which they note the importance of virtual schooling to the Bloomberg-Klein administration: "At [iZone's] core is a heavy emphasis on expanding online learning, a major focus of Klein's tenure at the Department of Education" (Phillips, 2010). These public statements about iZone fit well as a response to the problem statement the city represents in the state's Race to the Top application:

> While most industries have experienced tremendous change over the past 50 years, our education system has remained remarkably static, adhering to the [a] set of 19th century assumptions that fail to fully engage and challenge students who have grown up in a digital world. . . . ("Race to the Top Application Assurances," 2010, p. 314)

When the state secured approximately $700 million in Race to the Top funding, nearly half of which was earmarked for New York City, city officials started a public relations campaign to promote its most "innovative" initiative. Chancellor Joel Klein and Deputy Chancellor of Innovation John White each address the city's educational innovation strategy. In Deputy Chancellor White's interview (White, 2010), he states:

> The day should be here when every child comes to school to receive an education that is customized to their needs. That's what the Innovation

Zone is about. It's about taking on the assumptions that for so have long forced kids into our box when really we should be providing them with an education that is tailor-made to them. (n.p.)

In another video on the same site, Chancellor Klein (2010) says the following:

If you don't build innovation into a culture you won't get innovation, and that's what we set out for ourself [sic] as a challenge. Innovation Zone, innovation culture, new ideas, using technology differently, focusing on the individual student, thinking about platforms that may help deliver content, thinking about teaching approaches. And we're doing all of those things right now. (n.p.)

When Joel Klein abruptly stepped down at the end of 2010, the mayor promptly appointed a vice president at Hearst publishing named Cathie Black to the chancellorship. Although Black served as chancellor for only three months before returning to the private sector, she spent the days before taking office touring schools around the city with an army of reporters in tow. In a memo to principals (leaked online), Chancellor Black shares her impressions from three school visits, emphasizing personalized and individualized instruction. She writes:

I've had the opportunity over the past few weeks to visit several schools already focused on innovations that personalize learning. At P.S. 262 in Bedford-Stuyvesant, students have personalized learning plans supported by online assessment systems. As a result, students have become significantly more engaged in their work and teachers are able to spend meaningful time with individuals and small groups. Global Tech Preparatory Middle School in East Harlem is supplementing the traditional instruction of a classroom teacher with online resources, allowing each child to progress at his or her own pace. And on a visit to the School of One pilot at M.S. 131 in Chinatown today, I saw students using technology to follow individualized class schedules and engage with interactive content online to enhance their learning. (Black, 2011, n.p.)

Black was pressured to resign after several embarrassing statements and slip-ups.

Applying Taubman's discursive taxonomy to the above artifacts from New York City helps demonstrate how the discourse of Race to the Top shaped the way leadership in the city ran a school system of over 1 million children. As Duncan situated his talk to conservative businesses by bemoaning the "factory-model" that calcified our schools, the authors of the city's section in the state's Race to the Top application refer to "19th century assumptions." In both cases, these tropes are used to appeal to neoliberal ideologies and logic—the secretary speaking to business leaders, the application authors arguing that because private industry had moved beyond the assembly line schools should consequently follow suit. Disregarding the flawed logic that equates public educational institutions with private industry, three excerpts echo the logic of Race to the Top with a common theme that technology can help students learn on their own and in their own ways. John White declares that the time has come "when every child comes to school to receive an education that is customized to their needs," insinuating that current students do not get the attention they require, which should be "customized." Customizing education is something that technology can do, he suggests; it isn't something we might expect from smaller class sizes or greater parental involvement. Joel Klein's syntax reveals much about his ideological bent when he places "platforms that may help deliver content" between the "individual student" and "teaching approaches." In his view, which he continued to manifest as vice president for Rupert Murdoch's education division called Amplify, technology is the key to shake up teaching by "empowering" students. Finally, the leaked email from Cathie Black is perhaps most telling. At first, it might seem that her stint as chancellor was so brief that she hardly merits attention. However, the brevity of her stay is why her words are important. Having had no experience in education aside from her own time as a student, Black was known to have been coached and handled by the communications office in the city after a few initial embarrassing incidents. This is why her email about school visits is so important— she was told precisely what to say. If you are the new chancellor, then, what is important to emphasize to the public? In the Bloomberg administration, now flooded with Race to the Top money, you echo the marching orders: using technologies in schools will allow students to learn on their own and get teachers out of the way. She doesn't say that, of course. She describes "innovations that personalize learning" like "learning plans supported by online assessment systems," "online resources," and "interactive content online." Personalization, individualization, and customization. These are the talking points around which city leadership rallied. These are the talking points that, without saying so, regards learning as a commodity students can receive through technology and commercial products with little intervention by a professional educator.

PEDAGOGICAL AND ADMINISTRATIVE SPACES

Present-ing the Absence of Software

In Chapter 2, I argued that one challenge in studying the impact of the ontology of software on education is its invisibility. Whereas it is the case that most of us engage with myriad forms of software everyday, it is not the case that we often have a critical awareness of how the nature of software affects us.

This should not be a surprise. What we engage with when we encounter software is often not software per se but devices that run on and host software applications as well as visual user interfaces that—by design—mask the complex inner workings of software and information systems. We experience software's influence while being unable to articulate what it is, who made it, and how it might do things to which we'd object. Something not dissimilar occurs when considering how software is positioned in the political discourse surrounding education. It is hard to study the role software plays in the discourse because it is seldom referred to by name.

Between 2009 and 2014, Secretary of Education Arne Duncan delivered nearly 200 speeches totaling over half a million words. He uses the word "software" only seven times. To put this in perspective, words we might associate with software, like *technology* or *data*, are used 350 to 400 times. Software is not a word that appears in the discourse with frequency by proponents or critics. It is not a word that Taubman uses explicitly either. He seems aware of the rising role of information technologies but does not call it software by name. This is the central problem we face as researchers and practitioners. We do not call software by name. As a result, we cannot possibly ask some of the most important questions about what these reforms are doing to our families and profession. If the tropes and words that comprise a significant portion of the education reform discourse (the political, economic, pedagogical, and administrative spaces), how do they traverse software space and with what effects? In an extended example exploring the city's use of online learning, I will elucidate precisely why theorizing and methodologizing software space is necessary.

Tracing the Spaces of K-12 Online Learning

iLearnNYC, part of the city's Innovation Zone, was funded for five years partially with Race to the Top money. The political and economic discursive spaces created by the Obama Administration directly impacted how software space was perceived and used within administrative and pedagogical spaces (see Figure 2.1). During that time, it grew from forty to over two hundred. When I worked for iLearnNYC, my responsibilities were to support and eventually oversee the implementation of the program. In a typical scenario, a school leader approached iLearnNYC because she wanted to offer online courses in her school. We asked about the teachers' curricular needs and recommend courses for the school to review. They received demonstration accounts, logged in to our learning management system (LMS), and clicked through courses provided by over a dozen different companies. They also had the option of creating their own courses, but this is not something our team could thoroughly support. The principal made final selections—say, an AP English course from Vendor X and a foreign language course from Vendor Y. The school paid a discounted rate for online course licenses through the city's procurement system and assigned licenses to staff and students through an elaborate license management system that pulled data from city systems and permissioned users to access the vendor content they chose. We had help desk support and a team of implementation managers who supported schools. The help desk tracked technical issues users encountered, escalating ones they couldn't solve to the companies with whom we contracted. Implementation managers each had schools with whom they met and visited to assist them in using the online courses well. Each manager had over ten schools spread out across the city. They visited schools approximately once every two weeks, not enough to develop deep relationships with all schools or to engage in nuanced conversations about pedagogy in online or blended models. Nevertheless, these were the resources we were allotted and we made the best of them. There were success stories, of course, but these successes were exceptions to the norm.

Schools frequently chose to use online courses to address peripheral needs in their schedules. Foreign language courses, Advanced Placement courses, and credit recovery models were popular in our schools. One school, for instance, had a single Spanish teacher but wanted to offer students choices of foreign languages to take. Using one vendor's product, the school allowed students to choose from half a dozen different languages and the teacher played the role of coach who monitored each student's progress. The iZone became so excited about this iLearnNYC success story that they created a promotional video trumpeting it as proof of innovation. The video neglected to mention that whereas the software that powered the online course could help students learn the rote basics of a language, it could not recognize whether they were speaking or writing in the language correctly. Eventually, the teacher was receiving written and recorded oral assignment she couldn't assess because she didn't speak all the languages. Another school selected an online Advanced Placement English Literature course to use with its few, but enthusiastic, students who felt ready for more challenging course work. The students were perplexed when they submitted essays to the online course but did not receive any feedback or assessment. The teacher responsible for the course at the school expressed her anger—directed at me—because she taught part-time and was not told by her principal that she would have to assess student work or actually log into the course. She unabashedly expressed no desire to do either. In a third model, schools used online courses for students who had to make up units from other courses they nearly passed in what was referred to as online credit recovery. In theory, the online course assessed students' knowledge and skills in a given area, determined what parts the student had not mastered, and required them only to complete those parts. Within months we had complaints that students were not being supervised by an educator licensed in the appropriate content-area. A news report broke that one of our schools had put a parent volunteer in a computer lab with students during credit recovery class. From afar, the school seemed to be personalizing learning for students the system had failed. The reality was that the students continued to go unserved, albeit more efficiently with technology's help. When the state learned of some of the credit recovery practices, they publicly admonished the city and schools involved (Cramer, 2012).

Whereas we as an implementation team did the best we could, the fact was we simply didn't have the time and resources to support the schools the way they needed. Ideally, each school would have received frequent consultation on how to determine the ways in which online learning might be best used, how to review courses for their curricular and pedagogical quality, and how to ensure the school's technology infrastructure could support online learning. Instead, we provided quick reviews of courses, tips on how to get started, and watched panicked emails and help calls flood in. In retrospect, I see clearly that the reason we struggled the way we did had to do with two main factors. First, the leaders responsible for iLearnNYC were more focused on the technical and consumeristic achievement of rolling out a complex digital system that forced vendors to change their business models than they were on the integrity of teaching and learning. Public perception trumped pedagogy, always. (When one traces where the leaders went after their stints in New York, it is a sad commentary on not just the past but the future of neoliberal reforms.) Second, when we sought guidance from educational research and practical guides, which was not encouraged by those ultimately in charge, we couldn't find quite what we needed. For example, there existed only a handful of frameworks to assist schools in determining the quality of online courses in K-12 settings. Even a cursory look at these frameworks, however, show that they offer only a nod toward the complexity of specific content-areas as well as the unique differences between offline and online pedagogies. Eventually, our implementation team was ordered to deflect professional development needs to the companies whose courses schools purchased. Rather than engage critically with teachers in schools about practice, we were increasingly pushed to put schools in touch directly with vendors who would send their "trainers" to classrooms.

Over time, we had many dispiriting encounters with the companies with whom the city partnered. Most of our encounters were limited to trainers and salespersons. When we began developing a course catalog, for example, we requested demonstration accounts to the companies' courses in order to assess the quality of courses. I was surprised to learn that companies often break up content in courses in ways that require students to frequently click on links. A colleague pointed out to me that companies do this because the way they measure "engagement" is often based on both the amount of time students log in as well as how often they click on links. Another measurement of learning we frequently encountered was multiple-choice quizzes, which would be automatically assessed by software. In addition, companies had different versions of "interactive" activities that required students to match definitions to words or group concepts according to the readings in the course. Whereas it is the case that video and audio text were used with regularity in many courses, to say that the presence of such multimodal elements signaled their sound use would be a stretch. The quality of courses routinely underwhelmed our team—whose experience in classrooms ranged from three years to fifteen.

Related to the quality of online courses sold to schools, we encountered two other things that made us pause. First, whereas all companies offered some variety of reporting features for teachers and administrators, what such reports consisted of and the form they took varied widely from vendor to vendor. One company would provide a PDF of students' last log-ins whereas another would visualize students' completion of activities and provide an option to export data into spreadsheets. In a climate so focused on data, it was discouraging to principals that they were forced to store and view their data in different places depending on the companies involved. Second, when in some cases the team found academic content that we thought especially poor, it was impossible to find out who actually developed the content in question. As we inquired further, it became clear that several (perhaps many) companies outsource the development of courses to consultants whose names and credentials appear nowhere on the companies' web sites. Compare this to textbook production in which it is common to list clearly what experts contributed to the book. When speaking with a friend who had formerly worked for large K-12 online learning companies, she shared that it was common practice for the bigger companies to buy courses from smaller ones. If you looked closely and hard enough, you would find cases of identical courses being sold by different companies because of the incestuous histories of corporate mergers and divorces.

The process of procuring courses from K-12 online learning companies seemed to vary from vendor to vendor. Some charged schools per student, per course. Others charged per student, per catalog (which contained many courses). Still others charged schools based on a total number of concurrent users, making it possible for schools to use one license for multiple students over time. The different cost structures often befuddled principals. There were some constants I observed across companies. One constant was that in all cases, the duration of a license was temporary. That is to say, after the term of the contract a student and teacher would no longer have access to their course work. Another constant was that all vendors seemed to offer some form of "training," the cost of which was included in the cost of licenses. Additional training could, of course, be purchased. One can see very quickly how online learning companies profit from schools. Once a company develops a course, its purely digital form and standardized structure means that it can be copied and sold to a near infinite number of users.

The state's Race to the Top application calls attention to the desirability of online learning. This is no surprise. Online learning is a software-powered technology that generates data on students and teachers with every click. The nature of online course design naturally lends itself to alignment with standards: each reading, each question, and each click can be digitally tethered to some metadata structure. Administrators and teachers, as I've described, too often turned to online learning and frequently lacked an understanding of both the infrastructure and processes needed to make online learning function. Principals could seldom articulate what quality online teaching and learning entailed. What they knew, however, is that they could run data reports from online courses and stretch teachers' time and abilities to meet unrealistic demands. These facts alone seemed to be enough to merit investment. What we see with iLearnNYC is evidence that federal and state policies can encourage the use of products and services that only producers and promoters of software can provide.

SOFTWARE SPACE

If, as I argue above, Race to the Top created conditions in which pedagogues and administrators in New York State and City came to view online learning as a solution to their problems, we must examine online learning as occupying a software space. What does software space consist of in the case of iLearnNYC? In what follows, I present a summary of each of the layers in software space as they relate to iLearnNYC and pose a series of questions we might ask.

Devices

Schools in iLearnNYC needed devices for their students. Depending on the courses the school purchased the technical specifications for devices might vary. Headphones were needed for most courses because audio and video were frequently used. The size of the devices mattered in some settings, where the age and average size of students made using smaller netbook computers challenging. When tablets surged in popularity, we began receiving help desk calls complaining that the courses didn't work properly on iPads, which couldn't play the Flash video files upon which so many courses relied. How did the specific devices a school purchased help and hinder students' learning? Did schools who invested in desktop computers better position their students to benefit from online courses? Did the heavy use of Flash video by some companies hinder students' learning because their devices were unable to process it? How did screen and keyboard size affect students' experience in online courses? When we move beyond the word technology and imagine software spaces, questions like these emerge rapidly.

Networking Infrastructure

Some courses required more bandwidth than others. Courses that relied on streaming video, as engaging as such videos might be for some students, drained bandwidth and made it difficult for other students to load web pages. In addition, the access point in most classrooms—access points are little boxes one sees in classroom corners that transmit a wireless signal—could only accommodate 15 devices at once. A teacher who asked her class of 34 students to go online simultaneously to complete their personalized lessons was quickly flooded by complaints about slow loading web pages and stalled media. In what unforeseen ways did bandwidth limitations impact pedagogy? How did teachers and students respond to slow connectivity, in both explicit and implicit ways? How did teachers and students attempt to control and resist technological inadequacies? How did class scheduling position some students to access online courses easily while forcing others to access the Internet during "bandwidth rush hours"? Schools in collocated and densely populated areas experience greater wireless interference. How did schools and students respond to this? How did the central office's policy of blocking and permitting certain access to web sites affect students' learning?

Interfaces

When students are able to successfully use their devices to connect to the Internet and access their online courses, what they actually "interact" with is the user interface of both the computer and the course itself through a web browser. From afar, students appear to be looking at a screen and periodically clicking on a mouse, trackpad, or touchscreen. In reality, students are navigating multiple systems' interfaces, including the computer, the operating system, the browser, and the online course. Orientating oneself to these different interfaces requires effort from students and teachers. Each online course, for example, places the course content in different locations, makes managerial functionality available to students like progress tracking tools, and uses different navigation logics to move around the course in general. Students frequently encounter a disproportionate number of managerial tools rather than academic content. In a study of an online English course used in schools, I calculated that of the entire web page, less than 40% contained academic content. Imagine if for every two-page spread in a textbook, less than half of one page contained academic content whereas the rest of the page space contained a floating table of contents, branding, and message boxes about how to turn the page. It wasn't uncommon to hear a vocal student ask if she could "just go back to regular class" after encountering a series of subtle frustrating clicks while navigating an online course. How does the design of user interfaces affect students' and teachers' motivation to learn and teach? How are buttons and links used in online courses and with what pedagogical and epistemological ramifications? What managerial tools are students forced to interact with and how do such tools position students as learners? How do students perceive the quality of online content and media when used in online courses in comparison to media they encounter in their non-school lives? How do students and teachers conceptualize the entities who created the online course? When do students and teachers feel like they are being controlled through the screenic elements of the user interface?

Code

User interfaces provide a way for human beings to engage with code, the world of computational languages. Languages, do note, is plural. To speak of code is often to speak of multiple languages used for myriad interlocking purposes. Many different people, with a wide array of familiarity with different programming languages, contribute to software, which in part contributes to the inherent social and unstable nature of software spaces. Tracing the role that code plays, especially for the non-programmer, is challenging because it is both greatly invisible to us and incomprehensible. In addition, code is something that runs through all of software space. Whereas there are ways to analyze code even for the novice, which we explored in Chapter 6, what is perhaps more important to consider is the way in which the ontology of code—the limits and affordances of what it is by its nature—potentially and really impacts teaching and learning. In the case of iLearnNYC, we often found ourselves asking why an online course would automatically assess student work glibly. For example, why reduce the interpretation of a poem to a handful of inadequate and oversimplified statements for the sake of code? In part, it is because code must be programmed in advance with acceptable responses; to ensure automation there must be a single clear answer. When one views "progress trackers" in online courses, one might ask how student learning has been codified in order to be representable as a point of a finite continuum. How are poems, videos, feedback mechanisms, and communication tools represented through code? Code demands defined categories and numbers within unforgiving linguistic syntaxes. And yet, although it hearkens images of a humanless world of mechanization, code is written, compiled, and maintained by human beings whose ideologies, pedagogies, and politics are infused throughout software space. How do the assumptions of those other human beings manifest themselves in curricula?

Information Systems

One of the key challenges for iLearnNYC was the integration of various information systems. For users, it appeared that they simply went to a web site, logged in, saw their online courses, and began. In reality, dozens of information systems were integrated and constantly working to make the simplicity of the user's experience possible. First, there were data feeds pulled from city systems, which included teachers' names and ID numbers, classes teachers were teaching that year, and students assigned to teachers. Second, iLearnNYC created two-way data feeds for each of over a dozen vendors with whom they partnered. These feeds updated each other's systems regarding who was registered for which online courses, whether or not licenses had been purchased, and in some cases provided input for administrative reporting. Finally, the city built a customized piece of software that allowed schools to purchase licenses to courses, assign those courses to students and teachers, and inform the vendors of the license assignments. What are the implications of representing teacher and student identities as data for information systems? How do teachers resist and comply with how they are represented through information systems? How do the ways data are structured convey the ideologies and pedagogies of developers and companies who create software-powered technologies? How does software process such data feeds and with what effect on users?

REIMAGINING SOFTWARE SPACE IN EDUCATION

Although the word software is seldom used, it is the case that the education reforms of which Taubman and I speak in New York City are positioning software as a silent partner. In fact, I submit that software is a meta-mode of learning today. By meta-mode I mean that the ways in which we represent and discuss pedagogy is increasingly in terms that are mediated and shaped by software. Taubman discusses the ubiquity of standards and accountability measures in education after the passing of No Child Left Behind. These have only increased in the wake of Race to the Top, where New York is experiencing the aggressive implementation of Common Core Standards, teacher evaluation standards, and new teacher preparation standards. Each of these sets of instructional standards has associated testing mechanisms provided by private companies. Further, in addition to "performance" standards, we also witness the emergence of informational standards for structuring data that are intended to make it easier for vendors to profit from the curricular resources as well as all the data generated by so many testing and reporting requirements.

There is a fundamental tension between the ends of education and the ends of the companies who sell software-powered technologies to schools. Others have articulated this tension better than I. Education philosopher Maxine Greene (1995) writes with sadness in her book *Releasing the Imagination* about the way "Young people find themselves described as 'human resources' rather than as persons who are centers of choice and evaluation. They are, it is suggested, to be molded in the service of technology and the market, no matter who they are" (p. 124). This act of molding occurs not only via the words we use to talk about education and the need for reform, but also through the languages of software spaces, which, in order to process the complexity of pedagogy must reduce human experience into categories and numbers. The less we know about software, the more we ourselves are molded by it. The more we allow ourselves to be molded in this way, the more useful we are to analysts and algorithms trying to sell solutions to our pedagogical inadequacies.

To be clear, I do not believe that the use of software-powered technologies in education is inherently errant or bad. Rather, I believe that the way we currently position software in education dehumanizes our children and educators in the gullible belief that by opening the doors and purses of our schools to private industry we will "fix" education: industry before instruction; profits before pedagogy. When I witnessed the mayor's joke about text messaging technology, the teaching profession, and multiple-choice exams, I regret I didn't resist and respond to the arrogance and laughter that engulfed me. When today I hear the same sound bites from policy makers about *personalizing learning* or making education *transparent* by feeding *accountability* data to public and private information systems, I question what it will take to shift the discourse away from these empty and detrimental themes. These sound bites and public relations campaigns are harming children and educators. This is not a joke. What our use of software is doing to education is not a joke. What we educators are experiencing as our unions are assaulted and our professionalism mocked is not a joke. What our students feel when they are forced to shove the beauty of their minds into empty bubbles so software can automatically measure their learning is not a joke. I have since witnessed lifelong teachers fret, feeling inadequate that they cannot possibly meet all of the unreasonable demands placed on them. I have engaged with young adults preparing to be teachers who assume that this is what our profession has always been and must be: crowded classrooms, competing standards and interests, a culture of stress and numbers. I have listened to district leaders ignore the role software is playing in education without the slightest awareness that their professional and personal worlds are increasingly commanded by it. One way to address our current situation is to raise our critical and collective awareness of the way software operates in educational settings in our research, to which we turn next.

WORKS CITED

Black, C. (2011, February 28). An exciting year ahead. Yahoo Group, NYC Education News. Retrieved March 3, 2011, from http://groups.yahoo.com/group/nyceducationnews/message/30653.

Cramer, P. (2012, February 23). City alters Regents grading, credit recovery policies after audit. *Gotham Schools*. Retrieved July 22, 2012, from http://gothamschools.org/2012/02/23/city-alters-regents-grading-credit-recovery-policies-after-audit/.

Duncan, A. (2009, October 22). Teacher preparation: Reforming the uncertain profession. U.S. Department of Education. Retrieved February 28, 2011, from www.ed.gov/news/speeches/teacher-preparation-reforming-uncertain-profession.

Duncan, A. (2010, November 17). The new normal: Doing more with less. U.S. Department of Education. Retrieved February 28, 2011, from www.ed.gov/news/speeches/new-normal-doing-more-less-secretary-arne-duncans-remarks-american-enterprise-institut.

Gonen, Y. (2010, April 7). City schools working on plan to offer online classes. *New York Post*. Retrieved August 11, 2010, from www.nypost.com/p/news/local/city_promotes_online_classes_TykZepBwl7J6sPZNnbIuVI.

Greene, M. (1995). *Releasing the imagination: Essays on education, the arts, and social change.* New York: Jossey-Bass.

Klein, J. (2010, September). Innovation challenges. Innovation Zone, New York City Department of Education. Retrieved from http://schools.nyc.gov/community/innovation/izone/Explore_More/default.htm.

"Meet the Press" transcript for Nov. 15, 2009. (2009, November 15). *Meet the Press.* Washington, DC: NBC. Retrieved December 12, 2014, from www.msnbc.msn.com/id/33931557/ns/meet_the_press/.

NYCDOE. (2010, April 14). Chancellor Klein launches NYC innovation zone. Retrieved August 11, 2010, from http://schools.nyc.gov/Offices/mediarelations/NewsandSpeeches/2009-2010/izone.htm.

Phillips, A. (2010, April 14). More schools to experiment with online work, schedule changes. *Gotham Schools.* Retrieved August 11, 2010, from http://gothamschools.org/2010/04/14/more-schools-to-experiment-with-online-work-schedule-changes/.

Quillen, I. (2010, September 14). Analysis notes virtual ed. priorities in RTT winners. *Education Week.* Retrieved December 2, 2010, from www.edweek.org/ew/articles/2010/09/15/03online_ep-2.h30.html?qs=race+to+the+top+online+learning.

Race to the Top Application Assurances. (2010, May 28). New York State Board of Education. Retrieved December 12, 2014, from http://www2.ed.gov/programs/racetothetop/phase2-applications/new-york.pdf.

Robelen, E. W. (2010, January 31). "Race to Top" driving policy action across states. *Education Week.* Retrieved December 12, 2014, from www.edweek.org/ew/articles/2009/12/23/16states.h29.html?qs=race%20to%20the%20top.

Taubman, P. M. (2009). *Teaching by numbers: Deconstructing the discourse of standards and accountability in education.* New York: Routledge.

Unknown. (2009, November). The school of one—The 50 best inventions of 2009. *Time.* Retrieved August 11, 2010, from www.time.com/time/specials/packages/article/0,28804,1934027_1934003_1933977,00.html.

U.S. Department of Education. (2009, July 24). President Obama, Secretary Duncan announce Race to the Top. Retrieved February 28, 2011, from http://www.youtube.com/watch?v=xsPGVO_4pkw.

U.S. Department of Education. (2010). *Race to the Top.* U.S. Department of Education. Retrieved December 15, 2014, from www2.ed.gov/programs/racetothetop/index.html.

White, J. (2010, September). The iZone Mission. Innovation Zone, New York City Department of Education. Retrieved December 12, 2014, from http://schools.nyc.gov/community/innovation/izone/Explore_More/default.htm.

7 Where the Machine Stops

"My attention turns back to the importance of wide-awakeness, of awareness of what it is to be in the world."
—Maxine Greene in "Imagination, Community, and
the School," Releasing the Imagination, p. 35

I completed my doctoral studies while working full-time for the Department of Education. The days were jammed with meetings and school visits; the evenings consisted of either taking or teaching classes. In one section of my dissertation, I describe the political and organizational structure in which the Innovation Zone and iLearnNYC existed. I had to walk a fine line. Whereas I was a taxpayer and budding academic, I also was employed by the city and needed to be sensitive to how I conveyed some of the goings on. In one section, I delicately tried to describe the philosophy of Joel Klein based on his public statements and documentation. I remember vividly the day I completed that section. Sitting in the library at my graduate school one evening, I smiled at my small accomplishment. Then I read a press release. Klein announced his intent to resign as chancellor. I couldn't believe it. After days of delicately writing about his tenure, I was now free to be a bit more specific. I also decided to add to the section as the new chancellor took office. Half way through Cathy Black's chancellorship, sitting in the same library, I found myself deleting parts of her section because she too was leaving. I became increasingly aware of not only what I was writing about, but who my imagined audience might be. I knew that many of the colleagues I worked with did read some research and that writing readable research could directly affect decisions in the district. And yet, district- and state-level education is deeply tied to election cycles and politics. What kind of research would they read and under what conditions? How can researchers be systematic and rigorous in their studies while also embracing their own positionality and voice?

The previous six chapters have developed a framework for the importance of accounting for software in educational research. I have attempted to frame the establishment of critical software studies in education as a response to the hidden ways software can affect the way we research teaching and learning. In what follows, I share two examples of how one might pull together the different concepts and methods into more coherent studies. The first example (not an exemplar) applies critical software studies to online learning in New York City schools. The second looks more narrowly at the role of software in value-added teacher evaluation initiatives as exemplified in New York State and City. My hope is that what follows provides examples of what critical software studies research might look like in action.

TWEED'S ENGLISH: A CRITICAL SOFTWARE ANALYSIS OF ONLINE LEARNING IN NEW YORK CITY SCHOOLS

Less than two weeks after Hurricane Sandy tore through New York City, schools chancellor Dennis Walcott issued a press release from the central offices adjacent to city hall. Walcott announced that the city would make online courses available to students whose schools remained uninhabitable. In part, the press release reads:

> The initiative is intended to prevent learning loss for students who have had to move from their homes or schools and whose school attendance has been affected. The courses are made possible through an extension of iZone, the Department of Education's program that supports innovative models of teaching including online tools for classroom learning, and through the donation of program licenses from partners Apex Learning, Desire2Learn and Powerspeak. Teachers experienced in online learning will teach the courses and be available to students throughout enrollment. (NYCDOE, 2012)

The chancellor states that online courses will help "prevent learning loss," yet nothing is said about how such courses foster learning. He names three companies whose "donation" made the option possible, yet he says little about the reputation of these companies and the quality of their courses. The chancellor's operating assumption—that online learning can help prevent the loss of learning—merits closer inspection. This is especially true as we witness the expansion of online learning in public schools across the country due in no small part to the support such "innovations" receive from those in positions of power.

Online learning is spreading rapidly in K-12 settings throughout the United States. Defining *online learning* as "learning that takes place partially or entirely over the Internet," researchers have claimed that "Online learning—for students and for teachers—is one of the fastest growing trends in educational uses of technology" (Means, Toyama, Murphy, Bakia, & Jones, 2010, p. xi), citing increases of up to 65% over a two-year period.

Others estimate schools will be altered dramatically over the next decade and that "by 2019, about 50 percent of high school courses will be delivered online" (Christensen, Horn, & Johnson, 2008, p. 98). There is supporting evidence that this expansion is indeed already being funded. Venture capitalists have begun feverishly pouring funds into K-12 education technology endeavors, many of them online learning-related platforms and services. In 2010, venture capital firms invested $130 million in the "market." In 2011, that number leaped to $334 million (Ash, 2012)—a 39% increase in just one year.

The educational research community has struggled to thoroughly analyze the impact of online learning in K-12 settings, as more research exists in higher educational settings (Barbour, 2013). The research that does exist tends to rely on theoretical and methodological perspectives and techniques that treat "technology" as an object of study (Cuban, 2001) while not thoroughly accounting for the ontological and epistemological aspects of the kinds of technology being used today, most of which are powered by software (Berry, 2011). Software affects the kinds of teaching and learning that are possible. It inherits the ideologies (Kitchin & Dodge, 2011) and pedagogical assumptions (Lynch, 2014a) of those who create it. Nevertheless, the lack of research and theory about K-12 online learning has not deterred districts like New York City from investing in it. We must ask: How do commercial online courses both enable and encumber learning in public schools while realizing the ideological agenda of neoliberal reformers? Without enough convincing scholarship, policy makers have tethered themselves to compelling discourses that dilute the complexity of both software-powered technologies and education. Too many policy makers subscribe, instead, to the notions that students living in an "information age" learn radically differently than previous generations of students and only technology can bridge the perceived digital divide, that our nation's economic problems are due to our schools having not prepared the work force we need, and that if we just have enough data on students (and teachers) we can fiddle with algorithms until a previously undiscovered solution to education is unearthed. What follows is an attempt to identify and begin filling the scholarly gap in support of policy and pedagogy.

Situatedness and Context

My approach to this question is based on my work in the New York City Department of Education for nine years under the Bloomberg administration—as a teacher, a coach, and schools official. New York City is home to over one million students and 80,000 teachers. One of the key levers to the reforms in New York City during this time was the role of "software-powered technologies" (Lynch, 2013, 2014b), which increasingly refers to online courses. A windfall of federal money through the Race to the Top competition, which was funded through the American Recovery and Reinvestment Act of 2009, changed the pace, size, and focus of that pilot program. New York State saw $700 million, about half of which was earmarked for New York City. In the state's winning Race to the Top application, the city was featured prominently with strong emphases on its plans to leverage online learning. The small pilot I worked for exploded into a super-funded program devoted to exploring ways to pilot and scale innovations in schools called the Innovation Zone or iZone, which the chancellor mentions above. iZone had a specific program "extension" devoted to the large-scale implementation of online learning called iLearnNYC. The *New York Post* referred to iLearnNYC as representing "a boom in online learning" (Gonen, 2010); another news agency called the expansion of online learning "a major focus of Klein's [Bloomberg, Walcott] tenure at the Department of Education" (Phillips, 2010). The city used multiple funding streams—including Race to the Top money—to procure a platform and curricular content from private companies. The procurement costs included (in part) $2.7 million dollars to Desire2Learn for the online learning environment itself, $3.2 to Discovery for online resources, and $4.5 million to Apex Learning for online courses across grade levels and content areas (Otterman, 2011).

What follows is an attempt to systematically trace the interplay between the educational reform discourse surrounding iLearnNYC via the artifacts that comprise its promotion (i.e. news interviews, press releases) and the effects online learning as a software-powered technology has on the way we teach and learn. I use *software-powered technologies* as a term to emphasize the fact that many of the uses of technology we talk about in education today are not the physical technologies of the past, but rather are software-based. For instance, the technologies of pen and paper are replaced by word processing software, textbooks are becoming digitized, and blackboards have been made "smart." More will be said about this below. In particular, I am interested in the ways corporate and neoliberal ideologies attempt to co-opt the use of software-powered technologies in order to control *official knowledge* (Apple, 1993). Given the growing enthusiasm for the use of software-powered technologies in schools like online learning, critically examining how software itself is imbued with the ideologies of its makers is of paramount importance.

Critical Educational Studies Examined
Technology and Textbooks

The above excerpts exemplify the neoliberal effort to control *official knowledge* (Apple, 1993). From Apple's perspective, a neoliberal agenda works at various levels of education to control what, how, and from whom students learn, steering the direction of our schools through strategic control over the knowledge included in curricula while seeking to reform schools by applying free-market logic to the "education crisis," thereby inviting for-profit companies' participation in public education. Textbook companies provide Apple's main example. Because it is the business of companies to sell to the largest market, the way in which they *reproduce* knowledge is slanted toward their bottom line. In short, the states that buy the most textbooks (i.e. Texas) are likely to have their viewpoint nurtured in the kinds of content that makes it to print. Importantly, content that ends up in textbooks, Apple argues, is *recontextualized,* meaning that it is pulled out of its original context, like in the halls of academia, in order to align with companies' business needs. The result is that business needs, more than educational ones, "influence textbook writers and adopters to order knowledge into bite-sized chunks that can be easily understood and mastered (and which are politically safe)" (p. 68).

One concept that recurs explicitly and implicitly in the critical educational studies literature is that of the growing presence of neoliberal *logic,* which refers to the parameters by which problems and solutions are defined and place the drive for profits over pedagogical integrity. Apple uses "logic" explicitly when he argues that schools are "ever more subject to administrative logics that seek to tighten the reins on the process of teaching and curriculum" (Apple & Jungck, 1998, p. 133). Bromley expresses a similar stance when he refers to "applying economic logic to schools" (Bromley & Apple, 1998, p. 8). When our driving logic is economic in nature, it means that the needs of our families, communities, and democracy pass through a commercial filter. The rationale for making decisions places the ends of education second to profits. Picciano and Spring (2013) make similar claims in their discussion of the *education-industrial complex,* a concerted effort by government officials, philanthropic groups, and companies to impose a certain neoliberal logic and create schools that "function like a business and that their balance sheets should be driven largely by accountability as measured by assessments and testing . . . students and parents are viewed as customers rather than partners in the common good" (pp. 4–5). This notion of a logic is key to understanding not just the institutional discourses but to understanding precisely how software serves as a vehicle for the infusion of neoliberal ideologies into the lives of teachers and students.

Apple and others (Altbach, Kelly, Petrie, & Weis, 1991; Luke, 1988; Metcalf, 2002) analyze the way in which neoliberal forces interplay in the production of curriculum materials like textbooks. In these cases, critical theorists treat as their unit of analysis the structural elements and discourses of social, political, and corporate institutions. I argue that with the expansion of software-powered technologies we need to introduce an additional factor that merits close critical inspection: the nature of software. Again, textbooks provide a useful starting point to understand why software merits attention. In the case of textbook use, Apple (1993) is right to ask, "*Whose* knowledge is of most worth?" (italics original; p. 46) as he unpacks the way both the content of textbooks and the process by which they are produced reflect the ideologies of both the publishers and their best customers. The neoliberal apparatus focuses its strategy on ensuring that what they deem to be appropriate content prevails as prevalently as possible. When it comes to online learning, which is entirely powered by software, we have to consider not only the curricular content or *knowledge* itself but also the degree to which software companies have programmed software to promote certain *pedagogies*. This is where our unfamiliarity with software leaves us vulnerable. Textbooks are a technology with which educators are familiar; software-powered technologies like online courses are less familiar and even disorienting. Whereas educators have been shown to be able to resist the official knowledge of textbooks in both subtle and pronounced ways (Apple, 1996), I submit that we are far less deft at resisting software if for no other reason than because we are not conscious of its ontology and epistemological effects. It is all too possible to allow pedagogy to be dictated by software and not educators. If we are to avoid a "redefinition of 'mind' down to a lower level that *can* be imitated by machines" (italics original; Bromley & Apple, 1998, pp. 17–18), we need more nuanced ways of understanding how software-powered technologies push back on our practices in ways that textbooks and other analogue technologies do not.

The Commercialization of Pedagogy Through Software

Despite rhetoric of personalization and innovation, online courses are built on database logic and demand students comply with the understanding of non-educator programmers and executives at companies. Whereas those in power have learned to reassure the public that teachers matter and have a role in the use of online courses (recall the chancellor's statement above), too many districts and schools have been content to under-support teachers in mastering this new technology and in doing so they are quietly handing pedagogy over to private industry. It is through software that this handing over of pedagogy is occurring, at least in part.

Software studies is an emerging field that examines how the nature of software—its ontology, its history, its politics, its functionality—impacts those who use it. A fundamental principle of software studies is the notion that software has an active presence in the world. Whereas more traditional technologies like textbooks are static and relatively inert, software directly mediates and shapes (Berry, 2011) the way we live our lives. Software is what makes a wide array of human creativity and destruction possible, from music production to architectural design to remote controlled military aircraft. Software studies is concerned with the social impact of software in both great and subtle ways, less so with the analysis of code and hardware we see in code studies or computer science, although both of these fields are referred to intertextually. Credit for naming software studies is often given to Lev Manovich, a visual artist and cultural theorist whose conceptualization of software and its impact on film and the arts I will draw on below. By combining concepts from software studies with multimodal analysis, we can arrive at a systematic approach to collecting and analyzing data from new media that accounts more explicitly for the way in which software and the companies who produce it impact teaching and learning.

One of the key elements of software Manovich (2001) develops in his *Language of New Media* is what he refers to as *database logic*. In order for software-powered technologies to create the "illusion" (p. 177) of interactivity and personalization we so often attribute to them, Manovich argues that the complexity of human experience must be *transcoded* into *quantities* in order to be *automated* via the logic of a database. An example helps to illustrate what these concepts mean and how they interrelate. When I take a picture of my son playing on the playground, the camera on my phone captures the complexity of that lived experience in visual form through sensors. What is a live and fleshy experience is transcoded, meaning the camera converts what I see into a digital format consisting of alphanumeric quantities. For example, the camera "reads" the color of my son's skin as #f2b692. Once digitized into a file consisting of sets of these kinds of numbers, the photo can be automatically stored, retrieved, and manipulated with ease via databases and algorithms. This ease of manipulation is what allows popular photography apps for smartphones to apply filters to our pictures and share them instantaneously. The logic of the database treats all this data the same, which makes for rapid processing of data, be it photos, videos, stock market trades, or data drawn from students' learning. When processing data, software relies on limited commands in order to function: if this/then do that, yes/no, 1/0. To transcode is necessarily to reduce lived experience into numbers and process them in fundamentally limited ways. The softness of my son's skin, its smell of smeared peanut butter, and the stickiness of grape jelly is lost because software has not been created or programmed to capture and transcode such things. Stickiness and scent are not easily captured by database logic, certainly not by my phone. It is a concern about this limitation that leads Manovich to warn that "Because new media is created on computers, distributed via computers, and stored and archived on computers, the logic of a computer [or database] can be expected to significantly influence the cultural logic of media" (p. 46). The same influence exists in the use of software-powered technologies in education.

This reliance on database logic means that software itself leans towards certain epistemologies. As Manovich describes, the need for software to quantify experience in order to automate processes through databases and algorithms relies on complex systems of dichotomies. At the deepest level, software demands a concrete number and to be told yes *or* no, right *or* wrong. Database logic cannot tolerate ambiguity. What feels to users like freedom when using software-powered technologies is an illusion. Video games exemplify this contradiction when player autonomy is the result of the game having been very tightly programmed to control the player's options at all times. "Behind the freedom of the surface," Manovich writes, "lies standardization on a deeper level" (p. 197). Whereas Apple describes how textbook knowledge is reproduced and recontextualized as the conservative and neoliberal entities officiate knowledge through ideological filters and strategic institutional manipulation, software-powered technologies recontextualize knowledge *and* also impose the logic of the database which carries with it an epistemological stance that demands standardization and binaries—two words that offer a hint as to the pedagogical impact software might have.

Although Manovich doesn't develop the educational critical implications of his theory, others do explicate the ideological nature of software. "Software," after all, "is not an immaterial, stable, and neutral product" (Kitchin & Dodge, 2011, p. 37). The fact is that software is developed by teams of people whose motivation for such development ranges from public good, to hobby, to profit. In the case of most software-powered technologies used in education, it is nearly always the latter. Companies create software and their motivation for developing software certain ways and not others reflects their ideologies. Consider this simple example. It is not uncommon for users of text messaging (SMS) to have an experience where in a rush to text they mistype a word, which the messaging software autocorrects. My phone, which is made by Apple Computers, will automatically correct my typo of the word "iPhone" but doesn't recognize my mistyping of the name of its competitor Google. It isn't a technical limitation that makes this the case. It would require the same effort from Apple Computers to program its messaging application to recognize Google and its products in the way it quickly recognizes and autocorrects its own. An ideological stance, not a technical limitation, prevents them from doing so. Although it might seem like an innocuous feature on a mobile phone, its implications are troubling. In its decision to make the word *Google* less available to its users, Apple Computer is using software to mitigate the presence of a very real word in our lives—a word that has been in the *Oxford English Dictionary* since 1998. Software, as this example illustrates, is injected with the ideologies of those who create it. When we consider the role that software plays in education, we must be wary of software's inherent epistemological and ideological leanings and their impacts on the integrity of pedagogy. The notion of official knowledge suggests that the kinds of knowledge conveyed in textbooks is the result of a neoliberal agenda seeking to control students' cultural literacy through partnerships with publishing companies. In the case of software, although there are ideological leanings of which we must be aware, the epistemological slant of software-powered technologies is in fact due to a foundational technical limitation. That is, software can only "know" that which complies with the logic of the database.

It should be clear why education reformers zealously promotes software-powered technologies. First, software-powered technologies satisfy neo-liberal desires to shuffle the responsibility for our children and citizenry to corporations while bolstering the economy. Software used in education is often developed privately and therefore requires that schools and governments pay public funds to private companies. Second, epistemological strengths and limitations of software align tightly with the conservative desire to control official knowledge (Apple, 1993). Whereas the content of textbooks had to be controlled prior to printing, in online courses the digitization of curricular content provides infinite opportunities for online course providers to "update" content to powerful clients' desires. In addition, software-powered technologies privilege certain epistemological stances that regard the act of learning itself as consumeristic, the consumption of correct content. The limitations of software play well into the hands of a reform movement that increasingly wishes not only to control knowledge but pedagogy as well, downplaying the importance of educators (increasingly by assaulting their unions) especially when online courses wait in the wings to automate the teaching process.

To discuss only official knowledge is not enough. We must now begin to discuss *commercial pedagogy*. As software-powered technologies continue to be funded and imposed on schools for both administrative and instructional purposes, we must be aware, as mentioned above, of the fact that software pushes back on human intentionality in ways that other technologies do not. What's more, the ontological limitations and epistemological prejudices of software lean toward a kind of learning experience that is inherently narrow and consumer-based.

Methods

How, then, do we critically study software-powered technologies like online courses in order to expose and critique the commercialization of pedagogy? The field of multimodal studies offers methodological guidance in unpacking the *multimodal ensembles* (Kress, 2011)—convergences of textual, video-based, visual, audial modes of communication—that comprise online courses. We can capture the material aspects of multimodal ensembles and transcribe these modes for analysis in ways that "accommodate [their] variability and reflect its [their] diversity" (Flewit & Hampel, 2011, p. 53). In the present inquiry, we are interested in the way the ontological and epistemological nature of software pushes and pulls against the *epistemological commitments* (Kress, 2003) students intend to make in response to curricular content.

In order to examine the way multimodal ensembles encourage certain ideologies and epistemological commitments we must consider the way in which User Interface (UI) design impacts how one interacts with the curricular content. The UI is a mostly visual representation presented to users and with which users interact. In short, it's what you see on the screen. The UI occupies an in-between space where the logic of the database (software) meets the logics of human social communication (multimodalities). UIs exhibit a fundamental tension that both enables and inhibits social experiences, including pedagogy. UIs are designed to convey freedom and ease of experience for users when what software demands is a set of predetermined inputs. In an educational setting, "predetermined inputs" suggests a view of students' creativity, inquiry, and knowledge that is potentially dim and soulless—students are positioned as consumers rather than producers. UIs are situated in a kind of modal crossroads where speech, writing, video, and other modes converge. I argue that we can study the material aspects of UIs in many ways, including attention to layout of the page, links, individual texts like writing or video, and buttons by analyzing pixel counts and the moments where students are required to click on the screen.

In her discussion of new media design, Murray (2011) notes that "design is always the conscious creation of a particular artifact within a longer cultural tradition of practice. It always involves a choice of conventions in a context in which there is not just one correct way of doing something" (p. 25). I would add that not only is what presents itself on the screen worthy of study, but so too might be that which is absent (Fairclough, 2001, 2003). In online courses, the modes of writing and image do not occur independently but rather in a tightly designed UI that facilitates a student's interactions with curricular content. Manovich (2001) goes as far as to suggest that "content and the interface merge into one entity" (p. 67). If this is true, that the interface is not merely a vessel for curricular content but in fact shapes that content while being shaped by it, the UI is uniquely positioned between the user and the software that powers the online course.

For this analysis, I focus on an online English course offered by one of the companies named in the chancellor's press release called Apex Learning. I chose an English course because my background is in English education. The course is one that would be offered to 11th grade students, which is the year in which students in New York City commonly take their state exam in English. I selected the Honors section because I expected it to represent the "best" of what the company's courses can be. The course is for the second semester of study, which I selected in order to avoid what often appear to be "introductory" or overly "review-based" units that often serve as the bookends of courses. The unit of analysis for this study requires brief explication. It is insufficient to measure traditional units of analysis like turns in speech or academic content alone. In a multimodal examination of an online course, we focus on the specific elements of the ensemble—text, video, audio, buttons, links, banners, menus—and how they converge within the UI. For current purposes, I will focus on two of these material aspects: 1) the high-level layout of an online course's UI as well as 2) diving more deeply into place on the page where students are forced to make epistemological commitments.

Data Collection and Reduction
Layout Analysis

Designers of online courses make very intentional decisions about what appears where and why in order to create a sense of "agency in navigation" (Murray, 2011, p. 159). The designers' goal is to frame the interface in such a way that users perceive freedom of action when navigating while strategically limiting their choices; UIs present to users only options that software can accommodate in accordance with the limitations of database logic, ideally in an aesthetically appealing and navigable way that results in students' engagement. UIs walk a fine line between the rigid and unfamiliar ontology of software and a sense of easy and familiar user experience. The former "sees" ones and zeros; the latter sees buttons, texts, and images. If UIs are "conscious creations" (Murray, 2011, p. 25) designed in specific ways to achieve specific ends, we can measure and quantify the number of pixels UI designers of an online course devote to different kinds of functions. Pixels refer to the discrete "dots" that together comprise the images we see on computer screens. It is common practice in web design to use pixel counting tools to generate precise measurements for various elements visible on the screen. In my analysis, I generate pixel areas (height x width) for different components of the web page template used in the course. The result is a view into what one sees on the screen as a series of "blocks" (Kress, 2003) that have been placed by designers, and their bosses. I pose the following questions when examining the UI:

1) How does the design of this UI position students as learners? What kinds of activities do the layout blocks privilege?
2) What does the design of this UI convey about the ideologies of those who created it? How else might the company have designed the site and with what effect on the students' experiences?

Button Analysis

If the UI is the primary site of study in the analysis of online courses, then I suggest the most crucial single component of UIs is the button. A common feature on web sites, buttons convey a sense of control, certainty, and confidence. Buttons represent the discrete moment when students intend to make an epistemological commitment. When one clicks a button on a web site it is an unambiguous commitment of a particular action, that is, "something well defined and predictable will happen as a result of the user pressing it" (Pold, 2008, p. 31). Any confidence a user has is at least somewhat illusory, however. The button achieves its purpose via a series of illusions. Users do not "press" buttons as we often say, rather we "click" on them. In fact, we do not even click on actual buttons. We click on a mouse or tap a screen which in turn prompts software to simulate the experience of pushing a physical button. Users hear the sound of a click, the simulated button icon changes appearance in an effort to create the look of having been physically pushed, and something then happens on the screen after the button has successfully been engaged. Buttons create a "functional spell" (p. 33), enchanting users into believing that in an environment that is so digital, so intangible, and so ever-changing, there is something definite and solid only a click away. The purpose of the button is to create a clear place and moment where users enact commitments: of purchase, of agreement, of desire, of learning.

We can employ what I call button analysis to tease out the interplay between software, academic content, user action, and ideologies. UIs use buttons to mark the moment of epistemological commitments students make in online courses. There are many kinds of buttons in online courses (i.e. a "help" button, "next page" buttons) as well as buttons available in the web browser in which the course appears (i.e. the "back" button, "forward" button, "search"). Much might be learned by thoroughly analyzing these buttons as well. However, for present purposes, I identified buttons that followed the presentation of academic content or assessment, which appear to require students to commit to an expression of their knowledge. I use the following four questions to guide the analysis of buttons:

1) What curricular content do students encounter and/or what are students asked to do?
2) What buttons are students required to click?
3) What happens on the screen when students click the button?
4) How does software respond to the "input" of the clicking of the button?

In Pursuit of Stability

My goal is to peel away the different layers of the student's experience clicking a button in order to expose and explore the ways in which learning might be affected in unforeseen ways. It is an attempt to "stabilize" what Kress (2003) notes is highly unstable media and what Manovich (2001) notes is, in part, an illusion. For example, the pixel measurements I take can change at any time if the company who created an online course makes an update, for instance. It is also the case that the same online course can appear to the user differently on various web browsers and computer screen sizes. Similarly, the analysis of buttons is necessarily a wobbly enterprise. They are not, in fact, buttons at all. Nor are they actually pressed. Nor is the sound one hears actually that of a button being pressed. This kind of instability is, however, a necessary part of software-powered technologies and the new media they create. The approach

I outline offers a way to capture stable insights into the relationship between software and learning that accepts instability and illusion as a fruitful presupposition.

Quantifying Site Layout Through Pixel Count

The online course under investigation has a layout that does not change significantly throughout the course. It consists of a banner at the top of the screen identifying the company and course, beneath which are "breadcrumbs." Breadcrumbs are a horizontal listing of pages that comprise the hierarchical location of the current page. For example, Home>pages>online course>Apex. On the left side is a window that remains in view at all times and contains an outline of the entire course. As students move through content and activities, the outline updates to reveal the scope of work for the current section, like a table of contents that shows users where they are. A single content display section near the center of the screen houses the curricular content for the course. The size of that section remains mostly stable, requiring that students click on buttons to continue reading or watching content. There are various "help" icons available in different places on the screen. The course appears not in the typical browser one might expect but rather as a smaller "pop-up" window that limits access to typical features of the web browser.

I begin by calculating the area in pixels of the entire web page students encounter. I then measured the pixel areas for the various blocks of the UI that the designer designated for specific user activities. Next, I identified them according to their main function, resulting in the following categories: branding (where the company is clearly identifying itself), management (features that are primarily intended for students to manage their own work in the course, like breadcrumbs and course outlines), support features ("help" icons, links to additional resources like vocabulary lists), and curricular content (that which appears in the central window as what students are to learn). Additionally, there is a significant amount of empty space in the course UI. This is important to acknowledge as it can affect how the measurements are interpreted. My calculations include empty space rather than calculating the components of the UI's filled space only.

The pixel analysis conveys the following about the online course UI design. The curricular content itself comprises less than half of what students experience on the screen (43.79%). In order for students to view all the academic content they frequently have to click a button, as many as a dozen times, in order for new parts of the content to load in the same window. The presence of support features, which can be vital to students receiving helpful tips at key times in a course in order to continue, amounts to less than 2% of the UI. Branding and self-management features comprise nearly a quarter of the screen (23.36%). Finally, nearly one third of the screen is empty (30.96%).

Articulating the Epistemological
Tension of Buttons

Given the modal density of online courses, by which I mean the great number of distinct modes that converge, I now focus my analysis on one part of one module in one unit of study, which is representative of what we see in other parts of the course as well. Students encounter curricular content and prompts related to the topic *modernism*. The main modes of content representation are: written words on the page, narrated slideshows in which students click through slides (some of which are animated) and listen to a voice recording, images (often chosen to emphasize something in the written text), and quizzes that have two main kinds of questions: 1) multiple-choice selection and 2) open text boxes for longer responses. Students engage with the interface by clicking on different kinds of buttons and/or links. The main kinds of buttons students encounter enable students to offer definitions of key words, to advance to the next slide or page, to select multiple choice options and submit responses via a "continue" or "submit" button, and a variety of icons used often to point students to support resources (i.e. clicking on an icon of a piece of paper prompts the system to read a poem aloud to the student).

In one part of a unit called "A New Direction: Modernism," the course presents eleven "pages" students click through to review the content. Students click a forward facing arrow each time. Pages in the study contain text related to the topic, often an image related to the content being discussed, and sometimes video presentations that include a narrative track and animations. Interspersed throughout the unit are two kinds of assessments for which I offer two examples. The first is a multiple-choice quiz. In one representative case, a quiz prompt reads, "You've had a brief overview of the three tenets fundamental to modernism. Do you remember what they were? Explore them further in the questions below." Then students read a question and select a multiple-choice answer. For example, "Before modernism, people saw reality as: (A) Objective and true, (B) Subjective." After three questions, students receive a score with the "right" answers explained. In order to move from one question to the next, students must click a button labeled "Continue." The second kind of assessment appears to be more open-ended. In a representative example, students are prompted as follows, "Now consider another poem by a different writer also associated with modernism, Edna St. Vincent Millay. Click the icon on the right to read the poem. Is this a modernist poem? Let's ask a few questions to find out." After reading the poem, students are then presented with the prompt: "What do you notice about the rhyme scheme?" Students type their response into a text box, clicking the button labeled "Submit" when complete. Immediately after submitting, students receive the following response from the system: "If you said that the rhyme scheme was regular, you're right. (It goes as follows: abbccaa deeffdd)." It is necessary that students click on buttons in order to do two main things: to continue their course work and to submit responses to assessments.

Findings

There are two main findings from the above analysis. First, the data suggest that online courses promote the neoliberal ideologies through the coordination of market-based and database logics. Second, the kinds of experiences that this company creates for students in its online learning environment twists students' learning experiences to align with the ontology of software rather than the needs and abilities of students.

Imposition of Corporate Ideology on Students

The data gathered from both the pixel and the button analyses presented above suggest that student learning experiences are transcoded to align with the logics of both the market and of the database. If we subscribe to what Murray (2011) writes about the conscious creativity involved in designing UIs, it is reasonable to conclude from the layout analysis that the designers of the course had a "choice of conventions" (p. 25) and chose to represent a screenscape heavily populated with managerial features. Most of the screen is dedicated to non-curricular content and functionality. Designers of the course chose to dedicate only 44% of the screen to content, a decision which betrays the ideological leanings of those in power. The creators of the online English course above embrace a disempowering view of learning and effect the managerialization of students themselves in ways that align tightly to the neoliberal reform agenda. Most of what students see on the screen positions them as managers, not constructors, of their own authentic learning: outline of content to be covered, buttons to click as a way of informing supervisors of one's productivity, automated scoring of assessments that puts the onus on students to fix what they don't understand.

The layout conveys the sense that students are responsible not only for grappling with the academic content, but also for autonomously monitoring their own progress. Forgetting for a moment that the "progress" a student monitors is dubious at best, the assumption that students should be responsible in this way is highly debatable. The effect of such "personalization" is to transfer the responsibility for students' learning away from adults (who are paid with public funding to assume precisely such responsibilities) and onto the shoulders of children. The fact is that students are not given the *full* responsibility of actually teaching themselves. They are given faceless adults' predigested knowledge and provided an interface through which they must comply. All under the banner of personalization and innovation, public officials who promote such online learning shift the responsibility for educating our children to a highly unregulated, unaccountable, and profit-minded entity. This assertion regarding the intentionality of UI design is supported by the analysis of buttons as well.

Students use forward-moving arrow buttons to navigate the curricular materials of the course. Recall that in order for students to read all the required content and to view videos, they must click through as many as a dozen mini-pages in the content window of the UI. It is strange that so many clicks are required for students to access content when it is common practice for web designers to create web pages that can scroll down endlessly. It would be easy, technically speaking, to include all the content for a unit on a single web page. One reason for requiring so many clicks is that each time an arrow is clicked, software captures that information and students' "progress" is tracked. This information can be made available to administrators who monitor students' progress. Importantly, students are not made overtly aware of this monitoring mechanism. Drawing attention to the way software acts in this case provides some explanation for the surprising percentage cited above—that just over 40% of the screenscape is curricular in nature. The fact is that the more frequently a student has to click through course material, the more data are available for computing their progress through the system. The forward-moving arrow, then, represents *not* students' educational progress, but rather represents the designer's—or more accurately, the company's—use of software to aggregate data that can be reported to administrators as thin evidence of learning. It is primarily a managerial, not a pedagogical, design decision.

Transcoding of Epistemological Commitments for Processing by Software

The system also employs two kinds of buttons with regard to assessments: multiple-choice questions and open-ended response questions. Multiple-choice questions clearly limit the kinds of responses students can give. There is a "Continue" button that appears at the top of the quiz question window, like the forward-moving arrow, impelling students to select answers and click ahead with a sense of necessity: students don't have a choice whether or not to click the button, they must to proceed or their "learning" stalls. Again, each click is a source of data software gathers. When a student clicks on their multiple-choice selection, software compares the student's selections with predetermined answers that were programmed into the system. In this case, it is clear to the student that there is already a "right" answer and they are expected to choose the proper one. The act of choosing a response and clicking "Continue," then, comprises a student's *epistemological compliance* rather than epistemological commitment. Their commitment is validated or corrected automatically by software.

Open-ended questions appear to provide a counterbalance to the closed nature of multiple-choice questions, prompting students to type an original response into a text box before clicking the "Submit" button. While the question itself is open-ended (e.g. "What do you notice about the rhyme scheme?") and the textbox is seemingly poised to accept longer responses, when the student clicks "Submit" software is programmed to provide the *same* feedback regardless of what student type. I tested two responses—one directly connected to the prompt and the other pure gibberish—and the "feedback" was identical. The result is that students get a closed-response to an open-ended question. Whereas the multiple-choice question makes transparent the limitations software requires to provide automated feedback, this open-ended question masks the role of software and deceives students by making them think that they are going to receive feedback that is unique to the original response they are asked to input. The epistemological commitments that students intend to make are, in fact, ignored as software imposes its own pre-programmed knowledge on their learning.

What we witness in the above examples is the *commercialization of pedagogy* that is taking root in public education through neoliberal endorsement and promotion of certain uses of software-powered technologies like online courses. In a comparable way that Apple describes textbook companies recontextualizing knowledge for their marketplace, I argue that the online course studied here transcodes the complexity of learning and creates a Manovichean illusion of learning that reduces students' epistemological commitments to database-friendly bits of data. This commercial pedagogy values the coverage of content as the pinnacle of learning, not only because it aligns with conservative desires to control knowledge but also because it aligns with neoliberal wishes to promote software's ontology and the corporations who create it.

In Sum

When the country's largest school district issued a press release announcing that online courses would be made available to students in the aftermath of Hurricane Sandy, their motives, I believe, were well intentioned. When the companies named in the press release agreed to partner with the city to offer their products for free, their motives, I believe, were decent. I have worked closely with leadership in the city and with online learning companies. Most of the people I have encountered care about how students learn and believe that what they are doing is good. As the analysis above demonstrates, however, there is nuance to the way software limitations can steer learning and there is a dearth of explorations of those limitations. In part, the paucity of critical conversations about the role software plays in education is due to the nature of new media, which resists the applications of old theoretical frameworks and methods. This has resulted in researchers being slow to frame the field in ways that policy makers and companies can understand. As a result, companies offer products for sale to our children that districts can increasingly purchase easily with public funding. Their products escape scrutiny, however, from researchers and educators. In the case of the online English course studied above, the result is that students' own critical insights and creativity are cast aside for the logic of the database and the limitations of software. It is the nature of software that demands our attention if we are to avoid the continued commercialization of pedagogy and the danger that our students, especially the most vulnerable who are disadvantaged by socioeconomics as well as storms, will grow up to mistake the clicking of buttons for learning.

CLICK TO REFORM: TRACING TEACHER EDUCATION REFORM THROUGH SOFTWARE SPACE

In his article on the state of teacher evaluation, Smagorinsky (2014) articulates what he sees as the limitations of current teacher evaluation reforms as well as offering a proposal for change. He situates his critique within the context of the agenda of the Obama Administration and its Race to the Top program, which he refers to as "educational drone strikes, designed to eliminate the teachers whose students test poorly, but aimed so broadly that they create widespread collateral damage to the whole of the teaching profession and the communities they serve" (p. 165). The metaphor is more apt than one might realize, as it alludes to an aspect of the reforms about which we as researchers and teacher educators say too little: the role of software-powered technologies in education. Smagorinsky alludes to the role that computerized assessments are playing in determining teachers' evaluations, but these represent only part of software's presence. In order to understand how these reforms impact teaching and learning, and in order to resist them, we must account more thoroughly for how software makes it all possible. Without software, these reforms cease to exist.

What role—explicit and implicit—does software play in realizing the current education reform agenda, especially with regard to teacher evaluation?

Smagorinsky hints at the key role software plays when he refers to the problem of "having a machine decide whether or not they can teach, as is the case when evaluation is driven by test scores" (p. 171). The word "machine" is significant, as is its oft-repeated cousin "technology." However, both words mask what is really at the heart of the matter: software. In his philosophical examination of software, Berry (2011) warns, "Computationality tends towards an understanding of the world which . . . cannot but limit the possibilities of thought to those laid within the code and software which runs on the tracks of silicon" (p. 169). Any freedom or creativity we experience through software is the result of our actions being strictly controlled. It is a motif that recurs throughout software studies. Kitchin and Dodge (2011) write that in some ways "software is a powerful force of homogeneity, rather than the diversity that marks creativity" (p. 123). Manovich (2001, 2013) analyzes the ways in which lists and menus on web sites and applications are used to limit users' choices and to ensure that their actions align with the predetermined paths of software developers. A prime example of the tension between the free will of the user and the essential predeterminism of software can be seen in the use of buttons, which Pold (2008) writes "signify a potential for interaction" (p. 31) that conceal more than they reveal. Software scholars seem to agree: using software means submitting to software. Other fields, however, say precious little about software despite the fact that they, including the field of education, are becoming veritable "coded spaces" (Kitchin & Dodge, 2011) that rely on software to function. If it is the case that software, by its nature, forces users to comply with the directions of its programmers, surely educators and researchers should possess a critical sense of the ways in which software might affect pedagogy in unintended ways.

Education Reform in the United States

Education policy in the United States has, in recent years, been framed in direct response to the economic crisis. It is through the American Recovery and Reinvestment Act (ARRA) of 2009 that federal funding for the current reforms is provided in the amount of over $4 billion, a staggering budget to support the nation's schools. In order to prepare for the economic needs of the future, it was argued, it is necessary to educate students differently today. There is a litany of books one can cite that argue for the importance of preparing students for the 21st-century economy. Such books corroborate the federal government's reform agenda, frequently featuring technology as a key lever. Christensen, Horn, and Johnson (2008) describe how the investment in computer technology in public schools has resulted in few gains and that to spark true innovation in education policy makers, educators, and companies must approach technology disruptively, including distance learning, social media-style platforms, and online learning environments. In his books on education reform, Harvard professor Tony Wagner (2008, 2012) supports the idea that the school system is locked in a model of teaching and learning inadequate for today's world. Our society is globalized, technology ubiquitous, and new skills and dispositions are required to succeed. The traits Wagner envisions for students include curiosity, collaboration, associative thinking, and initiative. This notion that preparing students for new jobs means integrating technology into education is one shared by others, whether discussing young people's propensity for digital learning (Prensky & Thiagarajan, 2007; Trilling & Fadel, 2009), curriculum planning (Jacobs, 2010), and the power of video tutorials to individualize student learning (Khan, 2012).

The hallmark program of the administration's education reform agenda is called Race to the Top. Rather than distributing equal ARRA funding to all districts, the administration created parameters for states and districts to compete with each other for it. The administration outlines four areas of focus of Race to the Top:

- Adopting standards and assessments that prepare students to succeed in college and the workplace and to compete in the global economy;
- Building data systems that measure student growth and success, and inform teachers and principals about how they can improve instruction;
- Recruiting, developing, rewarding, and retaining effective teachers and principals, especially where they are needed most; and
- Turning around our lowest-achieving schools. (U.S. Department of Education, 2010)

Successful applicants interwove these various components and agreed to aggressive timelines to implement the reforms. Although not mentioned explicitly, it is also the case that states who received Race to the Top funding adopted a new common set of standards called the Common Core, chose a set of teacher evaluation and teacher preparation standards from a shortlist of options, and agreed to feed student achievement and teacher performance data into a data system managed by a non-profit entity called inBloom. More about each of these components will be said below.

Theoretical Framework

The present study is an attempt to trace the presence of software in the discourse of the education-industrial complex (Picciano & Spring, 2013) in which the neoliberal reform agenda justifies the officiating of knowledge (Apple, 1993) and the commercialization of pedagogy. The neoliberal reform agenda argues that increasing schools' use of *software-powered technologies* (Lynch, 2013, 2014a), a term intended to draw attention to the issues of power embedded in the production and use of software, is necessary to prepare students for the 21st-century economy and for the country to compete globally. In fact, as others have begun to articulate, software itself bears the ideologies (Bromley & Apple, 1998), epistemologies (Kitchin & Dodge, 2011), aesthetics (Manovich, 2001), and pedagogies of those who fund, promote, and develop it.

In conceptualizing what they call the education-industrial complex, Picciano and Spring (2013) argue that technology is a key lever for reformers to impose corporate ideologies on education. They trace in some detail how the same individuals move across public offices, private companies, and philanthropic administration. They explicate the degree to which technology companies who build data systems and whose products have become promoted in schools—student information systems, online learning,

e-readers, assessment technologies, tablets, laptops—have been systematically positioned to reap the rewards from education policies and legislation.
What they describe is in many ways a manifestation of what Apple (1993)
refers to as an alliance between neoconservative and neoliberal entities who
seek to co-opt education by controlling what is learned and by shifting the
responsibility for teaching the young away from educators and toward companies. As Apple and others (Bromely & Apple, 1998) have pointed out,
technology companies are strengthened in the field of education by public
officials and philanthropic groups. I would add that this is increasingly the
case because what we mean by "technology" has become synonymous with
software and that software-powered technologies have become ubiquitous
in our lives. When we consider software in this way, we see the disturbing
potential for software-powered technologies and the companies who create and control them to commercialize pedagogy, dismissing the expertise
of educators and humanity of learning for computational approaches to
education that mistake innovative approaches to information systems for
innovative learning.

Unlike analogue technologies of the past, software has an active and ideological quality (Kitchin & Dodge, 2011). By active, I mean software can
be programmed to automatically do things in our world. For example, our
mobile phones autocorrect our perceived misspellings when we send text messages, regardless of the actual correctness of such actions. Software is considered ideological insofar as the world views, epistemologies, and pedagogies
of the companies and communities who create any given software are infused
into the software itself (Berry, 2011; Kitchin & Dodge, 2011; Lynch, 2014a,
2014b). It is worth considering how the ontology of software—its need to
digitize experience, quantify, store and retrieve data, execute algorithms,
and to control users' behaviors—fundamentally impacts the ways we live,
know, create, and learn (Adams, 2006, 2010).

Manovich (2001) posits that software culture is infused with *database
logic*. Defining a database as "a structured collection of data" that are "organized for fast search and retrieval by a computer" (p. 218), Manovich argues
that the more human beings create, share, and consume media through
software-powered technologies the more the undergirding logic of the database shapes their process and product. Database logic demands clearly
predefined terms and all data must be put in their place. One of the ways
software developers control the kinds of inputs users can provide—which
eventually feed into and draw upon databases—is by imposing a logic of
selection. When engaging with software, users are constantly forced to select
from prescribed options: through links, through menus, through buttons,
and through toolbars. Manovich tersely states, "in computer culture, authentic creation has been replaced by selection from a menu" (p. 124). Software
shapes human behavior and creativity in ways that we do not necessarily
intend and of which we are not necessarily aware—an important cautionary
note in times of unbridled political enthusiasm for all things digital.

Methods

The current reforms demand greater use of software in teacher education. One way to conduct examine how software is positioned in the educational discourse is by collecting speeches delivered by Secretary of Education Arne Duncan and analyzing such texts for the explicit presence of the word software as well as tracing the implied role software plays even if left unsaid.

Data Collection of Speeches

For the purposes of this study, I chose to focus on public documents related to Race to the Top and speeches Secretary of Education Arne Duncan gave between February 2009 and August 2013. There are limits and affordances to my choice to focus on speeches. One limitation is that speeches represent only part of the discourse. Other studies could be done that look not only at speeches but also at transcripts of television and radio appearances, press releases, and quotations from media reports. Speeches, by their nature, are prepared in advance and are often longer than, say, television interviews. So whereas other texts would certainly contribute to our understanding, speeches are arguably the most prepared, public, and sustained discursive texts available.

In order to compile the speeches, I wrote a basic scraping program that automatically searched for and retrieved the web address, title, date, and content of all speeches archived on the U.S. Department of Education web site. Next, I reduced the scope of analysis in two ways. First, some speeches in the federal archives that initially seemed attributed to Secretary Duncan were sometimes delivered by his associates. I withheld these speeches from the final corpus. Second, I cleaned that data by removing unnecessary text (i.e. the titles of recommended web pages) and correcting errors that occurred in the retrieval (i.e. apostrophes being replaced by ampersands). All speeches were then saved according to their date of delivery, compressed, and uploaded to an open-source text analysis application called Voyant Tools for analysis. This left me with 185 speeches and nearly 500,000 words, controlled for Taporware stop words (i.e. *a, the, and, 1, 2, 3*).

On Text Analysis

Text analysis can be associated with several other scholarly traditions, including literary study, content analysis, discourse analysis, digital humanities, and linguistics. I employ a "grounded qualitative paradigm," which uses "quantitative content analysis to establish the basic data and qualitative analysis to interpret it" (Huckin, 2004, p. 22). For my study, I use text analysis software to conduct initial data collection, reduction, and pattern identification across the corpus. I then use a technique I refer to as *critical software analysis* to unpack the hidden role software plays in the secretary's agenda.

Critical Software Analysis

I refer to *critical software analysis* as a method for making visible the unseen role of software. I use this term as a hybrid of other methods suggested by scholars in software studies. Kitchin and Dodge (2011) argue that in order to unpack the hidden role software plays in every day life, it is necessary to "trace software through the figuration of space" (p. vii). Berry (2011) articulates the need for software's role in society to be "fully mapped" (p. 169), especially as "streams" of data become increasingly generated by both human users and software. Finally, Manovich (2013) describes his analytical method as his attempt "to trace *a particular path through this history* [of media authoring software]" (italics original; p. 43). Critical software analysis begins with a clear point of departure—data gathered, social problems, an experience—and systematically and transparently investigates the degree to which that which seems absent is in fact present. What appears to be invisible becomes bold, what appears to be peripheral becomes ubiquitous.

Explicit References to Software

The data collected reveal that Duncan (2009, 2010a, 2010b, 2011, 2012a, 2012b, 2012c) refers explicitly to software only seven times in the over half a million words he uttered. Due to the surprisingly few times software is referred to, I list the excerpts in which the word occurs in their entirety (with the word software emboldened):

- "Make No Small Plans," October 7, 2009: "In a way, the Harlem Children's Zone is to community schools what FedEx is to the U.S. Postal Service. FedEx uses all of the same basic technologies that the post office does—trucks, planes, and tracking **software**. / Yet FedEx combined those technologies with a new strategy to fill an unmet need—overnight mail service."
- "Using Technology to Transform Schools," March 3, 2010: "This initiative will create new demand from colleges and universities for online courses. It will open a new market for supplementary materials—one that you are uniquely positioned to fill. Our online skills program will create new opportunities for you as publishers and **software** developers—and will deliver the best possible education for students in the 21st century."
- "Rural America Learning Opportunities and Technology," July 21, 2010: "In Iowa, the Heartland Area Education Agency serves 54 public

school districts and 29 accredited private schools. Across its large geographic area, Heartland is providing professional development to teachers and principals. Using free **software**, these teachers and leaders communicate in real time in video conference. They don't need to be in the same room, let alone in the same country. These online courses give them opportunities for collaboration that they've had difficulty accessing before."

- "Beyond the Iron Triangle: Containing the Cost of College and Student Debt," November 29, 2011: "Working with faculty, NCAT helped to redesign whole courses, not single classes. And they introduced innovative uses of instructional **software** and Web-based learning resources to assure that students mastered specific learning goals."
- "The New Platform for Learning," March 8, 2012: "First of all, President Obama is deeply committed to STEM education. His goal is to create an education system that produces more people like you—with the creativity and technical skills—not only to invent new educational programs and **software**—but to help us lead in every other field."
- "Broadening the Spirit of Respect and Cooperation for the Global Public Good," May 3, 2012: "Finally, our joint work on the U.S.-China e-language project produced positive findings in an evaluation of student performance. Students with the lowest performance at entry made the largest gains when using a jointly-created supplementary, open-source gaming **software** program. They also gained increased motivation to learn a foreign language."
- "TIME Higher Education Summit," October 18, 2012: "We still have a lot to learn and perfect about online learning, adaptive **software**, analytics, simulations and gaming, and other uses of technology in higher education. But there is no question that a digital revolution is already underway in higher education, and its vast potential has only begun to be tapped."

There are three ways in which the secretary refers to software above. First, Duncan refers to software in the context of instructional uses. For instance, he describes teachers using "adaptive software," "gaming software," and "free software" in classrooms. In one instance, he prefaces his litany of software-powered technologies with the disclaimer, "We still have a lot to learn and perfect . . ." suggesting that software's use for instruction, although full of "vast potential," should be approached with enthusiastic caution. Second, the secretary uses the word software in the context of its explicit development—aware that he is talking to an audience of business community members who are responsible for creating the very kinds of software applications in which the secretary sees so much potential. Third, Duncan uses "software" to refer to the kinds of information systems companies like FedEx use to track packages, strongly suggesting that if schools only used information systems and analytics software with a "new strategy" their students would perform better. This reference is an important one as it alludes to an often hidden role that software plays in education reform.

Implicit References to Software

A review of the language of both the secretary's words and the Race to the Top criteria suggests that software—although unstated—is essential to effect change. We can trace the necessary presence of software for assessment, reporting, and analytical purposes. The tests that are being created and implemented by for-profit companies to assess students based on the "common set of standards" are intended to be taken on computers. The data schools are required to gather cannot be pulled without software, nor can schools do anything with that data—analyses, reporting, data feeds—without software. The process of certifying and evaluating teachers has become deeply technologized as data systems gather teacher and testing data, algorithms recommend curricular resources for teachers, and preservice teachers increasingly have to take computerized exams and upload portfolios to the Web for their certification—the servers for which, in some cases, belong to for-profit companies.

Let us examine briefly the way in which one state that received Race to the Top money is implementing key components of the reform agenda. New York State received over $700 million in Race to the Top money. As a result, state officials committed to implementing a common set of standards to measure student achievement (i.e. the Common Core Standards), standards to measure teacher effectiveness (most districts adopted the Danielson Framework for Teaching), and required districts to feed student achievement and teacher performance data to state-level information systems where they would then be fed to a nationally networked information system called the Shared Learning Collaborative, which was later renamed inBloom. A teacher's effectiveness score in New York is based on a formula of various measures, including student test scores and evaluation based on in-class visits by a supervisor. Both the student test scores themselves and the final teacher effectiveness scores are fed to the state's central database where the data is cleaned, organized according to new schema requirements, and fed to inBloom. The goal is for teachers to be able to log in to software applications (provided by companies that partner with inBloom) and find recommendations for teaching resources, including ones made by for-profit companies who have limited access to the data.

STUDENT TEST SCORES

In order for test questions to be automatically assessed, it is necessary to significantly limit the kinds of answers a student can input into the system.

One sample question ("Grade 10 Sample Items," 2013) made available to New York State asked students to read an excerpt from Ovid's *Metamorphoses* called "Daedalus and Icarus." Students are then asked to answer the following question:

> In "Daedalus and Icarus," what do the lines "he turned his mind to arts unknown / and nature unrevealed" (lines 9–10) imply about Daedalus and his invention?
>
> a. that his invention will bring him wealth and fame
> b. that his invention will be something beyond common understanding
> c. that the primary motive for his invention is revenge
> d. that he is nervous about the success of his invention

TEACHER EFFECTIVENESS RATINGS

An English teacher whose students take the above exam would be deemed effective or ineffective based not only on students' performance on the exam but also based on his or her supervisor's in-class observation, often a principal or assistant principal. The principal uses a rubric to assess the teacher, which in the case of New York is referred to as the Danielson Framework (Danielson, 2013). For example, a principal might assess the teacher's ability to employ discussion techniques in studying a poem like the one above. In this case, a principal has to determine at what level of effectiveness the teacher is doing so. Here is an example of how two (out of four) levels differ:

> Level 3 (Proficient): While the teacher may use some low-level questions, he poses questions designed to promote student thinking and understanding. The teacher creates a genuine discussion among students, providing adequate time for students to respond and stepping aside when doing so is appropriate. The teacher challenges students to justify their thinking and successfully engages most students in the discussion, employing a range of strategies to ensure that most students are heard.
>
> Level 4 (Distinguished): The teacher uses a variety or series of questions or prompts to challenge students cognitively, advance high-level thinking and discourse, and promote metacognition. Students formulate many questions, initiate topics, challenge one another's thinking, and make unsolicited contributions. Students themselves ensure that all voices are heard in the discussion.

Note that each level includes not only a numerical category (i.e. 3 or 4) but also a qualitative descriptor (i.e. proficient or distinguished) and description.

inBLOOM REPORTING

When the state prepares student achievement and teacher performance data to be fed to and ingested by inBloom's information systems, it has to do so according to a preordained schema. That is, if inBloom is going to receive a long list of information from the state, it has to be organized in a way that inBloom's systems can instantly understand. inBloom's schema ("Developer Documentation," 2013) is organized under "domain entities." Domain entities include CourseOffering, EducationOrganization, Learning-Objective, LearningStandard, School, Student, Teacher, and more. Each domain entity then breaks down into a list of possible categorical types of information that a state can feed to inBloom. For instance, the category Student contains the following fields: address, birthData, cohortYears, disabilities, economic-Disadvantaged, homeLanguages, learningStyles, name, race, sex, student-UniqueStateId, and many more. Within these structures, only some attributes are "key fields," meaning they *must* be reported. In the case of student-related reporting, the following are some key fields: studentUniqueStateId, schoolYear, session (which refers to the grades for classes the student attended during a specific grading period), administrationDate (when an assessment was given), assessment (which assessment is being reported), assessmentItem (which item on an assessment a student answered), studentCompetencyObjectiveId (which competency the student is being assessed on), learningObjective, disciplineIncident, and the list goes on. Teachers' data feeds follow a similar schema. Key fields for teacher-related reporting include: teacherUniqueStateId, programAssignment (i.e. regular education, Title-1), school, and section (i.e. the class and students a teacher is assigned to). To underscore, the fields listed above are non-exhaustive and only represent key fields. Other data fields that inBloom's schema support districts reporting teacher and student phone numbers, email addresses for parents, and even the kind of weapon used in a discipline incident.

Analysis

Our critical software analysis has to account not only for the expressed pedagogical and political ends of the education reforms, but also for that which is hidden. As we see above, the discourse places great emphasis on the use of information systems. It is into information systems that all measures of performance—for students as well as for teachers—must eventually be entered. It is reporting and analytics from information systems that policy makers and companies point to as evidence of the effectiveness of the public school system. To trace the role of software in education we must accept the primary importance of information systems, the database logic that drives them, and the pivotal role selection plays.

The exams students take in New York State have been created by a consortium of public, private, and non-profit organizations to align with the

Common Core Standards. It is no surprise that the sample question above focuses students' attention on a couple lines of poetry. The test question asks students to interpret what the lines "imply." The test fabricators offer four options from which the student must select. The options reflect the test fabricators' interpretation of the lines of poem. The task for the student is not, as the question suggests, to interpret an implication of the lines of the poem. Rather, the task of the student is to figure out how the test fabricator read and interpreted the poem—or, at least how the test fabricator did *not* interpret the poem in which case a process of elimination might result in a correct answer.

The format of multiple-choice questions on computer-scored exams like the one above reigns in popularity, in part, because it meets the needs of database logic. It is debatable that a question such as the one above achieves the ends of the Common Core Standards, which seek to raise students' active ability to read and respond to challenging texts. In a question like the one above, all we know is that a student read a challenging text and question well enough to guess at how a faceless adult read and responded to a challenging text and question. (It is also worth noting that volumes of research on the teaching of literature would argue against the soundness of the pedagogy reflected in the question above.) Students are forced into a moment of selection—a kind of computational corral, a false choice—where an opportunity to capture authentic evidence of students' learning is abandoned for the sake of the database. In the end, the student's answer to the question is correct or incorrect—categories ripe for data entry.

When teachers are evaluated using a rubric like the one above, we see another way in which the complexity of pedagogy is reduced to something a database can receive and retrieve. Again, selection is used to achieve this. If our English teacher is teaching a poem by employing discussion techniques, his principal might sit in the back of the room and take notes using the evaluation rubric as a way to articulate what she sees. The principal might find herself trying to determine if, in the end, the teacher's performance merits a Level 3 or a Level 4 score on the rubric. To be clear, she must select only one score for the teacher in this category. The information system into which she enters the final evaluation will not accept ambivalence. And yet, the difference between the Level 3 and Level 4 scores is not a simple one to delineate. For example, a key difference between a Level 3 and a Level 4 is the role that students themselves play in engaging in "high-level thinking and discourse." In a Level 3 performance, it is the teacher who is leading the discussion greatly by using multiple teaching techniques and "stepping aside" as needed. In a Level 4 performance, the discussion is driven by "students themselves." The issue with separating the two levels of performance the way the rubric does is this: It is completely possible, even desirable, that a teacher would differentiate instruction in a classroom so some students have more teacher-led conversations whereas others lead their own.

Because of the way the rubric is positioned politically, however, a principal might value such teaching but would have no way to enter it into a database. The database requires a 3 or a 4. That's it. It is important to note, however, that if the rubric is used as a device in classrooms to guide shared conversations between teachers and administrators, that is a very different case. In that case, we can trace the use of the rubric back to the improvement of one's pedagogy. It is a private, professional conversation. But when we position rubrics as devices to force choices as in the example above, it becomes an extension of software—little more than a menu option, a link, a button that we click on.

When the student's test scores and the teacher's evaluation are entered into district and state information systems, the data have to be prepared for their next incarnation. They have to be structured in a way that aligns with a schema created by inBloom. Based on the key fields, inBloom will receive data about students that include the identification number the state provides, any learning disabilities, second languages spoken, history of disciplinary incidents, and assessment data like the exam being reported and details about what questions the student did well and poorly on. (These assessment data are then mapped to another schema of "learning objectives" and "competencies," which is beyond the scope of the current discussion but well worth rigorous attention.) inBloom also receives data about teachers, including their identification number with the state, the school at which they teach, the classes they teach, and the students for whom they are responsible. With this information, that inBloom can quickly facilitate the processing of information to determine how well or poorly a specific teacher's students did on an exam, drilling down to the level of specific test items. As long as teacher evaluation data are fed to inBloom or sister systems via the same schema, it is technically simple to generate a score for a teacher's performance based on the state's formula ("Guidance on New York State's Annual Professional Performance Review," 2013): the teacher's students' test performance (40%) and the results of the principal's classroom evaluation (60%).

DISCUSSION

The analysis above suggests that the needs of information systems—and those who produce, maintain, and rely on them—is potentially influencing pedagogy. When we consider the degree to which private companies profit from these endeavors—creating and selling large-scale assessments, selling computers on which to take assessments, updating networking infrastructures at schools to ensure Internet connectivity, building district- and state-level information systems, selling professional development coaching and materials—it leads me to say we are witnessing the neoliberal commercialization of pedagogy through a sophisticated software-powered education-industrial complex. As we see above, regardless of what language we use to discuss teaching and learning, or what rhetoric we hear from our policy makers, the real discourse that comprises education reform is the one driven by information system schemas like inBloom's and the database logic it promotes. It merits mentioning as well here that there are many more fields provided by inBloom that are not identified as "key fields," yet. We could rightly assign significance to these other fields based on the fact that inBloom has articulated the fields in the first place. This might be a hint as to the direction of their long-term agenda, including the degree to which learning is constructed (i.e. as competencies) as well as the role of parents.

We can have excellent teachers differentiate class instruction and immerse students in experiential learning, we can have lessons about poetry that guide students through imaginative experiences, and we can have rich human conversations with our school leaders about how to sharpen the craft of teaching, but in the end all that will be valued, counted, and publicly reported has already been defined. This is a problem. It is a problem not because the categories offered by inBloom are necessarily poor, but because 1) they are created mainly by non-educators, 2) they are mostly unknown to educators and certainly not commonly discussed publicly, and 3) the primacy of their place in education means that what it means to teach and learn is predetermined by those who are least qualified to define it. As in the example of the principal's use of the teacher evaluation rubric, it isn't the rubric itself that is problematic—rich conversations can occur through a common framework. The same is true of the current lust for information systems. It is not to say that using data in this way could not be very helpful to school leaders and teachers; it is to say that if education officials position these kinds of systems in ways that demoralize educators and implement them in ways that are slanted to the best interests of companies who can profit from student and teacher data, we have fallen far short of our highest aspirations for democratic education—and will not likely be preparing students to cope with the unknown challenges of future economies.

Implications and Further Research

In Race to the Top, we witness the imposition of neoliberal ideologies on our schools at every level: the tests students take, the evaluations teachers receive, and the ways in which information is packaged and shared beyond the district. And yet, the secretary of education hardly uses the word at all. It is not that we are "having a machine decide whether or not [teachers] can teach" as Smagorinsky writes. Rather, it is that we are allowing our policy makers to shift the responsibility of pedagogy to those who promote and produce software—all without saying the word. Software is capable of much sounder pedagogical use, but it has been overtaken for political and economic purposes that are both misguided and delusional.

How can we respond to such efforts that are coordinated across federal, private, and philanthropic organizations? One step is to organize and engage in the discourse. My hope is that the present study will be of use to some who choose to do so. In addition, more research is needed from the field to articulate precisely how the ontology of software contains the ideologies of its creators, how those ideologies can be recognized and analyzed, and what the direct impact on teaching and learning is. Methods of multimodal analysis would benefit from applying critical frameworks to account for the nature of software and how it is used by the neoliberal apparatus to control education. Researchers who study the implementation and effectiveness of technology, as another example, can account for the ideological influences at play in classroom settings, including the degree to which software embodies such ideologies and the ways pedagogy is subtly commercialized. Our schools cannot rely on reformers to approach the use of software critically. The profits to be gained are too great, the rhetoric preached too easy to agree with, and the scene populated by too many whose enthusiasm is naïvely misplaced. Disrupting the scene requires new ways of articulating the issues and staunch scholarly refusal to allow the education of our children and professionalism of our teachers to be reduced to the selection of a menu option or the click of a button through which we submit.

CONCLUSION

The above studies attempt to demonstrate what critical software studies looks like when applied to single sites of study: online learning and teacher evaluation. While far from perfect examples, they do, I hope, begin to add concreteness to what critical software studies can look and feel like for researchers who might apply concepts and methods to their own work. There is another audience, however, who also might find critical software studies valuable to their practice: teachers. Helping teachers see how software operates in schools is an essential part of critical software studies, although it requires scholars to think beyond the typical genres of research writing and to adopt a tone and style that is both critical and accessible.

WORKS CITED

Adams, C. (2006). PowerPoint, habits of mind, and classroom culture. *Journal of Curriculum Studies, 38*(4), 389–411.

Adams, C. (2010). Learning management systems as sites of surveillance, control, and corporatization: A review of the critical literature. In D. Gibson & B. Dodge (Eds.), *Proceedings of society for information technology and teacher education international conference 2010* (pp. 252–257). Chesapeake, VA: AACE.

Altbach, P. G., Kelly, G. P., Petrie, H. G., & Weis, L. (1991). *Textbooks in American society: Politics, policy, and pedagogy*. Albany, NY: SUNY Press.

Apple, M. W. (1993). *Official knowledge: Democratic education in a conservative age*. New York: Routledge.

Apple, M. W. (1996). *Cultural politics and education*. New York: Teachers College Press.

Apple, M. W., & Jungck, S. (1998). "You don't have to be a teacher to teach this unit": Teaching, technology, and control in the classroom. In H. Bromley & M. W. Apple (Eds.), *Education/Technology/Power: Educational computing as a social practice* (pp. 133–154). Albany, NY: SUNY Press.

Ash, K. (2012, February 1). K-12 marketplace sees major flow of venture capital. *Education Week*. Retrieved July 22, 2012, from www.edweek.org/ew/articles/2012/02/01/19venture_ep.h31.html.

Barbour, M. K. (2013). The landscape of K-12 online learning. In M. G. Moore (Ed.), *Handbook of distance education* (3rd edition, pp. 574–593). New York: Routledge.

Berry, D. (2011). *The philosophy of software: Code and mediation in the digital age*. New York: Palgrave Macmillan.

Bromley, H., & Apple, M. W. (Eds.). (1998). *Education/Technology/Power: Educational computing as a social practice*. Albany, NY: SUNY Press.

Christensen, C. M., Horn, M. B., & Johnson, C. W. (2008). *Disrupting class: How disruptive innovation will change the way the world learns*. New York: McGraw Hill.

Cuban, L. (2001). *Oversold & underused: Computers in the classroom*. Cambridge, MA: Harvard University Press.

Danielson, C. (2013). The framework for teaching evaluation instrument. The Danielson Group. Retrieved December 15, 2014, from www.danielsongroup.org/userfiles/files/downloads/2013EvaluationInstrument.pdf.

Developer Documentation. (2013). inBloom. Retrieved January 4, 2014, from www.inbloom.org/developer-documentation.

Duncan, A. (2009, October 7). Make no small plans. U.S. Department of Education. Retrieved December 2, 2010, from www.ed.gov/news/speeches/make-no-small-plans.

Duncan, A. (2010a, March 3). Using technology to transform schools. U.S. Department of Education. Retrieved June 27, 2014, from www.ed.gov/news/speeches/2010/03/03032010.html.

Duncan, A. (2010b, July 21). Rural America learning opportunities and technology: Secretary Arne Duncan's remarks at the national rural education summit. U.S. Department of Education. Retrieved December 20, 2014, from www.ed.gov/news/speeches/rural-america-learning-opportunities-and-technology-secretary-arne-duncans-remarks-nat.

Duncan, A. (2011, November 29). Beyond the iron triangle: Containing the cost of college and student debt. U.S. Department of Education. Retrieved December 20, 2014, from www.ed.gov/news/speeches/beyond-iron-triangle-containing-cost-college-and-student-debt.

Duncan, A. (2012a, March 8). The new platform for learning. U.S. Department of Education. Retrieved March 8, 2014, from www.ed.gov/news/speeches/new-platform-learning.

Duncan, A. (2012b, May 3). Broadening the spirit of respect and cooperation for the global public good. U.S. Department of Education. Retrieved December 20, 2014, from www.ed.gov/news/speeches/broadening-spirit-respect-and-cooperation-global-public-good.

Duncan, A. (2012c, October 18). *Remarks of U.S. Secretary of Education Arne Duncan at the TIME Higher Education Summit*. Presented at the TIME Higher Education Summit, Washington, D.C. Retrieved May 3, 2014, from www.ed.gov/news/speeches/remarks-us-secretary-education-arne-duncan-time-higher-education-summit.

Fairclough, N. (2001). *Language and power.* New York: Longman.

Fairclough, N. (2003). *Analysing discourse: textual analysis for social research.* New York: Routledge.

Flewitt, R., & Hampel, R. (2011). Multimodal data collection and transcription. In C. Jewitt (Ed.), *The Routledge handbook of multimodal analysis.* New York: Routledge.

Gonen, Y. (2010, April 7). City schools working on plan to offer online classes. *New York Post.* Retrieved August 11, 2010, from www.nypost.com/p/news/local/city_promotes_online_classes_TykZepBwl7J6sPZNnbIuVI.

Grade 10 Sample Items. (2013, October 28). Partnership for Assessment of Readiness for College and Careers (PARCC). Retrieved January 7, 2014, from www.parcconline.org/sites/parcc/files/Grade10SampleItemSet10.30.13.pdf.

Guidance on New York State's Annual Professional Performance Review. (2013, November 23). New York State Education Department. Retrieved January 7, 2014, from www.engageny.org/sites/default/files/resource/attachments/appr-field-guidance.pdf.

Huckin, T. (2004). Content analysis: What texts talk about. In C. Bazerman & P. Prior (Eds.), *What writing does and how it does it: An introduction to analyzing texts and textual practices* (pp. 13–32). Mahwah, NJ: Lawrence Erblaum Associates.

Jacobs, H.H. (2010). *Curriculum 21: Essential education for a changing world.* Alexandria, VA: ASCD.

Khan, S. (2012). *The one world school house: Education reimagined.* London: Hodder & Stoughton.

Kitchin, R., & Dodge, M. (2011). *Code/Space: Software and everyday life.* Cambridge, MA: MIT Press.

Kress, G. (2003). *Literacy in the new media age.* New York: Routledge.

Kress, G. (2011). Discourse analysis and education: A multimodal social semiotic approach. In R. Rogers (Ed.), *An introduction to critical discourse analysis in education* (2nd Edition), New York: Routledge.

Luke, A. (1988). *Literacy, textbooks, and ideology: Postwar literacy instruction and the mythology of Dick and Jane.* New York: Falmer Press.

Lynch, T.L. (2013). The secretary and the software: On the need for integrating software analysis into educational spaces. In J. Gorlewski & B. Porfilio (Eds.), *Left behind in the race to the top* (pp. 129–142). Charlotte, NC: Information Age Publishing.

Lynch, T.L. (2014a). Holy interfaces and the sanctity of software: A critical software analysis of rubrics as vehicles of conservative reform. In M. Tenam-Zemach & J. Flynn (Eds.), *A rubric nation: A reader on the utility and impact of rubrics in education* (pp. 125–141). Charlotte, NC: Information Age Publishing.

Lynch, T.L. (2014b). The imponderable bloom: A multimodal social semiotic study of the role of software in teaching literature in a secondary online English course. *Changing English, 21*(1), 42–52.

Manovich, L. (2001). *The language of new media.* London: MIT Press.

Manovich, L. (2013). *Software takes command.* New York: Bloomsbury Academic.

Means, B., Toyama, Y., Murphy, R., Bakia, M., & Jones, K. (2010). *Evaluation of evidence-based practices in online learning: A meta-analysis and review of online learning studies.* U.S. Department of Education. Retrieved January 7, 2014, from www.ed.gov/rschstat/eval/tech/evidence-based-practices/finalreport.pdf.

Metcalf, S. (2002). Reading between the lines. In A. Kohn & P. Shannon (Eds.), *Education, Inc.: Turning learning into a business* (pp. 49–75). Portsmouth, NH: Heinemann.

Murray, J.H. (2011). *Inventing the medium: Principles of interaction design as a cultural practice.* Cambridge, MA: MIT Press.

NYCDOE. (2012, November 20). Chancellor Walcott announces new online courses for students impacted by Hurricane Sandy. Retrieved December 28, 2012, from http://schools.nyc.gov/Offices/mediarelations/NewsandSpeeches/2012-2013/new_online_courses.htm.

Otterman, S. (2011, March 29). Amid layoffs, city to spend more on school technology. *New York Times*. Retrieved April 1, 2013, from www.nytimes.com/2011/03/30/nyregion/30schools.html?pagewanted=all&_r=0.

Phillips, A. (2010, April 14). More schools to experiment with online work, schedule changes. *Gotham Schools*. Retrieved August 11, 2010, from http://gothamschools.org/2010/04/14/more-schools-to-experiment-with-online-work-schedule-changes/.

Picciano, A. G., & Spring, J. (2013). *The great American education-industrial complex: Ideology, technology, and profit*. New York: Routledge.

Pold, S. (2008). Button. In M. Fuller (Ed.), *Software studies: A lexicon* (pp. 31–36). Cambridge, MA: MIT Press.

Prensky, M., & Thiagarajan, S. (2007). *Digital game-based learning*. St. Paul, MN: Paragon House. Retrieved January 17, 2014, from http://books.google.com/books?id=e-CjQAAACAAJ.

Smagorinsky, P. (2014). Authentic teaching evaluation: A two-tiered proposal for formative and summative assessment. *English Education, 46*(2), 165–185.

Trilling, B., & Fadel, C. (2009). *21st century skills: Learning for life in our times*. San Francisco, CA: Jossey-Bass.

Wagner, T. (2008). *The global achievement gap: Why even our best schools don't teach the new survival skills our children need—and what we can do about it*. New York: Basic Books.

Wagner, T. (2012). *Creating innovators: The making of young people who will change the world*. New York: Scribner.

U.S. Department of Education. (2010). *Race to the Top*. U.S. Department of Education. Retrieved December 15, 2014, from www2.ed.gov/programs/racetothetop/index.html.

8   Soft(a)wareness

"The dialogue can be generated and enriched by the writing some of us try to do, the journals we keep along with others. Even now, it helps me to be in search of words, to break with immersion by seeing and saying."

—Maxine Greene in *"Teaching for Openings,"*
Releasing the Imagination, p. 115

Before becoming director of implementation for iLearnNYC, I spent a number of months working as an "innovation coach" with several new small schools in Manhattan. I met with teachers and principals, tried to understand their vision for teaching and learning, and tried then to develop a plan for how software-powered technologies might be able to support their vision. Time and time again, I encountered two main kinds of responses to using technology in the schools. The first response was one of enthusiastic embrace. This did not mean that teachers knew deeply how to leverage technology, just that they were open to it and believed that it would improve their practice and increase students' engagement. The second response was one of eye-rolling dismissal. Some teachers, for instance, had experienced too many other waves of new technologies and consciously chose to stick with the analogue methods they knew and upon which they could rely. In both cases, there was something missing.

As I have been outlining in this book, researchers, policy makers, and educators must adopt a critical stance with regard to software-powered technologies. In fact, my hope is that the book itself provides some guidance to the former two stakeholders. When it comes to reaching educators, however, a book of this length and tone might not be sufficient. I am, however, fortunate to edit a column in a widely read journal for English teachers called *English Journal,* which for over a century has chronicled the teaching of secondary English in the United States. In that column, I write brief essays that seek to convey to English teachers just how software works in education and raise their awareness of critical ways to leverage and resist its presence. In what follows, I present six installments of the column. My hope is that these columns will provide an example to other researchers of how one scholar frames his work for an audience of educators and how the ideas expressed in this book might appear to a broader—and vital—audience.

PECS SOVIET AND THE RED UNDERSCORE

Pedagoguery is a word. It's not one I use very often, but it is a word. An old word. Three hundred years ago it referred to the act of teaching. A century later its meaning shifted to refer negatively to empty or dogmatic instruction. When I type it in my word processor, however, something unexpected happens: a red squiggly line appears. The word appears to be floating on a crimson sea of incorrectness and I am left questioning myself. Puzzled, I pick up my phone to text my friend.

"Hey. Isn't pecs soviet a word??" I send.
"What on earth are you talking about?" he replies.
"Not pecs soviet. I don't know why it did that. I meant pedagoguery."
"Oh. That's a word. I prefer pecs soviet, though."

I return to my word processor, click the red underscore, and ignore the error.

What I describe has become commonplace. In both instances, the use of a word is called into question by software. In the first case, the word processor has a spell check feature that is programmed to underline words that are not in its dictionary. In the second case, the phone's software is programmed to automatically correct words that are mistyped or unrecognized. Software makes both of these functions possible; they are "software-powered" (Lynch, 2013). Software powers our computers and phones. It also has the power to impact our choices, to steer our behaviors in ways we do not always see. This is especially the case in education where what it means to teach and learn is becoming increasingly tied to software.

Software Is Neither Passive nor Neutral

We use various digital tools in our classrooms and lives—from web sites to word processors to smartphones. These digital tools are not technologies in the "traditional" sense. These technologies are powered by software. Unlike simpler technologies—like chalk, for instance—software is active; it pushes back on those who use it. Consider the active nature of the squiggly line in my opening example. Chalk doesn't zap corrections onto the blackboard as you write. Misspellings must be found by the human beings in the room. Software, however, makes it possible for a typo to be automatically exposed.

The ability of software to prod us into correcting our spelling (indeed, to fix misspellings for us automatically) hardly seems like it merits a column in a widely read teaching journal. The fact is, software does much more than play the part of grammarian. In an age of data-driven education reform, Common Core Standards, and teacher evaluation systems, official uses of software abound. Software powers many of the programs and devices we use, whether for administration or instruction: student information systems, attendance and scheduling programs, digital gradebooks, new Common Core curricular web sites and resources, the uploading and evaluation of teaching videos, myriad testing and assessment systems, online courses, e-communities, automated essay scorers, reading intervention programs, plagiarism detection tools, interactive whiteboards, e-readers, response systems or "clickers," educational apps for tablets and mobile phones, and, of course, email.

Given its ubiquity, it is important to note that software does not merely appear out of the ether. It is developed. Software does what it does because it has been programmed to do so. Product development teams, programmers, and executives at companies make decisions about what it is software will do for reasons that sometimes appear to have more to do with making a profit than with enacting sound pedagogy. A company's worldviews, ideologies, and assumptions about what constitutes learning are infused into the software-powered technologies they create and promote with each invisible line of code, each design choice on the screens we see. In my case with *pedagoguery,* the two different companies that designed my word processing software and mobile phone made very intentional choices to mark as misspelled or autocorrect some words and not others. The brand names of both companies are recognized; a word referring to teaching gets flagged as incorrect. This seemingly simple choice has real-world consequences, albeit minor. The companies' software decisions interfered with my moves as a writer, blurred my meaning, and confused my friend.

Software Has Limitations Inherent to Its Nature

Over the last several years, a collection of video tutorials for students posted on YouTube has surged into a "model" of innovative use of technology in education. Khan Academy receives millions of daily viewers and has received millions in philanthropic funding. As a testament to the site's success, the Academy's founder, Salman Khan, graced the cover of Forbes magazine under the headline, "The $1 Trillion Opportunity" and a byline that reads, "No field operates more inefficiently than education. A new breed of disruptors is finally going to fix it. Here's how to join them." The allure of Khan Academy, at least for the editors at Forbes, is that it is an innovation that can "disrupt"—and cash in on—the lucrative educational marketplace.

Khan Academy consists of thousands of videos that visitors can click on to hear Salman Khan, or one of his team, explain a topic while watching him draw on a digital blackboard. For many videos, there are quiz-like questions students take as their "progress" is tracked by software. From a pedagogical perspective, one could argue that there is something far from innovative about Khan Academy, however. Whereas there are benefits to giving students access to video tutorials (they can, for instance, re-watch them infinitely), at their core they represent a traditional banking model of teaching. The adult is the expert who imparts his wisdom to students. Students are not positioned to create knowledge or to work collaboratively to solve real-world problems, qualities that often appear as essential 21st-century skills (Alvermann & McLean, 2007; Moje, 2009; Tierney, 2007), or, as the Common Core Standards themselves state, "the ability to gather, comprehend, evaluate, synthesize, and report on information and ideas, to conduct original research in order to answer questions or solve problems, and to analyze and create a high volume and extensive range of print and nonprint texts in media forms old and new" (Common Core Standards Initiative, 2010).

The problem of the fanfare for something like Khan Academy is critical to be aware of: It confuses an innovative use of software to *develop content* for an innovative use of software to *improve pedagogy*. Software can be of great use for the former, but has significant limitations when it comes to the latter. Those limitations are inherent to the nature of software itself, which is something the growing field of software studies has been exploring (Berry, 2011; Kitchin & Dodge, 2011; Manovich, 2001, 2013). Software relies on binaries like 1/0 and if/then (i.e. if the user is not logged in to Facebook, then send the user to log-in page). It requires definitive inputs that can be neatly stored in database folders and forces users to provide narrow kinds of information (i.e. are you married *or* single?). It quantifies human experience in order to process it (i.e. all colors in digital media have a unique six digit "hex code" that designers use). The list goes on. What is essential to note is that the limitations that are inherent to the nature of software must be critiqued and leveraged to improve teaching and learning. Holding up Khan Academy as a model of improved pedagogy rather than of improved content development is a case in point. To be clear, this is not to say that video tutorials cannot be used well in classrooms. Imagine what might happen if a teacher gave students the knowledge and skills to create and share similar tutorials in response to real-world questions the students themselves generated. Same basic idea, same software used. The pivotal difference is that students are the ones who engage in the creative work of learning.

In the months to come, we will continue delving into the relationship between the nature of software and its effects on teaching and learning. Each column will consist of an educator's experience from the field using software-powered technologies, including a critique of the kinds of instructional practices such software enables and inhibits. Readers who are interested in submitting to the column are invited to contact me. Our humble hope is that these columns will help us see more clearly how software functions and in what ways we can be empowered to resist and wrangle it. It is only by raising our collective critical awareness of the active role software plays in shaping our experiences, our teaching and learning lives, that we can protect our craft from subtly drifting into a state of software-powered pedagoguery.

REASSESSING HOW WE "SEE" STUDENTS

The word *rubric* appears in the English language in the 1400s, etymologically rooted in a similar French word meaning *red*. In this early usage, the word rubric referred to annotations in clerics' liturgy books—written by church officials. Writing in fiery crimson, the marginalia were intended to guide priests through the mass to ensure human error did not interfere with the sacred event (OED, 2014). Today, rubrics have become a controversial mainstay in education. Several years ago, *English Journal* ran a pairing of columns to surface the debate on rubrics with Vicki Spandel (2006) arguing for the use of rubrics and Alfi Kohn (2006) arguing against. In essence, those in favor of the use of rubrics say that outlining expectations and providing a shared language for assessment is beneficial to both students and teachers. Opponents offer counterpoints, including the fact that providing students with rubrics, for instance when teaching writing, results in students suppressing their own voices in order to comply with the preordained tenor the grid provides. Today, we must add that rubrics are used not only here in the land of human beings who say mass and teach students, but are an instrument to generate data for the world of software.

Rubrics take many forms, but their primary function has changed little over the last seven centuries. Rubrics are devices created to limit the scope of messy social events in order to generate consensus, which in modern terms often means quantitative data. We identify *six* traits (plus one, of course) to assess writing or teacher evaluation rubrics that distill the complexity of pedagogy into *four* domains. This act of breaking apart phenomena into predetermined discrete elements is fundamentally computational. Similar to the way software developers define for us the ways we can engage with software space—we click on buttons, links, check boxes, bubbles—rubrics reduce the wide open plains of human creativity and choice to mere selections that accord with the ideological and technical needs of those who create them. Like software, rubrics can be used to serve very human and socioculturally responsive ends or they can be used to serve what Taubman (2009) calls "audit culture" and the needs of sophisticated computational assemblages, including information systems (Lynch, 2014b).

Allow me to walk you through a brief example from a longer study (ibid.) to demonstrate how rubrics function as software. When preparing to implement the Danielson Framework (Danielson, 2013), one district in New York State posted a video of a principal and assistant principal using the popular rubric to assess teachers. The video shows the principal observing pedagogy, taking notes, and using the rubric with the teacher to discuss how he can continue to grow as a professional. Whereas the video shows the rubric being used primarily to facilitate a shared conversation between educators, the reality of how the rubric is used is quite different. Months later, when the same district rolled out the new teacher evaluation system to all educators, they required principals to enter teacher evaluation data into a software application. The same principal who might have used the rubric to engage in professional dialogue with a new educator was given the additional—and not innocuous—step of distilling the teacher's pedagogy into a number and entering in that number into software space.

There is a subtle but important difference in the two evaluation scenarios above. In the first, the rubric is used to facilitate a shared social conversation of which the educator is an active part. Data that are gathered are social-ized and contextualized. In the second scenario, data that are gathered are inputted to software space where they are parsed, aggregated, disaggregated, manipulated via algorithms, and rendered back into the world in a form that is politicized and sadly distant from their original human context. When we use rubrics to generate discrete data out of complex lived experiences, how are those data rendered out of software space and back into the social world? In the case of teacher evaluations in New York, rubrics are used as/with software to create reports for newspapers of teachers' effectiveness, using a "value-added" metric based on student test scores. The data that were socially gathered and computationally analyzed were subsequently rendered publicly in the form of admonishment and shame.

When we consider the debates around rubrics, we must account for the fact that we use rubrics today to generate data and data eventually find their way into software space. How data are *rendered* when they return from software space to the social world merits scrutiny and creative reimagining.

An example from writing assessment will help illustrate this point.

In her study of trends in large-scale writing assessment research, Behizadeh (2014) argues for socioculturally responsive approaches to large-scale writ-ing assessment that values portfolio models, the writing process, students' choice of topic and genre, students' native language fluency, and multi-modal expression. Large-scale portfolio assessment, Behizadeh notes, is often rejected because opponents say it is too costly and lacks reliability. She challenges such naysaying writing, "Instead of rejecting large-scale portfolio assessment, the key is to avoid the conflation of reliability with standardization and to reframe reliability" (p. 5), which should be reached by "local consensus among qualified evaluators" (ibid.). One way we might reframe reliability, I think, is not only in the way in which consensus is reached, but how that consensus is rendered back into our lived worlds. As the example of publishing reports on teachers suggests, we must con-sider the act of rendering beyond the realm of pedagogy and in terms of the political. I believe we can create large-scale methods of assessment that better represent the learning process, the voices of students, and the feed-back of communities.

It is completely possible to leverage software space for the sociocultur-ally responsive ends of which Behizadeh speaks. Let's translate her example into software space. Imagine students composing a portfolio, as Behizadeh describes, with multiple examples of writing in several different genres, different styles and dialects (including academic), and providing a writing process reflection for each piece. Then, imagine their portfolios being assessed by different people in their lives—a peer, a teacher, a family or community member—who use a shared process- and skills-based rubric that students themselves help create. Each assessor enters their evaluation data into software space via a shared portal where the data are parsed, stored, and algorithmically manipulated. Finally, imagine if that data are rendered beautifully and informatively as sophisticated data visualizations. There are possibilities in leveraging data visualization in education that are desperate for exploration and examination. How might students respond to feedback rendered spatially/visually? What impact does students' contribution to assessment language have on their willingness to revise writing?

It seems to me that we not only need to reframe reliability, but also what constitutes data (Golden, 2014) and the acceptable ways in which reliable data are rendered for the benefit of our students, educators, and communi-ties. Software, data, and rubrics are capable of far more than we think, far more than the many paltry products and policies shoved our way would sug-gest. Red annotations written in powerful letters might carry the weight of the institution be they churches, corporations, or state legislatures, but they cannot dictate pedagogy. That schoolish sacrament belongs to us.

BARDS AT BAT

In his bestselling book, *The Signal and the Noise*, statistician Nate Silver (2012) writes about the prizes and pitfalls of statistical predictions, from the stock market to congressional races to his great love of baseball. Silver writes, "If the quantity of information is increasing by 2.5 quintillion bytes per day, the amount of *useful* information almost certainly isn't. Most of it is just noise, and the noise is increasing faster than the signal" (italics origi-nal; p. 13). In baseball, analysts have volumes of data about virtually every aspect of every player to have played the game. And yet, somehow, they cannot predict with much accuracy how players will fare year to year. We too are awash in data nowadays, made all the more prevalent as software-powered technologies and information systems have become requirements in school districts and, increasingly, classrooms. It can be challenging, even vexing, to discern the signal from the noise. For English teachers, I sug-gest there is much we can gain by welcoming software into our classrooms through an approach to literary study some call *distant reading*. In the spirit of sport, we begin with a poetic match-up: Shakespeare versus Milton. Let's look at the stats.

A Numbers Game

Using free web-based text analysis software, I analyzed both *Hamlet* (Shakespeare, 1603) and *Paradise Lost* (Milton, 1668). When we look at *Hamlet* quantitatively, we see that Shakespeare's play contains 32,259 words, 3,479 sentences, averages of 9.27 words per sentence, 4.1 characters per word, 1.34 syllables per word, and has a Flesch-Kincaid reading level of nearly fourth grade (not accounting for the archaic nature of the language, of course). When we quantify Milton's work, we learn that his epic has 80,139 words, 1,871 sentences, averages of 4.5 characters per word, 1.41 syllables per word, 42.83 words per sentence, and a reading level of late college (17.78).

Although the works are of drastically different lengths—*Paradise Lost* is more than double the length of *Hamlet*—we can make some initial inferences based on averages. Both authors write words of comparable characters and syllabic length. Milton, however, writes in the Latinate and so his sentences are exponentially longer than Shakespeare's, which likely explains the difference in grade level reading as well. Milton's long sentences (or lines, more accurately) might also explain why, despite Shakespeare's play being half the length of Milton's epic, he writes nearly twice as many sentences as Milton. These are interesting findings but not too surprising. The genre of both works, not to mention a consideration of audience, would quickly explain why the numbers reveal what they do.

Before reading further, what do you predict the numbers will signal about the authors' writing when we conduct a similar analysis on two speeches in the play: Hamlet's "To be or not to be" and Satan's "What, though the fields be lost"? Consider what message the respective characters are trying to convey. Hamlet is contemplating, among many things, life and death. Satan is trying to rally his troops to continue the revolt against God. Look at all that literary data above once more and make a prediction.

A quantitative breakdown of the Prince of Denmark's soliloquy contains 277 words, 8 sentences, an average of 34.62 words per sentence, 4.23 characters per word, 1.35 syllables per word, and has a Flesch-Kincaid reading level of nearly 13.85. Satan's galvanizing speech to his fallen troops contains 312 words, 8 sentences, an average of 39 words per sentence, 4.58 characters per word, 1.4 syllables per word, and has a Flesch-Kincaid reading level of 16.11. When we look at these numbers, are we lost in the noise or is there a signal to be heard? In this case, I am struck by how similar the two excerpts are based on the numbers. This is especially notable when we see that the two passages contain the exact same number of sentences and very comparable average number of words per sentence. Shakespeare averages 9.27 words per sentence for the entire play, but over 34 words per sentence during Hamlet's meditation. This signals something worth asking: Why does

Shakespeare write significantly longer sentences when Hamlet is in the pivotal scene? Can I say, as I am tempted to, that when Shakespeare is overtly developing his lead character, he writes more like Milton?

What Distant Readings Afford

I would suggest that what we experience above is what Moretti (2000) calls distant reading. To read distantly, in my view, is to foreground computational or quantitative readings of texts in our meaning-making process. As Moretti (2007) reminds us elsewhere, "Quantitative research provides a type of data which is independent of interpretations . . . and that is of course also its limit: it provides *data*, not interpretation" (p. 9). When we regard quantitative readings of texts as a valid and complementary type of reading, we see that there are only certain patterns and insights we can gain from the high analytic altitudes that quantitative readings provide. Milton might at first seem like first runner-up in the canons of our classrooms, yet our distant reading suggests that Shakespeare at his best writes like Milton. As Moretti notes, we do not stop with such readings. They are not valuable, I don't think, in and of themselves. But their unique distance makes new kinds of close readings possible, readings we in English education might consider in terms of the efferent and aesthetic (Rosenblatt, 1978), the authorized (Rabinowitz & Smith, 1998), or what I referred to elsewhere as *new literatures* (Lynch, 2015).

In Our Classrooms and Beyond

Using distant reading techniques in our classrooms affords us and our students nontraditional ways to access the meaning-making experience, to transact with the text (Purves, 1993). In addition to the kinds of quantitative analyses demonstrated above, there are a number of tools available online that allow us to create instant word clouds, compendia, and visualizations of texts. Importantly, these tools are useful not just for studying literature. They can also be used to help students examine and improve their own writing. Imagine if we worked with students to quantify their writing assignments, interpret the numerical data, and set goals for their growth as writers. I have done this with secondary and graduate students, finding it especially useful when teaching sentence variation, changing the lengths and rhythm of their sentences in order to emphasize points and engage readers. When we read "average number of words in a sentence," as in the examples above for Shakespeare and Milton, we can use that information as reflecting an author's sentence variation. Students can be taught to analyze their writing quantitatively and, in essence, play with the numbers they generate in order to refine it. To support teachers interested in exploring distant reading in their classrooms, I have created on my web site a short list of what I find to be the most valuable ones like using online readability engines, color-coding texts, and simple text analysis methods.

Finally, exploring distant reading methods is especially important in today's reform climate. The Common Core Standards, in implementation more than as a document, falsely separates quantities from letters, informational from literary texts. We are led to believe that reading fiction is somehow less valuable and useful than nonfiction, that we shouldn't "give a shit about what [students] think or what they feel" (Coleman, 2011). And yet, when we resist these false dichotomies and categorizations, we see that calculating numbers can open up new opportunities for reading letters and that what we feel when reading a literary text is perhaps the result of our astute ability as readers to detect humanistic signals from the political noise.

READERS AND WRITERS REBOOTED

In the last several issues, this column has begun to explore how the nature and ubiquity of software both enables and inhibits teaching and learning. Other contributors considered how the default settings of e-readers sway our literary interpretations (Griswold, 2013), how lecture-style videos must be counterbalanced with social engagement (Bach & Watson, 2014), and how users of speech recognition can bend their voices so software can understand them (Mountain, 2014). Several readers have also expressed interest in learning more about the use of software to automatically assess student writing. In order to understand the effects of such software, we have to imagine software as *a reader that can only respond to texts in certain ways*.

NCTE's Position Statement on Machine Scoring

Last year, NCTE released a position statement (Anson et al., 2013) on the growing use of machine-scoring software in assessing student writing (often referred to as automated essay scoring or AES). The position statement was deftly researched, thoroughly annotated, and clearly written by a task force of educators and researchers. The report argues that the use of software to automatically assess student writing contradicts sound pedagogy, undermining the importance of the writing process. As an alternative, they suggest investing in online portfolio systems rather than AES software. That NCTE took such a rigorous and public stance on the issue is to be applauded.

If we are to determine the proper place of software-powered technologies, however, we must understand with greater nuance what software does with student essays. Specifically, the report twice refers to the fact that machines or computers, once "programmed," can execute assessments automatically. This is true, although reference to such concrete objects like machines and computers mask the fact that it is *software* that produces the effect with which the report is concerned. Software is *written* (that is, programmed) by teams of developers to *read* essays in certain ways. The way software reads essays is the product of two worldviews: 1) the world according to software and 2) the world of the companies and developers of software. Let's look at each of these more closely.

How Software Reads Writing

Software reads quantitatively. It can quickly recognize, organize, tally, and report on any text it encounters: number of words, frequency of words, and how many periods there are (and, therefore, numbers of sentences). Were we to assign software to read *Moby Dick*, it would do so in less than five seconds. Software could quickly tell us the most frequently used words in the novel or any other unit of analysis it is programmed to read for, such as punctuation, paragraph breaks, and so on. In Melville's book, the most frequently used words (excluding functional words like *and* and *the*) are: whale, old, man, Ahab, and ship (see Table 8.1). Software can take this information and visually represent how these words appear over the course of the entire book (see Figure 8.1). At first, it might feel that the way software reads the text—in this case a work of literature—is at odds with our own teaching values. However, there are compelling voices that argue for leveraging software to gain new insights into literary interpretation and instruction. Some talk about the merits of *distant reading* (Moretti, 2000, 2007) as not just a complement to close reading but as a method of reading texts that reveals new understandings impossible to achieve otherwise. Others discuss an *algorithmic criticism* (Ramsay, 2011), arguing that the act of literary criticism and the nature of software align quite well. In the case of Ahab and the whale, consider what kinds of questions arise from seeing the numbers and graph. Isn't it worth discussing with students the fact that Ahab's name soars in frequency after he perishes, that quantitatively we might say he wins his battle with Moby Dick? Notice that the role of software's reading is to provide a kind of distance to spark closer analysis, analysis that demands a critical understanding of the text in order to proceed. Some observations can only be made at the high analytic altitude of software, but the hard work of meaning making must be done by barefoot human beings on deck.

Table 8.1 Most frequently used words in Melville's *Moby Dick*.

Word	Frequency of Use
Whale	979
Man	448
Old	443
Ahab	440
Ship	393

Ahab's Lexical Victory over Moby Dick

This line graph depicts the interplay between the terms "whale" and "Ahab" throughout the novel *Moby Dick* based on relative freqency of word use. The whale might drag Ahab to his demise, but the captain's name is never used more frequently than at the book's end. Quantitatively, Ahab wins.

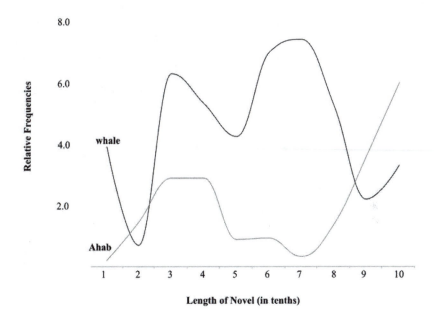

Text Source: Project Gutenberg | Data parsing: Voyant Tools

Figure 8.1   Graph depicting the interplay between the words *Ahab* and *whale* in Melville's *Moby Dick*.

How Software Is Written to Read

When the authors of the NCTE position statement mention that software has to be "programmed," they refer to a quality of software that merits pause. Software reads the way it does because there are inherent limitations to what software can and cannot do. More accurately, human beings program—that is, they write—software to read and respond to the world. When it comes to AES software, we must note that for-profit companies are writing the software. In a recently published chapter (Lynch, 2013), I examined how one company's essay-scoring software reads students' writings. Programming software to read in sophisticated ways is not easy, nor is it cheap. For instance, if a company wants software to read essays and place value on keywords like *characterization* and *Ahab,* its programmers must take the time to instruct software what to look for and how to calculate the value of what it finds. They have to tell software to accept a student's spelling of *Ahabb* and *whela*. Imagine all the misspellings that have to be anticipated if software is to forgive them.

The most robust AES software includes in its calculations a database of human-scored anchor essays. As long as the rubric and task is the same across students, software can recognize profiles of what strong essays look like. In seconds, it can determine according to its logic whether a piece of student writing is strong, good, or weak. We have to ask ourselves: What kinds of learning does this software both enable and inhibit and to whose benefit? In my experience, companies that develop such software make decisions based on their fiscal bottom line. Moreover, the trainings they provide educators to use their products often lack sophistication, common sense, and rigor. The products we are increasingly encouraged (or forced) to use are developed by non-educators who themselves do not question the pedagogical merits and limitations of software. It is not in their interest to do so.

Rebooting

My stance is that all software both enables and inhibits elements of teaching and learning. Our collective responsibility is to sharpen our understanding of the nature and politics of software so we can make informed decisions regarding pedagogy. Whereas some insightful work has identified how AES software can be used well in classrooms (Myers, 2003), such work does not make explicit the world view of software and the companies who create it. My fear is that if we don't continue to discuss knowledgeably and critically the ways in which software impacts how we teach, learn, and think, we will find ourselves bending our daily behaviors to suit its limitations and acquiesce to the companies who develop it. Pedagogy is our expertise, our responsibility. It is something of which software itself is fundamentally incapable without us. We must make clear that despite outward appearances in these digital times, deep learning is never merely a click away.

FEELING WALT WHITMAN

> *"Having pried through the strata, analyzed to a hair, counsel'd with doctors and calculated close, // I find no sweeter fat than sticks to my own bones."*
>
> —Walt Whitman, *Song of Myself*, line 20

The advent of the Common Core Standards raised to the surface an age-old tension in the field of English education between informational and literary texts. With pressure placed on teachers to put nonfiction texts before students, there emerged a loud counterpoint from those who fear that fiction is falling by the wayside (Unknown, 2012). For some English teachers, the implementation of the standards seems to devalue the importance of the literary experience, favoring logic over feeling, science over art, factual argument over fictional emulation, and the strata over one's own bones. Such concerns have some basis. The lead author and spokesman for the Common Core crossed a line when he demeaned the subjectivity of student voice in writing, saying to a crowd of state education officials, "as [students] grow up in this world [they will] realize that people don't really give a shit about what you feel or what you think" (Coleman, 2011). Amidst such polarizing rhetoric, we might be tempted to view software-powered technologies as the mere bedfellow of reformers who seem to put spreadsheets, rather than students, first. I see a unique opportunity for us to grow as a field. I suggest we can use software-powered technologies to read and interpret literature with us, blurring the lines between fact and fiction, numbers and letters. I propose *new literatures* as a way to harness software in order to deepen our practice and resist the co-opting of our craft.

New Literatures

New literatures refers to the practice of inviting software into literary meaning-making experiences with students. In a recent article (Lynch, 2015), I explain how using software to teach literature can open new opportunities for students to wrest meaning from the text while simultaneously shining a critical light on the issues of power embedded in the software-powered technologies shaping so much of our world. To use software-powered technologies in our schools well, we must have a more nuanced understanding of how these "software spaces" function. They include things we see like devices and user interfaces, as well as things we don't see like networking infrastructure, code, and information systems. New literatures examines and leverages the characteristics of software space that can add richness to teaching literature. For example, there are many ways to quantify literary texts that, when engaged with thoughtfully and creatively, can provide new entry points for interpretation and classroom discourse. I demonstrated a simple example previously when I plotted the word frequency of *Ahab* and *whale* in *Moby Dick,* the result being a graph that makes the posing of new questions possible (Lynch, 2014c). In another column, I used openly available software to profile Shakespeare's writing in *Hamlet* and compared it to Milton's writing in *Paradise Lost.* By using a common technique to quantify texts, I was able to observe some surprising patterns in the authors' character development that a group of readers might richly explore and critique (Lynch, 2014a). When we add to quantitative literary study the creation of data visualizations—graphs, charts, tables—we render quantities in a way that quickly encourages literary analysis. Importantly, to engage in new literatures is not to succumb to the easy belief that quantification is itself the end. Rather, as Moretti (2007) reminds us, "Quantitative research provides a type of data which is ideally independent of interpretations . . . and that is of course also its limit: it provides *data*, not interpretation" (emphasis original; p. 9). To make any real sense of the numerical data, no matter how aesthetically pleasing the visualization is, requires students to grapple with multiple interpretations of the text.

Song of Myself

As an illustration, I invited software to read Whitman's *Song of Myself* (1855) with me. I took an e-text version of the poem located online, copied it, and pasted it into a spreadsheet. I then organized the text so each line of the poem had one cell in one row, labeling the verse of the poem in a separate column. The next step was to generate a quantity associated with each line. I could, for instance, have used a simple formula to tally the number of words per line, but that would not have been very interesting in this case. Instead, I used a proprietary tool to calculate a sentiment score for each line of the poem, a process called sentiment analysis. Sentiment analysis is an increasingly popular way for companies to determine whether people are speaking positively or negatively about them online, especially via social media. In the end, each line of the poem received a score from –1 to 1 based on how negative or positive the words contained therein appeared to be. I then used that data to create a visualization that shows the sentiment analysis score for each verse in chronological order (see Figure 8.2).

What does this quantification and visualization convey? First, I was struck that there were sequential verses that software read as drastically positive and negative. What are the topics of those verses and why might Whitman have written with such extremity? Is there a clear aesthetic effect he might have been trying to achieve? Second, it was surprising that there were a couple instances of verses that were either perfectly neutral or very close to it. What are these verses about and why are they placed where they are? If students are afforded the opportunity to analyze the data visualization, dive into the poem to look more closely at the text, and present their insights, it seems to me a sound use of time. Further, I encourage students to question the validity of the numbers. Do you agree with how the sentiment analysis engine scored the verse? If you agree, what is the logic that the analytical engine seems to be using? What kinds of words are being counted as positive and negative? How might the fact that such analytical engines are used by companies for social media be affecting the kinds of scores it generates? The goal is not for students to place their faith in pure quantitative objectivity. It is to explore the fact that the divide between numbers and words is a false one, that numbers are used all the time to tell stories, and that those stories can be as fictional as they are factual.

Feeling Walt Whitman

Each bar in the visualization below represents one stanza from Whitman's *Song of Myself*. The 52 stanzas are listed in chronological order as they appear in the poem, top to bottom. The quantity represented is the sentiment analysis score per stanza: the more positive the sentiment, the further to the right the bar extends; the more negative to the left.

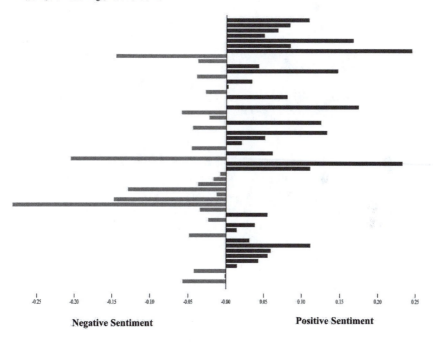

Negative Sentiment   Positive Sentiment

Text Source: Project Gutenberg | Data parsing: Excel & Semantria| Visualization: D3

Figure 8.2 Negative bar chart depicting the sentiment score for 52 verses from Whitman's *Song of Myself*.

Close and Distant Futures

The more software-powered technologies find their way into our classrooms and pockets, the more essential it is that we make critiquing its active presence in our world a priority. Consider what it would mean to invite software to read with you and your students: experiment with using spreadsheets and e-texts to see what new questions about texts emerge, challenge students to use quantitative evidence when writing literary analyses in addition to linguistic excerpts, or use some of the samples I refer to here with your students to see what ideas they drum up. I have created a page for new literatures on my web site where you can find more examples, tutorials, and free materials. As Whitman reminds us, we can both pry the strata *and* our bones. The two are not mutually exclusive. Critically integrating quantitative and literary readings of texts have the potential to expose our students to poetic songs that are as grounded in numbers as they are in the sweet fat of their fleshy selves.

SPREADSHEETS AND SINNERS

> *"The chief parallel to compare one great thing with another—is the power over us of a temple of some alien creed. Standing outside, we deride or oppose it, or at the most feel sentimental. Inside, though the saints and gods are not ours, we become true believers, in case any true believer should be present."*
>
> —E.M. Forster, *A Room with a View*

In the last column, I shared an example of how quantitative literary analysis and data visualization might be used to provide students new entry points into the interpretation of literature. I referred to the act of critically inviting software to read with us as *new literatures*. In what follows, I extend the conversation, arguing that not only can new literatures deepen and extend our own classroom practice as English teachers, it also challenges enthusiastic supporters of STEM education to uncouple their agendas from the acronymic content areas. The kinds of competencies that are heralded in STEM education, like teaching students to systematically gather real-world quantitative data for analysis and gaining familiarity with programming languages, do not belong to science or technology or engineering or mathematics. They are *human* ways of engaging with the world, not some alien creed.

A View of *A Room with a View*

For purposes of illustration, let us look at a quantification of a novel—longer than a single poem although more manageable for classroom practice than corpora. I have chosen a favorite book I read in high school, reread in college, and taught many times: *A Room with a View* (Forster, 1923). Forster's novel chronicles the story of young Lucy Honeychurch's excursions in Italy with her chaperon Charlotte where their adventures are as sociocultural as they are geographic. I located an e-text copy of the novel online and pasted it into a spreadsheet, giving each paragraph its own row and cell. I then calculated the word length and sentiment analysis for each paragraph (see Tables 8.2 and 8.3). Sentiment analysis, as I described previously, is a method of automatically calculating how positive or negative a text is based on a dictionary of predetermined quantities for individual words and phrases. It is used by companies, for instance, to track the popularity of their brands in social media. The final spreadsheet has over 2,100 rows. Next, I used openly available web-based software called Raw to convert the data into

Table 8.2   Quantitative data from Chapter 20 of Forster's *A Room with a View* showing the sentiment score for several paragraphs, including Lucy's exclamation, "Nonsense!"

Chapter	Paragraph Number	Source Text	Sentiment	Paragraph Length (in words)
Chapter 20	08	"Oh, bother Charlotte," she said thoughtfully. "What can such people be made of?"	–0.033079788	13
Chapter 20	09	Same stuff as parsons are made of.	0.200000003	7
Chapter 20	10	Nonsense!	–1.200000048	1
Chapter 20	11	Quite right. It is nonsense.	–0.600000024	5
Chapter 20	12	Now you get up off the cold floor, or you'll be starting rheumatism next, and you stop laughing and being so silly.	0.019999996	22

a visualization, which I then customized to clearly show the sentimental ebb and flow for the novel's 20 chapters (see Figure 8.3). Each chapter has a graphic showing how positive or negative the software has read its paragraphs. Longer chapters have longer graphics, shorter ones are shorter.

At initial glance, I see something surprising in Chapter 20. Whereas I expected that the final chapter would be mostly positive or sentimentally neutral given how pleasant I feel upon its completion, we see two extremely negative paragraphs, according to software. What is the cause of these negative dips and how accurate is software's reading?

The two negative paragraphs occur as Lucy and her lover George are reflecting on their life together after meeting in Italy. The first line is Lucy responding "Nonsense!" to George comparing the ever-loyal and overbearing Charlotte to a clergyman (see Table 8.2). The second line, "Oh, bother that man!" is uttered likely by George in response to someone interrupting the couple while sharing a quiet intimate moment (see Table 8.3). Quantitatively, these two lines are extremely negative. Qualitatively, the extremity of their numerical score might not be compelling to readers. In the context of the characters' interaction, the exclamations represent feelings of playfulness

A View of *A Room with a View*

This visualization shows the ebb and flow of each chapter--paragraph by paragraph--for E.M. Forster's novel *A Room with a View* based on modern sentiment analysis. The colors are purely aesthetic.

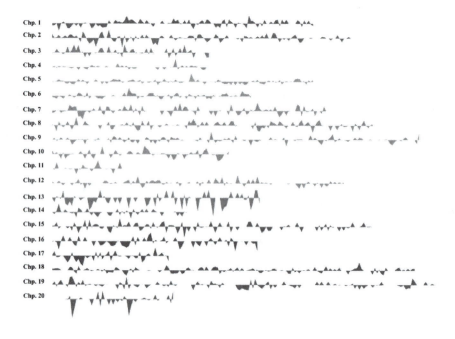

Figure 8.3   Area graphs based on the sentiment score for each paragraph in each chapter of Forster's *A Room with a View*.

and disbelief conveyed in moments of peaceful tenderness. Students might be quick to conclude that software is misreading the lines, and I would agree. This presents an opportunity to better understand software as a reader. *How* is software reading those lines? We know that the words are read by software and compared to some kind of sentiment dictionary which uses a combination of statistical analysis and algorithms to return a single numerical score. It appears that the line might be read as negative because 1) key words are predetermined to be of negative sentiment, i.e. *nonsense* and *bother,* and 2) that exclamation points affect how much weight is applied to those predetermined metrics. Further, it is worth noting that the brevity of both exclamations is the result of Forster's choice to give them their own paragraphs. In doing so, the author chose to emphasize the content of those lines through paragraph breaks and punctuation. Little did he know that it would also mean those lines would be analyzed

Table 8.3 Quantitative data from Chapter 20 of Forster's *A Room with a View* showing the sentiment score for several paragraphs, including George's exclamation, "Oh, bother that man!"

Chapter	Paragraph Number	Source Text	Sentiment	Paragraph Length (in words)
Chapter 20	34	Perhaps. Then he said more gently: "Well, I acted the truth—the only thing I did do—and you came back to me. So possibly you know." He turned back into the room. "Nonsense with that sock." He carried her to the window, so that she, too, saw all the view. They sank upon their knees, invisible from the road, they hoped, and began to whisper one another's names. Ah! it was worth while; it was the great joy that they had expected, and countless little joys of which they had never dreamt. They were silent.	0.19335714	94
Chapter 20	35	Signorino, domani faremo—	0	3
Chapter 20	36	Oh, bother that man!	–1.057319164	4

by software as weighted independent units rather than as part of a more comprehensive scene.

Critical Implications

In recent years, the volume of the cries to bolster STEM education has continuously increased. Its thump engulfs us. We hear its beat in many forms: calls to prepare students for the "21st century," a crisis narrative that predicts the nation's fall from economic grace if legions of young people cannot launch Martian drones and code, an abundance of funding for science and math education, and a new set of common standards that, in implementation if not in copy, positions "informational" texts as more important than "literary" or "fictional" ones. After prolonged exposure to such certain and rhythmic thumping, even the most open-minded and creative educators can find themselves swaying to the beat.

Cover your ears.

Our field is not defined by the convenient binaries of others. It is not informational or literary, scientific or artistic, quantitative or qualitative, objective or subjective. There is a skill set, a knowledge base, and a process that drives STEM education and there are many ways to teach into such things. Teaching students to quantitatively analyze literary texts and render their analyses via data visualizations is one example of how students can learn so-called "STEM" curricula in English classes. To say it is possible is one thing, but why bother? My answer to this question is simple: Ours is the field of teaching students to master the use of languages to make sense of and contribute to their communities. Software space is comprised of languages and these languages must be understood, manipulated, and put to good work in the world. Teaching students to approach software space with a deep understanding of its humanitarian limitations and affordances should be a significant part of our daily work. If we don't do so, we risk creating a nation of what Martha Nussbaum (2010) called "technically trained people who do not know how to criticize authority, useful profit-makers with obtuse imaginations" (142).

Conclusion

By engaging in new literatures in our classrooms, we can teach our students to regard software as a kind of reader and writer with limits and affordances. In doing so, we prepare students to critique the ways software responds not only to literature, but to our everyday worlds—which it reads and writes more ubiquitously and quickly day by day. "New literatures" is not the only way, of course. We can approach software space critically in our work with digital writing processes (Hicks, 2009), video games (Gerber & Abrams, 2014), and the production of multimedia (Rozema & Webb, 2008; Vasudevan, 2010). As teachers, we must escort our English students into the temple of STEM so they can see for themselves that its saints and gods are neither ours as humanitarians nor "theirs" as scientists. We are all believers in learning and are most devout when in each other's presence.

IN SUM

Critical software studies is not intended to be a field limited to researchers. Whereas the way key concepts are conveyed and applied might differ when the audience is one of educators rather than researchers, the critical spirit remains the same. I wrote the above columns with a particular imagined reader—someone who is passionate about teaching English but has a mostly ambivalent stance when questions of technology arise. The effect, I hope, is that more teachers are questioning the inherent value of software-powered technology while also gaining sober confidence in new ways such technologies can be of value in the classroom. If we are to move beyond dichotomous responses to software—enthusiasts and Luddites—we have to add nuance to the discourse and meet educators where they are, the classrooms in which they teach and the journals they read.

WORKS CITED

Alvermann, D.E., & McLean, C.A. (2007). The nature of literacies. In L.S. Rush, A.J. Eakle, & A. Berger (Eds.), *Secondary school literacy: What research reveals about classroom practice* (pp. 1–20). Urbana, IL: NCTE.

Anson, C., Filkins, S., Hicks, T., O'Neill, P., Pierce, K.M., & Winn, M. (2013). *Machine scoring fails the test.* Urbana, IL: NCTE. Retrieved January 7, 2014, from www.ncte.org/positions/statements/machine_scoring.

Bach, J., & Watson, J.A. (2014). What's worth sharing? *English Journal, 103*(3), 108–111.

Behizadeh, N. (2014). Mitigating the dangers of a single story: Creating large-scale writing assessments aligned with sociocultural theory. *Educational Researcher, 43*(3), 125–136.

Berry, D. (2011). *The philosophy of software: Code and mediation in the digital age.* New York: Palgrave Macmillan.

Coleman, D. (2011, April 28). *Bringing the Common Core to life.* Talk at the Chancellor's Hall, New York State Department of Education, Albany, NY. Retrieved December 15, 2014, from http://usny.nysed.gov/rttt/resources/bringing-the-common-core-to-life-download.html.

Common Core Standards Initiative. (2010, June 2). Common Core Standards for English Language Arts & literacy in History/Social Studies, Science, and technical subjects. Common Core Standards initiative. Retrieved January 7, 2014, from www.corestandards.org/assets/CCSSI_ELA%20Standards.pdf.

Danielson, C. (2013). The framework for teaching evaluation instrument. The Danielson Group. Retrieved June 20, 2014, from www.danielsongroup.org/userfiles/files/downloads/2013EvaluationInstrument.pdf.

Forster, E.M. (1923). *A room with a view.* New York: Quality Paperback Book Club.

Gerber, H.R., & Abrams, S.S. (2014). *Building literate connections through virtual worlds: Practical ideas and applications.* Rotterdam, The Netherlands: Sense Publishers.

Golden, N.A. (2014). Education reform and Potemkin villages: Expanding conceptions of "data." *English Journal, 104*(2).

Griswold, M. (2013). Rekindling reading: On the use of e-readers in the English classroom. *English Journal, 103*(2), 101–104.

Hicks, T. (2009). *The digital writing workshop.* Portsmouth, NH: Heinemann.

Kitchin, R., & Dodge, M. (2011). *Code/Space: Software and everyday life.* Cambridge, MA: MIT Press.

Kohn, A. (2006). The trouble with rubrics. *English Journal, 95*(4), 12–15.

Lynch, T.L. (2013). The secretary and the software: On the need for integrating software analysis into educational spaces. In J. Gorlewski & B. Porfilio (Eds.),

Left behind in the race to the top (pp. 129–142). Charlotte, NC: Information Age Publishing.

Lynch, T. L. (2014a). Bards at bat: The sport of quantitative literary analysis. *English Journal, 104*(1), 89–91.

Lynch, T. L. (2014b). Holy interfaces and the sanctity of software: A critical software analysis of rubrics as vehicles of conservative reform. In M. Tenam-Zemach & J. Flynn (Eds.), *A rubric nation: A reader on the utility and impact of rubrics in education.* Charlotte, NC: Information Age Publishing.

Lynch, T. L. (2014c). Readers and writers rebooted: Teaching software to read the world. *English Journal, 103*(5), 86–88.

Lynch, T. L. (2015). Where the machine stops: Software as reader and the rise of new literatures. *Research in the Teaching of English, 49*(3).

Manovich, L. (2001). *The language of new media.* London: MIT Press.

Manovich, L. (2013). *Software takes command.* New York: Bloomsbury Academic.

Milton, J. (1668). *Paradise lost.* E-Text. University of Virginia Library. Retrieved March 22, 2013, from http://web.archive.org/web/20080922193133/http://etext.lib.virginia.edu/toc/modeng/public/MilPL67.html.

Moje, E. B. (2009). A call for new research on new and multi-literacies. *Research in the Teaching of English, 43*(4), 348–362.

Moretti, F. (2000). Conjectures on world literature. *New Left Review,* January–February, 54–68.

Moretti, F. (2007). *Graphs, maps, and trees: Abstract models for a literary history.* New York: Verso.

Mountain, L. (2014). Can you here me now? Speech recognition software in educational settings. *English Journal, 103*(4), 104–106.

Myers, M. (2003). Automated essay scoring: A cross-disciplinary perspective. In M. D. Shermis & J. C. Burstein (Eds.), *What can computers contribute to a K-12 writing program?* (pp. 3–20). New York: Routledge.

Nussbaum, M. C. (2010). *Not for profit: Why democracy needs the humanities.* Princeton, NJ: Princeton University Press.

Purves, A. (1993). Toward a reevaluation of reader response and school literature. *Language Arts, 70*, 348–361.

Rabinowitz, P. J., & Smith, M. W. (1998). *Authorizing readers: Resistance and respect in the teaching of literature.* New York: Teachers College Press.

Ramsay, S. (2011). *Reading machines: Toward an algorithmic criticism.* Urbana, IL: University of Illinois Press.

Rosenblatt, L. M. (1978). *The reader, the text, the poem: The transactional theory of the literary work.* Carbondale, IL: Southern Illinois Press.

Rozema, R., & Webb, A. (2008). *Literature and the web: Reading and responding with new technologies.* Portsmouth, NH: Heinemann.

"rubric, n. and adj.". OED Online. March 2015. Oxford University Press. http://www.oed.com/view/Entry/168394?rskey=WeKqA3&result=1&isAdvanced=false (accessed December 07, 2014).

Shakespeare, W. (1603). *Hamlet, prince of Denmark.* E-Text. University of Virginia Library. Retrieved March 22, 2013, from http://web.archive.org/web/20080913171731/http://etext.lib.virginia.edu/toc/modeng/public/MobHaml.html.

Silver, N. (2012). *The signal and the noise: Why so many predictions fail—but some don't.* New York: Penguin Press.

Spandel, V. (2006). Speaking my mind: In defense of rubrics. *English Journal, 96*(1), 19–22.

Taubman, P. M. (2009). *Teaching by numbers: Deconstructing the discourse of standards and accountability in education.* New York: Routledge.

Tierney, R.J. (2007). New literacy learning strategies for new times. In L.S. Rush, A.J. Eakle, & A. Berger (Eds.), *Secondary school literacy: What research reveals for classroom practice* (pp. 21–36). Urbana, IL: NCTE.

Unknown. (2012, December 10). Common core nonfiction reading standards mark the end of literature, English teachers say. *Huffington Post*. Retrieved December 10, 2012, from www.huffingtonpost.com/2012/12/10/common-core-nonfic tion-reading-standards_n_2271229.html.

Vasudevan, L. (2010). Literacies in a participatory, multimodal world: The arts and aesthetics of Web 2.0. *Language Arts, 88*(1), 43–50.

Whitman, W. (1855). *Leaves of grass*. E-Text. Project Gutenberg. Retrieved March 22, 2013, from www.gutenberg.org/files/1322/1322-h/1322-h.htm.

9 Imagining Education After Software

INTRODUCTION

I was on a plane when I received a text from my wife. Maxine died today, it read. I stopped fidgeting in my seat and paused. Maxine Greene passed away after years of declining health. The educational philosopher introduced me to the field of education. As a young aspiring teacher, I was fortunate to spend a month during my first summer at graduate school in a tutorial with Maxine. Just the two of us in her apartment. We read Forster's *Passage to India* together and philosophized about what it meant to teach literature, about the power of the aesthetic experience, and about the state of education. I knew so little about all those things. Since then, I have reread Maxine's collection of essays, *Releasing the Imagination* (Greene, 1995), several times and continue to be struck by her powerful prose, a masterfully woven textile of the philosophical, the aesthetic, the literary, and the critical. During the summer days I spent studying with Maxine, seeds were sown. I could not have known it then. Today, I attribute my deep belief in pedagogy as a beautiful creative art to Maxine.

IMAGINATION AND INFORMATION

I sat on the tarmac in Denver reflecting on the impact Maxine's work had on my life. For the previous two days, I had attended a conference organized by a philanthropic group supporting the city's professional development pilot program. Forty-eight hours filled with discussions about information systems, metadata, and search functionalities with technology leaders from other large districts across the country. What would Maxine say about who I was becoming as an educator a decade after our summer sessions? What would she say about software and how it is positioned in education? In education today, we are experiencing a slow and ceaseless battle between information and imagination. If Maxine implores us to imagine things as "if they could be otherwise" (p. 22), educational policy demands we "see things as data dictates." There is a fundamental difference between these two perspectives.

Put most simply, imagination is driven by that which is not yet, data by that which appears to be already.

One of the ways this tension between imagination and information becomes clear is by considering the way the Common Core standards position informational and literary texts. To the authors of the standards, there is a clear and unproblematic relationship between texts that are written to primarily inform readers and those that are more literary, the purpose of which might be to entertain or to create some artistic experience. In Chapter 5, I associate these terms to Rosenblatt's distinction between efferent and aesthetic readings. In her well-known example, she describes efferent readings as those primarily concerned with garnering useful information from a text, like reading the instructions on a medication bottle to save the life of someone who might have overdosed. Aesthetic readings, on the other hand, are primarily concerned with creating an ecstatic experience for readers that is necessarily informed by one's own history and social context. When the Common Core standards were implemented, teachers and administrators around the country scrambled to find "informational" texts for students like newspaper and science articles while literary texts were deemphasized if not cast aside.

A related dichotomy discussed in software studies that helps frame the relationship between information and imagination is the distinction between the logics of database and narrative. Manovich argues that the primary form of collective human knowledge production for the last two thousand years has been narrative. That is, human beings capture and catalog what it is they know in logical sequences that are explicitly or implicitly narrative. For example, Homer's catalog of ships in his epic poems or in songs or film that serve to express aspects of culture. Today, he thinks, it is the logic of the database that is mediating and shaping human culture. The more software is layered over all aspects of society, the more the demands of databases are essentialized. In contrast to the logic of stories, which value the sequencing of events and information in particular ways, database logic fundamentally treats all information the same, which makes it rapidly retrievable. Databases might be said to be anti-narrative, at least at first glance.

Greene might fear that as information, databases, and technical logics are privileged over other forms of knowing and being, we run the risk of dehumanizing education—what she refers to as *blankness*. Again, "Without some knowledge of connective details, it is extraordinarily difficult to overcome abstraction in dealing with other people. A fearful oversimplification takes over: in blankness, we see only 'Russia,' 'student movement,' 'ethnic minorities.' We are likely to chart things in terms of good/bad, white/black, either/or. We become pawns in a Manichean allegory of good and evil" (p. 95). I share Maxine's fear and wish to qualify her statement in terms of software space. It is ontologically true that software space, including information systems, are driven by a binary language of machine code. Ones and zeros dictate computers' actions. However, ones and zeros, while abstract, are not themselves good or evil. It is the social use of software that determines whether the result is one of beauty or blankness. When such systems are used to generate, organize, and analyze teacher performance data in a manner that ignores the sociality of pedagogy and the complexity of our communities, then blankness should be expected. If, however, such systems are used to gather different kinds of data and to facilitate communication processes across stakeholders, there emerges new possibilities for the use of software. To do so demands that information is wrangled and reined with imagination. Two examples from the preceding chapters are worth reference. First, I described how large-scale writing assessment could be reimagined by using the technicity of software to make human communication more efficient rather than using software to thinly automatically assess student writing. In this case, the use of software deepens rather than dries the sociality of learning. Second, I reprinted columns that explore what it means to invite software to read literature with us in our classrooms. Rather than using software to produce a digital version of traditional literary response practices, there are ways to regard software itself as a reader and to cast light on the value of its readings in efforts to refine and sharpen our own interpretations. The result can be thoroughly "informational" readings and even analyses of students' interpretations of literature that both honor their subjectivity while also holding them quantitatively and qualitatively accountable to the text itself. Information and imagination are not incompatible. They are two essential ingredients in the creation of knowledge. Until it is sequenced and imagined upon, information falls well short of knowledge. All knowing is ultimately narrative.

ABSTRACTION AND DEMOCRACY

When reading *Passage to India* with Maxine, we spoke frequently about the tension between the culture and humanity of 19th-century Indian people and attempts by British colonialists to "civilize" their subjects. Forster captures this tension by reminding the reader of the rawness of India's natural landscapes and the power of its ancient oral poetry. There are some things that defy language, we discussed. Hollering English words into caves returns only a defiant "Boum," not an English-speaking echo as expected. Like attempts by the novel's British protagonists to replace memories of Indian history and culture with their own, Maxine writes in one of her essays that ". . . much of education as we know it is an education in forgetfulness. Distracting the young from their own perceived landscapes and shapes, we teachers insist on the givenness of predetermined explanatory frames" (p. 74). These explanatory frames are ones of abstraction. In software space, such abstractions are necessarily predetermined to some extent. How are we to understand the interplay between abstraction, predetermination, and public education? I turn to an aesthetic text for guidance.

Walking through Manhattan's City Hall Park during the summer of 2014, one would have noticed scattered sheets of copper on the lawn. Some upright, some flat upon the grass. The half dozen wavy metal squares seemed both hauntingly familiar and strikingly alien. I crossed the park for weeks before stopping one day to investigate what artistic intentions there were behind the exhibit. A sign attributed the work to artist Danh Vo. It was called "We the People." The placard explains that Vo took the French blueprint for the Statue of Liberty, re-fabricated the sections of the statue in China, and established exhibits throughout the world featuring a handful of pieces at a time. The entire statue, the artist vowed, would never be reconstructed. I stared at the sign in the park for what seemed like an hour, occasionally looking up to glance at the pieces of the sculpture that surrounded me. I then turned around, looked just past city hall, and fixed my eyes northward to the top of Tweed Courthouse—the home of the city's education department. In education, we are doing to learning what Vo artistically argues we are doing to liberty: We are abstracting ourselves out of our own highest aspirations for our children and world. The Statue of Liberty is an icon of freedom. Its symbolization overshadows the sum of its own parts. Its visceral structure is also composed of over 200 separate abstracted pieces that represent liberty—but only when assembled. Left unassembled, what is rendered is not liberty but rather a challenge to whether the United States is living up to liberty's ideals. By dispersing the abstracted parts of the statue and erecting them individually all over the world, Vo draws our attention not only to the delicate nature of liberty today, but also to the dispiriting and even dehumanizing effects of abstraction.

I have since meditated upon the exhibit many times. It strikes me that the aesthetic effect of Vo's project is at least partially tied to the fact that I am able to read a description of his intentions. I might not, for instance, have realized that the copper structures were elements of the Statue of Liberty. Without some sense of the artist's imaginative intentions, I might well have felt only blankness: just another pretentious art show wasting taxpayer money and leaving the lawn disheveled. For me, in order to have that aesthetic experience, I needed some "knowledge of connective detail." That is, I needed some sense of the human being who imagined and created something that she or he believed could cut through the "givenness of predetermined explanatory frames" in our daily lives. For the original creator of the statue, Frédéric Auguste Bartholdi, abstraction is a necessary part of achieving the aesthetic and political goal. If what they wished for was to erect an unabashed symbol of liberty—a commitment to the ideals of democracy—its largeness and complexity demanded that it be conceived and built in smaller manageable sections. Vo's work makes me ask: In a democracy, how do we ensure that abstraction is put to good use, specifically in public education? What enables both Bartholdi and Vo to achieve their respective aesthetic effects, albeit in two distinct ways, is that there is some common consensus around the ultimate representation: a reminder to the public of our collective commitment to liberty. Of course, there might be many interpretations of what liberty means for both artists' audiences, but enough shared belief exists amongst those who see and are moved by the statues.

In education, we do not have such agreement. We do not have a shared sense of why children go to schools, what constitutes learning and, consequently, teaching. Ask a dozen people what they think the purpose of public education is and prepare for two dozen answers. This creates a problem for educators when so much of our world is mediated by software and the demand for data to make transparent to the public how its institutions are serving the greater good grows. We abstract pedagogy through rubrics, tests, and reports and have no way to reassemble such information into a noble and inspiring symbol. We achieve neither liberty nor art, only blankness. In absence of an educational ideal, alternative ideologies have taken hold. Some, if not many, are well intentioned in their view that the purposes of schools are to prepare young people for economic and social needs. Maxine saw this phenomenon as well 20 years ago when she wrote, ". . . the demands being made of education today have far more to do with 'world-class' technical achievement than with creating a community of citizens" (p. 64). Like Nussbaum's (2010) warning that present-day education is focused on "producing greedy obtuseness and a technically trained docility that threaten the very life of democracy itself" (p. 142), Maxine posits the notion that in addition to the three r's of education—reading, writing, and arithmetic—our public schools must prepare students for the three c's: creativity, community, and citizenry. In my dissertation, I argued for my own three c's that should constitute the focus of education: the collaborative creation and critique of texts (Lynch, 2011). It is these kinds of competing definitions that swirl in the discourse about education that has fueled efforts by others outside of education, some with ignoble motives, to become so influential in education reform. Listen to the way our policy makers and business leaders talk about education and you will hear confidently spoken declarative statements like, "We are falling behind other countries and need to teach students more science and math like when I was in school." Reading such a sentence in a book like this one might seem glib and trite. I assure you when uttered in other contexts it is accompanied by nodding heads. This lack of common definition makes even living up to Maxine's charge to imagine things "as if they could be otherwise" really challenging. We cannot agree on how things are in the first place, leaving our different definitions scattered about the grass like chunks of copper.

EDUCATION AFTER SOFTWARE

The previous chapters have framed what I refer to as critical software studies, which is a theoretical framework and methodological lens that I like to think Maxine would have appreciated. In what follows, I wish to review what I intended my argument to be—aware that my best efforts might have been read as confusing, contradictory, or much worse: irrelevant. In Chapter 1, I argue that the current education reforms emphasize accountability metrics, which require increased use of standards and the generation of data (i.e. tests, rubrics). Such accountability culture lends itself to the use of technology to collect, store, analyze, and report on data. Technology, as Selwyn (2014) argues, is not to be regarded as the neutral handmaiden of accountability but rather a complex and ideologically charged entity. In Chapter 2, I draw attention to the inadequacy of the word *technology* and claim that only by exploring software theory can researchers more accurately frame and analyze the role of what I call software-powered technologies in education. I introduce concepts from software studies and propose a critical software studies conceptual visualization that frames software space as the mediator and shaper of political, economic, pedagogical, and administrative spaces. Specifically, I argue that software space consists of at least five layers: devices, networking infrastructure, interfaces, code, and information systems. I then bridge software studies with what I broadly refer to as critical education studies in Chapter 3, claiming that if we are to examine the role of software in education we must do so from a critical perspective that is sensitive to issues of power, profit, and equity. It is here that I formally mark my belief that the purpose of public education must, fundamentally, be to strengthen democracy and demonstrate how reformers' reliance on software space position students and teachers as abstractions. Chapter 4 offers an operationalization of the concepts in the preceding chapters. It is not enough, I argue, to simply conceptualize critical software studies. Researchers must also have methods of systematically gathering data that allows them to demonstrate the hidden role software plays in education. The methods include a software-sensitive form of critical discourse analysis, functionality precedent, pixel analysis, click commitment protocols, source viewing, inferred algorithmic logic, and data structure analysis. With new methods in mind, I turn to a series of research and scholarly articles in Chapter 5 in order to explore how they would have been affected if a critical software studies framework had also been considered. I demonstrate that different kinds of questions, insights, and findings might well result from theoretical and methodological applications that explicitly attend to software space. In Chapter 6, I conduct a more thorough analysis of how one might critically examine the political discourse for the hidden role software plays. I look at a series of documents, including excerpts from speeches and public documents associated with Race to the Top. Chapter 7, then, offers two examples of what extended critical software analysis might look like, focusing on the use of online learning in New York City public schools and in reforms of teacher education and evaluation. Both examples try to pull together concepts and methods discussed in preceding chapters in coherent—albeit imperfect—models. Because critically examining software in education is the work of classroom educators as well as researchers,

I share in Chapter 8 how I have attempted to convey key concepts and considerations to an audience of secondary English teachers in a widely circulated teaching journal. The sections of the chapter contain columns from my recurring column. Although the spirit and ideas of Maxine's writings are present throughout the book, in both the explicit and implicit stances I take, I have spent more time above trying to make clear just how vital equity, creativity, and imagination are to our highest aspirations for public schools. Danh Vo's project provides a poignant case in point of the importance of imagining things as other than they are—as learners, citizens, and artists. With an eye toward the future, I now consider just how software might serve the needs of public schools and policy makers differently than we currently witness.

AS OTHER THAN THEY ARE

I believe that software space can serve the goals of democratic education, albeit less strongly when those very goals are contested. The language of Race to the Top and its associated initiatives suggests that the official goal of education is to prepare students for college and a career by teaching numeracy and literacy in ways that align to the Common Core Standards. Standards come and go, however, as do alliterative sound bites. I have offered perspectives on what a democratic education means, with special emphasis on warnings that the tension between economic and educational ends must be articulated and limited to ensure that we do not reduce education to a "pale reflection" of economic models. Our collective commitment to ensuring that our children have jobs does not necessitate the reduction of learning to training manuals nor the generation of assessment data that even the most scrupulous corporate executive would dismiss if provided by her own research and development team. We are capable of more. So is software.

Software theorists highlight the importance of more rigorously assessing the limits and affordances of the ontology of software. Many of these same theorists are themselves deft users of software, often for creative and critical purposes. Manovich (2001, 2013), for instance, gained some popular notoriety in 2014 for his analysis of millions of selfie images (Dewey, 2014). He is also himself a digital artist and programmer. Berry (2011) also situates his criticism and philosophy of software in his own experiences in software development. I point this out because it is important to balance the critical perspective articulated here with creativity. Software can be used for great good as we have seen in classrooms that connect students to others across the world, and the use of social media to organize political movements. It is the intentionality behind software's use that is of primary importance.

In schools, this means having clear pedagogical ends in mind when using technology. When using technology in classrooms, we must support teachers and students in critically understanding what software can and cannot do.

Educators must not assume that students are comfortable with technology simply because of their age. Students often need much assistance in both knowing how to use technology at a basic and advanced level for learning. There are valuable frameworks to assist teachers, principals, and coaches in using technology for instructional purposes. Both the TPACK framework (Koehler & Mishra, 2009) and the ISTE standards (International Society for Technology in Education, 2014) offer some sound guidance. However, both of these resources fail to account critically for the ways software mediates and shapes teaching and learning. They should be supplemented accordingly. School-based educators might consider creating reading groups about educational technologies, choosing texts that avoid the orthodoxy of optimism Selwyn describes. I am fond of starting meetings about technology in education with a premise: "Assume that using technology for teaching and learning is almost certainly a colossal waste of time and money. Now, let's see if this proposed use of technology proves itself to be otherwise." Don't drink the educational technology Kool Aid. It has too much sugar. In addition to reading groups, teachers who are interested in using software-powered technologies in their classrooms might consider simple and high-value uses. For example, teaching students to create screencasts in which they demonstrate something on their computers while recording their own voiceover is a kind of technology use that both positions students as creators of media and can be used for myriad classroom purposes. My own students have created screencasts of themselves walking me through drafts of their writing to which I respond with my own screencast in which I both discuss and demonstrate ways to refine their work. A math teacher in California runs a site called mathtrain.tv with his students in which students create math lessons for each other. Both examples use the same software-powered technology, but the number of ways it can be used is limitless. We don't need software to automatically correct student writing or to deliver some faceless, profiting adult's lectures to us. We can use software to create our own learning experiences.

In school districts and states, it is vital that we begin to think critically about the role of software-powered technologies ourselves and stop outsourcing insight and strategy to think tanks and companies. The case of inBloom in New York State serves as an informative case study. State education officials partnered with inBloom to receive data feeds on both teacher performance and student achievement data. They did so, in part, to comply with the requirements of the Race to the Top application. It became clear as parents protested the sharing of their children's data as well as when the state legislature admonished the education department for acting on their own that state school officials were making decisions that aligned with neither voters nor many elected officials. The point of contention in the inBloom case was not the manner in which teacher and student data were collected, which is a point worth underscoring. The internal and external outcry education officials received was not in response to the ways teachers are evaluated or students assessed through standardized tests. The outcry focused on making student data available to a third-party entity (the comparable sharing of teacher data did not emerge as a major concern). If the state education department's primary goal was to use teacher and student data to gain insights into teaching and learning in New York in order to better support schools, they might have responded to the outcry with a mea culpa and compromise. One thing inBloom provided, for instance, was a schema for organizing thousands of data inputs in a uniform way. If districts across the state all agreed to use a shared schema, it would make conducting comparative analyses across districts more effective. Perhaps, then, the state could broker cross-district support partnerships based on cleaner data. And, rather than making such data public in disaggregated and humiliating form, they could rely on the respectful anonymizing of individual schools and teachers that aggregate data provides. However, because the primary impetus of the state's partnership with inBloom was to partner with inBloom was political pressure, they lost track of their North Star: the people of New York. Whereas I encourage state and district leaders to look beyond their own schools for ideas and collaborations, it does not absolve them from possessing a vision for their schools that is cogenerated with principals, teachers, students, and families.

I also recommend that state officials seriously consider how software-powered technologies might be used to empower schools and districts to rigorously coordinate their assessments rather than outsourcing assessment mechanisms to private companies whose methods and infrastructure is a century old. For nearly one hundred years, large-scale assessments in the United States has changed very little. Whereas it might appear that with the advent of software-powered technologies we are witnessing more "adaptive" kinds of assessments that provide customized questions to students based on their previous answers, the fact is that these assessment methods resemble practices of the early 20th century more than they do 21st-century innovations. Educational technology scholar Paul Saettler (2004) argues that the history of technology in schools is inextricably tied to the Edward Thorndike's use of large-scale testing methods, which used predetermined questions and acceptable answers to sample what students learn. He writes, "Thorndike is the historical starting point for any study or analysis of modern educational technology" and that his "impressive demonstration of empirical-inductive means in the development of a science and technology of instruction unquestionably marked him as the first modern instructional technologist" (p. 56). I have argued elsewhere that one of the reasons Thorndike's approach to education was as successful as it was is due to the fact that the technologies available during the early 1900s aligned well with his pedagogical and epistemological values. Unlike John Dewey, who believed that learning was a social construct that emerged from students engaging in authentic inquiries and real-world settings, Thorndike believed that learning was a cognitive act the prowess for which was genetic. Prewritten tests with answer keys were easily manufactured on industrial printing presses. No technology at the time, however, could be used to scale more Deweyan approaches to education.

This is not true today, however. Today, software-powered technologies can support constructivist models of learning in which students pose their own questions, communicate with others, and generate collaborative and individual artifacts of their own learning. Consider the platforms used by journal editors to facilitate the peer-review process. These products—some open-source and others proprietary—leverage software space to allow authors to anonymously share their work with peers, for reviewers to offer quantitative and qualitative feedback aligned with standards editors create, and to return that feedback to authors. Software in this case is used to enable a social evaluation process across time and space. What prevents states and districts from using such platforms for large-scale assessment of students' writings? It is questions like these that both states and researchers should be asking.

Families and communities have an increasingly vital role to play in education, not only in the private lives of individual children but in the public discourse. Using software-powered technologies in schools—whether for instructional or administrative purposes—necessarily raises questions about curricular quality (how is technology being used?), privacy (what kinds of data are being gathered about my child, by whom, and how is it encrypted?), and our children's ultimate development (is the school using technology to teach my child to be a software engineer or a critically thinking and contributing citizen?). Elected officials rely on input from families and communities and listen to such input when it directly correlates to votes. The more families and community members discuss the kinds of educational experiences they imagine for children and engage with their educators in dialogue, the clearer it will be when external influences are compromising our children's education. As we have seen, software-powered technologies excel at putting geographically dispersed people in contact with each other. Families and communities should take to software space as a way to organize and act. When news about the state education department's pilots with inBloom came to light, parents around New York organized online. There were regular updates about what the state was doing, commentary pieces by a handful of concerned parents, communications to elected officials, and coordinated efforts to attend public hearings. As a parent and researcher, I viewed a three-hour hearing streamed online in which state legislators questioned education officials and inBloom representatives. After I received an email from a friend asking for a summary of what happened, I decided to create a three-minute mashup video that pulled together what I considered the highlights (and lowlights) to be. Within two days, other parents viewed the video. It received hundreds of hits and was written up in other blogs. Families and communities must become more critical consumers and users of software-powered technologies if they are to hold elected officials accountable for our children's education while participating and supporting efforts in their local schools.

ON RESEARCH AND LANGUAGE AND ARTS

At an educational research conference, I presented some of the concepts and methods in this book alongside other far more well-known and accomplished literacy scholars. All of whose work I had read and admired. During the question and answer portion at the end, an audience member asked one of the other scholars a question about the challenges of researching the role of technology in literacy and education more generally. The scholar responded that part of the nature of emerging technologies is that they are always emerging. In addition to the subjects of our research changing frequently (new technologies come out perpetually), the theories and methods we have to research such phenomena are in need of ongoing adjustment. It is the nature of the beast, she said. I hadn't intended to respond to the question the way I did. But, I stood up and respectfully disagreed with my colleague. It is not the case, I said, that the technologies are in such constant flux. It might appear that they are, but part of what we must do as researchers is to identify the aspects of technology that are more foundational to its ontology and build upon such ontological stability. This is why I work with software theory. I believe that by better understanding the nature of software—not technology—we can isolate concepts and methods of data collection and analysis that will provide us with greater confidence as researchers and sounder epistemological footing.

It is appropriate that this occurred at a literacy research conference. As has been pointed out throughout the book, software is a linguistic space to a great extent. I imagine that if researchers began to learn about how programming languages are derived, written, and read, we would see a flood of new epiphanies in our field. In an effort to explore the use of quantitative text analysis and data visualization in secondary English classrooms, I began teaching myself some different programming languages: Python, R, Javascript, and D3. I bought books about the languages, read blogs and community posts, and watched video tutorials online. I became aware of just how different and similar learning these languages was to reading and writing in human languages. On the one hand, as languages there is a logic and syntax, with some grammatical conventions applying across languages. On the other hand, there was one difference that continued to strike me: audience. When writing for software space, I had to imagine how my reader would read my writing. Feedback from the reader was immediate. Error, it would say. Novelist (and part-time coder) Vikram Chandra (2014) writes about this relationship between human and computational forms of writing. He writes, "I was writing fiction steadily, but I found that the stark determinisms of code were a welcome relief from the ambiguities of literary narrative. By the end of a morning of writing, I was eager for the pleasures of programming" (p. 17). There is much room for exploration here. What does it mean to think of software space as possessing a specific kind of audience(s)? What might it look like to teach students introduction to computer programming not by dropping them into an oversimplified game-like environment, but by comparing Python to poetry? Much of what seems to be emerging in the drive to teach students to program seems focused on pulling students away from the letter-based languages themselves and instead using highly visual or even mathematical methods of instruction. These might or might not be effective. It is certainly worth examining what a more poetic and even literary approach to teaching computer programming would look like. In addition to blurring the traditional line between arts and sciences, information and imagination, it could be a way to bolster students' literacy skills while simultaneously exposing them to critical approaches to reading and writing.

Ultimately, I imagine a future where stakeholders in education—students, teachers, administrators, officials, and families—engage with software space in both critical and creative ways. Lev Manovich (2014) makes an astute and useful observation about the societal significance of software: "If software is indeed the contemporary equivalent of the combustion engine and electricity in terms of its social effects, every type of software needs to be taken into account. We need to consider not only the 'visible' software used by consumers but also 'grey' software, which runs all systems and processes in contemporary society" (p. 21). By comparing software to the combustion engine and electricity, the theorist succeeds in raising software to a level of significance many of us might otherwise overlook. However, there is one way in which software is radically unlike such previous technologies. Software is something anyone can create. The effort and skill it takes to write a simple program is decreasing steadily. Educators should be teaching students to create with programming languages not because it will prepare the next generation of software engineers, although it might. We should be teaching students to create with code because in doing so they will become more critically aware of how software acts in our world. I am reminded of the work of literary theorist Robert Scholes, whom I read while in graduate school. In his book *The Rise and Fall of English*, Scholes (1998) argues that there should be a kind of reciprocal pedagogy between the teaching of reading and the teaching of writing. That is, students should write the kinds of genres and styles of the texts they read. Read what you write, write what you read. The rationale for this approach is that by attempting to emulate an author's writing, students have to "imagine themselves as other writers than they are," to paraphrase Maxine. With creativity comes critical thinking. The traditional gap between the arts and science must be closed if we are to prepare our students for participation in our democracy, which includes their contributions to the economy. There will be no technological innovation without artistic imagination.

CODE IS POETRY, POETRY IS CODE

The popular technology company Wordpress provides the software that powers web sites all over the world. Their tagline has always struck me and seems a fitting way to begin the ending of this book: Code is poetry. To those who are fluent in programming languages, there is poetry and elegance in even the most functional code. It seems appropriate that an inquiry into the hidden role of software in education should reach into the lines of poetry for final insights into the nature of technology and learning. I recall Walt Whitman's short poem, "I Was Looking for a Long While" (Whitman, 1855). It reads:

> I was looking a long while for Intentions,
> For a clew to the history of the past for myself, and for these chants—and
>   now I have found it,
> It is not in those paged fables in the libraries, (them I neither accept nor
>   reject,)
> It is no more in the legends than in all else,
> It is in the present—it is this earth to-day,
> It is in Democracy—(the purport and aim of all the past,)
> It is the life of one man or one woman to-day—the average man of to-day,
> It is in languages, social customs, literatures, arts,
> It is in the broad show of artificial things, ships, machinery, politics, creeds,
>   modern improvements, and the interchange of nations,
> All for the modern—all for the average man of to-day.

Whitman describes his search into the meaning of history and its significance to his present poetic purposes. He seeks historical intentionality and discovers that while it might exist in books or "legends," it is also in his very time and place. He finds Intentions in presence: presence in his natural surroundings, presence of the democratic ideal, presence of others, presence in the cultural gifts of language and art, presence in the "broad show" that includes technological developments like "artificial things, ships, machinery. . . ." The poet's affirming stance challenges me—us—to reflect upon where we too seek and find Intentions, especially for our children in our public schools. If we, like Whitman, choose momentarily to focus only on where we are here and now, if we examine the gifts of the earth, of liberty, of an increasingly diverse population—what do we envision for our children? When we observe the way computer languages affect our customs, literature, and arts—what do we envision for our children? When we picture our versions of the "broad show of artificial things"—what do we envision for our children? In a society that requires public schools to compete for federal education funding and insists on quantitatively ranking our teachers and students, are we losing an appreciation for averageness? That is, do the meritocratic ideologies that infuse our educational discourse and policies blind us to the simple truth that averageness should be celebrated?

When I first considered this poem as a focal point for reflection, I associated software-powered technologies with the "artificial things" Whitman references. He does not reference such things with any kind of criticism, just a fit of presence. As I reread the poem, I began to think of software-powered technologies as belonging more to "languages, social customs." The linguistic nature of software and its inherent reliance on human direction seem to fit software's ontology more accurately than the ambiguity of artificiality and thingness. Many minutes passed by as I deliberated whether software belonged to one line of the poem more than the other. My eyes were then drawn back to the first line. To *Intentions*. I imagined that I felt for a moment the same combination of discovery and embarrassment as when the poet found for his "chant" what I found for my own. It is our present intentions for the use of software-powered technologies that will offer us the clues we need to act wisely. There are numberless pages of opinion pieces, success stories, and how-to books on the merits of using software-powered technologies in schools. But they are just "paged fables." If we are to invite software into our schools, we must examine thoroughly the simple realities that surround us. We must fix our eyes and ears on "all else." I write this not only with policy makers and educators in mind. I write this as a parent with a child in public schools and a researcher fearful that if the academic community does not devise more nuanced and creative ways to study the role of software-powered technologies in education, the void will be filled by others who offer confident advice to politicians, pedagogues, and parents that distracts our schools from a democratic commitment to critical thinking, equity, and public engagement. My hope is that we might replace the drumbeat of arrogant surety we hear thumping in speeches and media reports with something more choral—harmonious whispers or, perhaps one day, an unstoppable bellowing chant.

WORKS CITED

Berry, D. (2011). *The philosophy of software: Code and mediation in the digital age.* New York: Palgrave Macmillan.

Chandra, V. (2014). *Geek sublime: The beauty of code, the code of beauty.* Minneapolis, MN: Graywolf Press.

Dewey, C. (2014, February 20). The surprising sociology of selfies. *The Washington Post.* Retrieved February 23, 2014, from www.washingtonpost.com/blogs/style-blog/wp/2014/02/20/the-surprising-sociology-of-selfies/.

Greene, M. (1995). *Releasing the imagination: Essays on education, the arts, and social change.* New York: Jossey-Bass.

International Society for Technology in Education. (2014). ISTE standards: Teachers. Retrieved November 26, 2014, from www.iste.org/docs/pdfs/20-14_ISTE_Standards-T_PDF.pdf.

Koehler, M., & Mishra, P. (2009). What is technological pedagogical content knowledge (TPACK)? *Contemporary Issues in Technology and Teacher Education, 9*(1). Retrieved September 20, 2014, from www.editlib.org/p/29544?nl.

Lynch, T. L. (2011, May). *The Tweed Effect: Theorizing the rise of online learning in New York City public schools.* Teachers College, Columbia University, New York, NY.

Manovich, L. (2001). *The language of new media.* London: MIT Press.

Manovich, L. (2013). *Software takes command.* New York: Bloomsbury Academic.

Nussbaum, M. C. (2010). *Not for profit: Why democracy needs the humanities.* Princeton, NJ: Princeton University Press.

Saettler, P. (2004). *The evolution of American educational technology.* Greenwich, CT: Information Age Publishing.

Scholes, R. (1998). *The rise and fall of English: Reconstructing English as a discipline.* New Haven: Yale University Press.

Selwyn, N. (2014). *Distrusting educational technology: Critical questions for changing times.* New York: Routledge.

Whitman, W. (1855). *Leaves of grass.* E-Text. Project Gutenberg. Retrieved December 4, 2014, from www.gutenberg.org/files/1322/1322-h/1322-h.htm.

Index